more big girl knits

more
big girl
knits

JILLIAN MORENO & AMY R. SINGER

25 DESIGNS FULL OF COLOR & TEXTURE FOR CURVY WOMEN

POTTER
CRAFT

New York

To all Big Girls, no matter what their size.

Copyright © 2008 by Jillian Moreno and
Amy R. Singer
Photographs © 2008 by Lise Varrette

All rights reserved.

Published in the United States by Potter Craft,
an imprint of the Crown Publishing Group,
a division of Random House, Inc., New York.
www.crownpublishing.com
www.pottercraft.com

POTTER CRAFT and colophon is a registered
trademark of Random House, Inc.

Originally published in hardcover by
Potter Craft, an imprint of the Crown Publishing
Group, a division of Random House, Inc.,
New York, in 2008.

Library of Congress Cataloging-in-Publication
Data is available upon request

ISBN: 978-0-307-58638-4

Printed in China

Design by Laura Palese
Illustrations by Erica Mulherin
Technical illustrations by Mandy Moore

Thanks to the Craft Yarn Council of America
(www.yarnstandards.com) for their Standard
Yarn Weight System Chart, which appears on
page 156.

10 9 8 7 6 5 4 3 2 1

First Paperback Edition

Contents

Introduction:
we're still
Fat &
we're still
knitting

It's been two years since we wrote our first book about learning to love and knit for your body—whatever shape and size it is—and big things have been happening in the knitting world.

It started slowly . . . an up-sizing revolution from established knitwear designers

and some of the biggest knitting magazines and yarn companies. Suddenly Big Girls are being embraced as part of the knitting community *at large.* (Oh, come on. How could we resist that pun?) Sweater sizes no longer automatically end at a 38- or 40-inch (97- or 102-cm) bust. We're seeing patterns with 45-, 48-, 52-, and 60-inch busts (that's 114-, 122-, 132-, and 152.5cm, if you speak metric). And not just 60-inch rectangles, but 60-inch sweaters with shaping. Hallelujah!

We're not accounted for in anywhere near the majority of patterns yet. But we deeply love that what we get to knit from isn't a *special section for women's sizes.* (Somebody cue the circus music, cause those sections tend to be full of tents. Ahem.) Instead, knitting patterns are being designed to cover a larger range of sizes, from extra-wee to big and bountiful. Sweaters for everyone. Can you imagine? The Big Girl revolution has begun. Viva la Revolution!

Our favorite thing that's happened since we wrote the first book is that we've gotten to meet plenty of round-rumped, big-bellied, and bountiful-boobed knitters who want to know even

Hint: **When a designer, publisher, or yarn company you love starts offering patterns in your size, especially if they've paid attention to shaping and fit, buying those patterns shows them that they've made the right choice and could encourage them to keep it up! If you're really feeling it, write a letter and tell them you appreciate that they're now including Big Girls in their knitting world. Help spread the Big Girl love!**

more about knitting for *their* bodies. So we figured it was time for us to get back to the measuring tapes, swatches, and ease charts.

Prepare yourselves, because we speak frankly about bodies, boobs, bellies, butts, and the styles and design features of knitwear we think will make the most of your unique Big Girl assets. If a sweater is going to make your ass look bigger, we'll tell you. We won't tell you something will make you look thin or "10 Pounds Lighter!", but we will tell you how to look your best.

The *Big Girl Knits* approach came out of our frustration with the fugly knitting designs we're still seeing offered to plus size, curvy women. Fluffy, froofy sweaters that turn you into a human muppet? Boxes or tents that give no hint of the actual woman-shape underneath? Eye-catching color and

ornamentation in exactly the *wrong* place? Huge cables and bobbles that make your own not-small bits feel and look like an overstuffed couch? It's a crime, and it's gotta stop!

We're dissed by society already because we're [insert the fat slur of your choice], but to get dissed by some practitioners of our favorite hobby, especially a hobby that talks all warm and fuzzy about community? Dammit, that's just wrong. It breaks our hearts to see big, luscious women following unsuitable patterns with blind optimism, knitting sweaters that can't help but look like crap on them, no matter how beautifully they're knit.

We want women to knit sweaters they love, sweaters that express who they are, and most of all, sweaters that look good on them. Not just good—fantastic. We want every plus-sized knitter to know the secret thrill of having a size 8 knitting friend say, "Hot sweater! Where can I get the pattern?" and getting to say, "Thanks! But sorry; it doesn't come in your size. Maybe you could do the math to get it to fit you." You know, like we've had to do our entire knitting lives?

So we offer you tools. We also offer you a carefully chosen bounty of patterns that you can sit down right now with—not do any math—to knit, wear, and look fabulous. We know it's hard to believe, but it's true. We think this is how it should be. (Here's a tissue.)

This book will teach you things, too—things that some skinny knitters might not know. (In fact, we heard rumors that sub-size-14 knitters bought our first book so they could learn the shaping secrets, too. That's cool with us.) We'll teach you what looks good on *your* parts. We'll teach you how to adapt almost any sweater pattern to curve, to undulate, to wrap *your* body in sweatery love.

Our first book, *Big Girl Knits*, has three great chapters full of our design suggestions (the great sweater designs are in the back), including how to figure out what will look best on you before casting on a single stitch, and what you should and shouldn't knit. There are charts that make intimidating math much more friendly, and a whole section on measuring yourself. If you haven't read it, we encourage you to get your hands on a copy and brush up on the key concepts. If you've read it and need a refresher, we're happy to oblige.

how to look Fabby, not flabby, in knit-wear

It's time to make friends with your mirror. Stand in front of a full-length one and really look at you—the body you are knitting for right here, right now. Not the pre-baby, pre-menopause, pre-metabolism-slowdown body you have in your mind. Not the body that used to be or is gonna be cute and sexy at some point in the future.

You don't get to knit for that other secret body you imagine you have, either—
the one that was created by years of people saying "You're too big. How about we get you something big that skims past your whole body so no one can see what you've actually got?" This secret body you imagine you have is actually *bigger* than you are, thanks to the possibly well-meaning but definitely useless advice the world, your mother, or some random a-hole has thrown at you.

Know Your Body

We ask you to look at yourself in the mirror, at all of yourself, not just a bit here and there. Take in the whole big, beautiful package. *This is you—* every lump, bump, and curve. This is the woman you're knitting for. You're the woman in the mirror; you're *not* the size tag in your pants. Look with love and tell the critical voices to shut the hell up.

You've Got Parts— We've Got 3 . . . B3

When you're knitting for your Big Girl self, it can make your brain hurt to imagine what might look superfine on *your* body. We make it easy. We break it down into three key body bits: Boobs, Belly, and Butt. We call them the B3.

Some of your Bs might be bigger than others, or maybe they're all the same. What parts do you like? What parts would you rather downplay? Looking good and feeling good in knitwear (or any clothing, for that matter) is all about balancing your overall silhouette. By using different sweater styles and shapes that work with your particular Bs, and avoiding the ones that work against them, you will knit sweaters that look killer on you.

And by the way, we don't employ the age-old fat-girl trick of attempted camouflage. Tents, smocks, and caftans only make you look as big as all that extra fabric. Fat girls in black don't look thinner, they just look like fat girls wearing black. Instead, we use practical prestidigitation, just like a magician. Magicians specialize in redirection—look here, not there.

So here's how to use the B3 system. Look in the mirror. Which one of your Bs is the biggest and most bodacious? Use the tips for that B to help you choose knitting patterns that will flatter you, or to know where to improve a knitting pattern (like adding short rows, if you're a Boob girl). If more than one B is bountiful, or maybe you're a B all over, choose a suitable tip from each, depending on which of your Bs you want to play up or down.

Let us say again that this is all about *you*. If we say, "show off your girls," and you don't want to, don't. We say, "cover that tush," and you think that's your hot spot? Well, rock it, baby. Our *rules* are more like guidelines that give you a place to start, but only *you* get to say what works for you. There is no knitting principal's office you'll get sent to if you don't play our way.

The 2 tips every Big Girl needs to follow

- Think skim—The fit of your sweater must skim your shape, not be loose enough to be a circus tent or so tight that people can see exactly what you had for breakfast. There's a wide and personal range between these two extremes, but it's your body and your sweater, so it's really all up to you. Think about outlining your curves.

- Go to waist—Celebrate your waist! Nip in a little at the waist of your garments, even if you think you don't have a waist, even by just an inch. It makes a huge difference! It defines the waist you have, creates the waist you didn't think you had, and mostly gives you a curvy, feminine, and tailored silhouette.

The 2 must-dos for each B

Boobs
- Show as much skin at your chest as you dare; if you're shy, at least let your collarbones peek out . . . collarbones are sexy.
- Add waist shaping so you don't just look round all over.

Belly
- Hems should hit an inch or two (2.5–5cm) below your biggest belly bit.
- Use dramatic neckline, cuff, and hem treatments to direct attention where you'd rather have it.

Butt
- Sweaters should stop above *or* below your biggest butt bulge . . . not right on it.
- Go for gentle shaping at the waist, then flare out to below your butt.

What size?

Sizes are the biggest joke in fashion. Every company has their own version of a size 16, and you'll have to look damn hard to find two companies that match. Year to year, companies change the measurements that correspond with each size, trying to please the population. You know a size 16 from 1950 is about the same as an average size 12 now, right? That's why Marilyn Monroe looks curvy-ish to us, but she sure doesn't look like a size 16 as we know it today. Sheesh. Seriously—if their numbers mean nothing, why are we paying attention to them?

The only numbers we need to know are *actual measurements,* not the number on the clothing tag or the size label in a knitting pattern. That's because measurements don't lie—unless you make them.

To figure out which set of numbers to follow in a knitting pattern, you need three things:

- a schematic of the garment showing the finished measurements
- a current set of your own measurements
- your favorite ease numbers

No moaning. We guarantee that when you knit a sweater to your own current measurements, you will be astounded at the results—you'll have a sweater that fits you!

Measuring kit:

- Nice new measuring tape
- Scrap yarn to tie around hips and waist

MAKE THE MOST OF MEASURING!

Our rule for measuring is the same as our rule for everything else: It's better with friends. You can't measure your own back. You can't see under your boobs. And the main reason not to go it alone is that you'll be tempted to pull the tape a little tighter, round your numbers down, and then beat yourself up afterward when nothing fits. Measuring with a friend keeps you honest.

- Use a new measuring tape, not the old stretched-out tape your mama found in the bottom of her sewing box.
- Do it every year: the whole shebang the first time, and then just the squishy parts every year after. Your bones are probably finished growing, but your butt, biceps, or boobs may not be.
- Don't hold your breath while you measure unless you don't plan on breathing when you wear the sweater.
- Make a party of it! Have a nosh, raise a glass, turn up the music!

- Don't be sad or angry or bummed out if the number on the tape is bigger than you expected. The number has no power over you—it's just a number. But it *is* a damned handy tool to help you knit stuff that will make you look much better than when you were guessing sweater sizes with your eyes closed and your fingers crossed.

WHAT DO YOU DO NOW?

Choose the size of the garment you want to knit based on your bust measurement plus the ease you like the best. And we're not sure why this is a secret, but it seems to be, so we're going to spell it out: *you can have different ease in different places*! Do you like your boob area a little leaner than your belly zone? Add 2" (5cm) of ease to the boob portion of your sweater but 4" (10cm) to the tummy part. You're knitting it; you might as well make it fit you exactly the way you like!

sweater chest 56"

My Measurements

NAME: _____   **DATE:** _____

CHEST CIRCUMFERENCE (B)	60	**LOWER LENGTH (LL)** *(favorite sweater length from hem to waist)*	9	
NIPPLE DISTANCE (ND) *(nipple to nipple)*	11½	**FRONT LENGTH (FL)** *(favorite sweater length hem to shoulder over boobs)*	28	
ARMPIT DEPTH *(top of shoulder to armpit crease)*	8½	**BACK LENGTH (BL)** *(favorite sweater length hem to shoulder over back)*	29	
PREFERRED ARMHOLE DEPTH (W) *(from top of your shoulder to just above your bra strap)*	13	**SHOULDER TO SHOULDER** *(cross back)*	18	
WAIST	54	**HIP (H)**	53	
BELLY *(only if it pokes out)*	57	**UPPER ARM**	25	
TANK STRAP WIDTH		**WRIST**	10	
SHOULDER TO FRONT WAIST *(shoulder to waist over boobs)*	24	**FOREARM**	13	
SHOULDER TO BACK WAIST	19	**SLEEVE LENGTHS**		
UPPER LENGTH (UL) *(waist to top of bra band)*	12	**SS:**		
SIDE LENGTH (SL) *(favorite sweater length, hem to bottom of bra band)*	9½	**¾:**		
PREFERRED SWEATER LENGTH, *from shoulder to hem*	29 a 30	**LS:**	26	

Knitting for yourself without using your current measurements is like driving in the dark without headlights: unsafe at any speed.

CHOOSING YARN

If you are fat, don't use fat yarn. It will make you look fatter.

This seems head-smackingly obvious, but how many times have we reached for the bulky yarn to get a sweater just *done* already? Just cause it's there doesn't mean it's there for *us*. (Sorry.) The most flattering thing we can knit for our big selves is something from the finest-gauge yarn possible. For handknitting,

use this simple guideline: 4 stitches to the inch (2.5cm) or finer will make you look most fine. For sanity's sake, do what we do, and purchase your superfine-gauge knitwear.

Got the itch to knit chunky for yourself, no matter what we say? Knit a wrap. An in-proportion, sized-for-a-big-bod wrap like Finagle on page 134. Amy loves hers.

FoBG

Friends of Big Girls (FoBG) are yarn store employees and owners who get us. Every yarn store should have one. They are the best friend a knitting Big Girl can have. They help us find flattering patterns and yarn, help with math, and generally make us feel like the fabulous knitters (and valued customers) that we are. Find yourself a FoBG and shop often.

IT'S TIME TO GO SHOPPING!

We've never seen a plus-sized yardage chart for shopping for yarn with abandon. For ours, we start with a basic pullover as the template in four different yarn weights, then we add

Yarn Yardage Chart

		GAUGE (PER INCH)	CHEST MEASUREMENT IN INCHES				
			40–42 (101.5–106.5cm)	44–46 (112–117cm)	48–50 (122–127cm)	52–54 (132–137cm)	56–58 (142–147cm)
VERSION 1	long-sleeved crew necked sweater, 28 inches long with a straight body, 4" (10cm) of ease.	7–7.5 sts	2180/1993	2370/2167	2630/2404	3050/2789	3320/3036
		6–6.5 sts	1920/1756	2070/1893	2300/2103	2690/2460	2910/2661
		5–5.5 sts	1660/1518	1820/1664	2000/1829	2340/2140	2530/2313
		4–4.5 sts	1420/1298	1530/1399	1700/1554	1970/1801	2120/1939
VERSION 2	short-sleeved crew necked sweater, 28 inches long with a straight body, 4" (10cm) of ease.	7–7.5 sts	1750/1600	1900/1737	2100/1920	2500/2286	2700/2469
		6–6.5 sts	1550/1417	1700/1554	1850/1692	2150/1969	2350/2149
		5–5.5 sts	1350/1234	1450/1326	1600/1463	1900/1737	2025/1852
		4–4.5 sts	1150/1052	1225/1120	1400/1280	1575/1440	1700/1554
VERSION 3	crew necked sweater vest, 28 inches long with a straight body, 4" (10cm) of ease.	7–7.5 sts	1525/1394	1700/1554	1850/1692	2150/1969	2325/2126
		6–6.5 sts	1350/1234	1450/1326	1625/1486	1900/1737	2050/1875
		5–5.5 sts	1200/1097	1275/1166	1400/1280	1650/1509	1775/1623
		4–4.5 sts	1000/914	1075/983	1200/1097	1400/1280	1500/1372
VERSION 4	heavily textured long-sleeved crew necked sweater, 28 inches long with a straight body, 4" (10cm) of ease.	7–7.5 sts	2850/2606	3100/2835	3425/3132	4000/3658	4325/3955
		6–6.5 sts	2500/2286	2700/2469	2990/2734	3500/3246	3800/3475
		5–5.5 sts	2175/1989	2375/2172	2600/2378	3050/2789	3300/3018
		4–4.5 sts	1850/1692	2000/1829	2210/2021	2575/2355	2775/2537
VERSION 5	elaborate collar/cuffs, long-sleeved crew necked sweater, 28 inches long with a straight body, 4" (10cm) of ease.	7–7.5 sts	2625/2400	2850/2606	3175/2903	3675/3360	4000/3658
		6–6.5 sts	2300/2103	2500/2286	2775/2537	3250/2972	3500/3200
		5–5.5 sts	2000/1829	2200/2012	2400/2195	2825/2583	3050/2789
		4–4.5 sts	1725/1577	1850/1692	2050/1875	2375/2172	2550/2332

* YARDS ARE IN PINK, METERS IN BLACK

embellishment or subtract sleeve length. Based on the gauge of the yarn you want to stock up on and the size you expect you'll be knitting, using this chart will give you a reasonable rough estimate of how much yarn to buy. But it's an estimate, so do what we do: get extra. If you shop at a friendly store that accepts exchanges on unused yarn with a receipt, you can cash it in for something good later on if you don't use it all.

3 Faces of Ease

Ease is the number you add to your body part measurement so your sweater fits the way you want it to. What kind of fit feels right to you?

BIG GIRL STYLE

Close fitting—add 2 inches (5cm)
Standard fitting—add 4 inches (10cm)
Loose fitting—add 6 inches (15cm)

FOR SOME OTHER GIRL

Very Close Fitting—use your actual measurements (a great way to show off back fat and belly rolls!)
Oversized—add 7 inches (18cm) or more (a knitted gazebo)

Fattening yarn

If it knits up to less than 4 stitches to the inch, you can see why it's called chunky or bulky. It adds inches and makes a stiff fabric. It doesn't drape, which would have flattered your curves—it tents, which makes your curves into a big block.

And say no-no to novelty. Hairy, fuzzy-wuzzy yarn that dingle-dangles or comes with its own fringe is a definite don't. Same with heavily textured thick yarns, because they add actual inches. There are lots of ways to get texture on your body that don't rely on too-thick-for-us yarn, and you'll read more about that in the next few chapters.

Flattering yarn

In a perfect world, all Big Girls would learn to love DK-weight yarn, but worsted works, too. The key number is 4 stitches to the inch or finer because it can do amazing things—it fits and shows your body and drapes beautifully.

(2) color & texture
Style secrets for big girls

Color and texture make for gorgeous knitting. It's beautiful to look at and so satisfying to knit, watching the design build between your flying fingers.

Big Girl knitters tend to belong to one of two camps: Some run screaming from colorwork and texture and only knit in stockinette stitch. Others knit sweaters with huge Aran ropes, wide swaths of Fair Isle, or big blobs of intarsia, thinking either, "Who cares what I look like in it?" or "This will hide me!" Bzzzzt! Sorry, wrong on both counts.

Curvy girls can look fantastic in all kinds of colorwork and textured knitwear, but you can't just close your eyes and pick a pattern. You've got to think about what you're knitting and where it will end up on your body.

Just how do you wrap your gorgeous curvy bod in color and texture and not look upholstered? How do you add flavor to your frame without adding the illusion of extra inches? How do you keep from looking as if you've rolled yourself up in an area rug?

It's all about balance, baby.

Just as shaping a sweater to get the best fit and silhouette for your body visually balances your Bs, color and texture can do the same. Always keep your Bs and the sweater shape in the forefront of your mind when looking at knitting patterns.

Colorwork and texture add layers to a garment, not only visually, but literally. In colorwork, you use two or more yarns to create a single layer of fabric. In textured knitting, you're crumpling up yarn into stitches and patterns you can feel. Both use more yarn per square inch, and that means you're creating a thicker and potentially stiffer fabric. But Big Girls look better in garments with a little drape, and we often don't want our sweaters to be any warmer than necessary. So use a little caution and clever planning when you incorporate the stuff we're going to teach you in this chapter. That way, your colorwork and textured sweaters will make the most of—not overwhelm—your body.

COLOR YOUR WORLD

Here's a quick word on color. You could study color your entire life and get fixated on hue, value, and saturation. But we don't

A few choice tips for your Bs

- Yoke sweaters are great for Belly girls. Check out the Bountiful Bohus sweater on page 34. The yoke adds visual interest up top to balance your beautiful belly. Are you a Boob girl? Unless you're aiming to look like Dolly, why paint your girls so bright?

- Huge rope cables are related to the long-and-lean kind, which are great for giving your knitwear some flattering verticals. But when cables get big, they get thick and bulky, and that adds literal feet to your literal frame.

- Horizontal motifs are hard for every B to work with. There's almost no way to avoid the fact that horizontals are gonna make you look wider. Note we said, "almost." We're sneaky, you know. See "Work a secret horizontal" on page 16 for details.

- A single large intarsia motif on the front is a huge (no pun intended) don't. You may think it's a shield to hide your body, but it's really a great big spotlight focusing attention on everything it covers.

think you should sweat the techie details. We're talking about our version of Big Girl style here, and heavy-duty color theory isn't part of it.

Two key things you need to know when picking colors to put on your body:
- Dark recedes and downplays.
- Light advances and showcases.

You know that thing we all have for black (or other dark colors)? Why do we reach for it when we know our skin glows when we wear deep pink and our eyes twinkle when we're in green? It's because clever use of dark colors can make things less noticeable. No, not your whole upper torso, but a nice pair of dark side panels in a sweater can visually slim you, and that's definitely a Big Girl *Do*.

Two more key things to know when picking colors to put on your body:

- Warm colors advance.
- Cool colors recede.

So if you're combining warm red with cool blue in a sweater, choose where the red goes wisely. The warmth of the red is the first thing people will notice.

The texture of a yarn contributes to the color too:

- Smooth and shiny make a color appear lighter.
- Fuzzy makes a color appear darker.
- Metallic is like a coastguard spotlight.

Contrast between colors can make us look bigger than we are:

- High contrast between colors emphasizes
- Low contrast between colors downplays

MIND THE GAP

When using two or more colors, think about the line you're creating between the colors when you change from one to the other. Look at our Butt girl above. She's made a gorgeous two-color sweater with an abrupt color change at her widest part. It's a horizontal she hadn't expected, and it's not pretty.

So she rips the thing out and starts over. This time, she thinks about what she wants to downplay (for her, it's her butt) and plans to put the dark color there. Then she decides to ease the color from light on the top to dark on the bottom so there's no hard horizontal. See how happy she is with the result?

HYPED ON STRIPES?

Quick! Close your eyes and imagine a striped sweater you'd like to knit. Are you seeing horizontal stripes? We command you (nicely, of course) to banish them from your mind! There is

---

Combo Platter

Does more than one of your Bs stand up and sing? You, my good woman, are a combo platter. The easiest way to balance your combo platter is to think about the B that doesn't stand out and put on a show there.

- **BOOBS AND BUTT?** Waist yourself.
- **BOOBS AND BELLY?** Rock the rump.
- **BELLY AND BUTT?** Up, up, and away.
- **ALL 3 BS?** Add the whisper of a waist and keep it smooth. The triple-B combo needs to think "skim" more than any other. Try just an inch (2.5cm) less ease than you usually use.

Remember you are balancing, so emphasize what you want to show off with your choice of shape, color, and ease.

---

almost nothing that looks worse on a rounded, Rubenesque woman than horizontal stripes. They make us look wider by filling in our curves.

The avalanche of self-striping yarns that have spilled into yarn shops over the past few years have made the unfortunate horizontal stripe ridiculously easy for us to knit. Still, we love those yarns—and won't stop using them. There are *smart ways* to use self-striping yarn that will work with your curves, not against them. And we're all about the smart.

Knit side to side and watch the horizontals go vertical.

Use a 2x2 slip stitch to create very narrow stripes that read as verticals, not horizontals (see Boo, Too on page 50).

Keep the self-striping yarn in a small area of intarsia on a solid color background.

Slip it good and use a self-striping yarn in place of one solid yarn in a slip stitch or Fair Isle pattern.

Work a secret horizontal, which really shows off self-striping yarn— a wide band at the front edges of a cardigan. How? Knit a section about 4 inches (10cm) wide (or narrower) in the self-striping yarn. It reads as a slimming vertical instead of a chunk-building horizontal.

Knit lace with a self-striping yarn and watch the horizontals break up. Caveat: This only works with *some* yarns in *some* lace patterns. You've got to swatch *big* to see how the color pools, clumps, and repeats. And it still might not work when you knit the full-sized piece. Be prepared to rip and rethink.

Use ombre yarns
(yarns that slowly shade from light to dark along the length of the ball), which can work as long as the gradation is going in the right direction for your bod. Remember to put the light portion on the part of you that you want noticed.

COLOR BLOCKING

The goal here is to keep the *colors* blocky, not you. To make it work, take advantage of the "light colors advance, dark colors recede" concept.

You can add blocks of color to any pattern. By block, we don't mean "a square of color." We mean *areas* of color. As a matter of fact, a curvy shape is more flattering on a curvy body than a square one, because the curvy bits work together rather than the curves fighting the squares.

One of the greatest uses of color blocks for curves is to knit in darker side panels. Voilà—instant waist!

Anything lighter and brighter will get noticed first, so think carefully about where you want the eye to go, and slip some color in there. Edge a neckline in a brighter shade of the body color. Or work a button band in a different color to add an instant vertical. Remember that it can work for you or against you: A brightly colored band around the hem would not be a happy thing for a Butt girl trying to focus attention elsewhere, but it could be brilliant for a Belly girl trying to direct the eye downward.

BEWARE OF MOTIF MANIA!

Repeat it once, repeat it twice. But repeating it all over ain't always so nice.

Motif knitting draws attention to both your mad knitting skills and to whatever part of your body the motif covers. You

---

Motif mantra

ATTENTION ATTRACTING
- Irregular spacing between motifs
- Strong contrast between motifs and background colors
- Inconsistently sized motifs

ATTENTION REPELLING
- Regular spacing between motifs
- Less contrast between the motif and background
- Consistently sized motifs

---

need to consider the size, frequency (if the motif appears more than once), your color choices, and how all these things work together. You will have to swatch to figure this all out, so rent some good movies—ones without subtitles.

Motif size should be in proportion to your body size: The bigger your body, the bigger your motifs should be. If you use a smaller motif, your body will look bigger than it is.

It's up to you to pick and choose between the two lists. Jillian likes high contrast between the colors and regular spacing. Amy likes her motifs in the singular and placed asymmetrically.

You *can* knit a block of mosaic into a solid-color sweater, but because of the potentially huge gauge difference between the mosaic patch and the rest of the sweater, mosaic is usually used as an all-over pattern. (If you can match the mosaic gauge to your sweater gauge, go crazy and use some of the self-striping tips above, like knitting half of the mosaic pattern with a self-striping yarn instead of a solid color.)

With mosaic patterns, you need to determine the feeling the pattern is going to create on the sweater (horizontal, vertical, diagonal) before you commit to it. Most of the time you can figure this out by looking at the chart in the printed pattern, but sometimes you've got to swatch, step back, and squint. If you are changing the colors from the originals used in the design, you *must* swatch before you launch into the sweater, because different colors can take your motif in a whole new or even opposite direction. And don't forget about contrast: If the colors are the same value (the same amount of gray), from a distance, they'll look more like an area of solid-color than a pretty two-color design.

Squinting is one of Jillian's favorite tools. If she can't tell if something feels horizontal or vertical—or if a particular color pops more than the others, or what the negative space between colors or patterns is doing—she squints at it. For her, squinting takes away the hard edges and presents the essence of the design details. It works for her; it might work for you, too.

INTARSIA: FIDDLY ON THE ROOF

When your Aunt Agatha asks for a sweater with a little kitty knit into the front of it, *that's* intarsia. It's also the way you can knit roses, stars, or any colored design into a solid-color sweater. Intarsia can be a block of solid color or a beautifully complex design made up of many colors like the knitted works of art Kaffe Fassett is famous for.

Yes, intarsia can be fiddly thanks to the multiple strands of yarn and the ends to weave in when you're done. But intarsia really rocks for curvy girls, because you can put the motifs *exactly where you want them*, so you don't end up with skulls, flowers, or whatever right on your nip tips. Sound familiar?

THE FAIREST ISLE

Traditional Fair Isle design creates strong widening horizontals. The effect it creates on a sweater can change drastically by the colors you pick, or the way the colors move within the pattern. On the other hand, traditional Fair Isle is great because when people look at you their eyes can't help but dance around the patterns. Why not use traditional motifs in a very Big Girl way instead?

- Use Fair Isle motifs on collars, cuffs, and front bands only (exactly where you choose to put your Fair Isle depends on the Bs you want to flatter).
- Use Fair Isle motifs as spots instead of bands.
- Knit your Fair Isle design from side to side so it goes vertical.

QUICKIE COLOR

Two quick and easy ways to add spots of color are embroidery and felting.

Embroider motifs exactly where you want them, without committing to the math or permanent sweater space. If you don't like how they look, pull 'em out! You can use any embroidery stitch or a combination: stars, flowers, cross stitch, chain. Unlike duplicate stitch (below), where the goal is to mimic knitted-in stitches, embroidery lets you create something you could never, ever knit into your work. Check out *Colorful Stitchery* by Kristin Nicholas for some great design ideas, but first, check out Kristin's felted and embroidered bag on page 152.

Felted motifs sewn or pinned on a sweater are quick and easy. Add a felted flower at the side of a gathered waist or cuff, or at the point of a V-neck. It's a great way to experiment with a spot of color you're not sure is "you" without the long-term commitment.

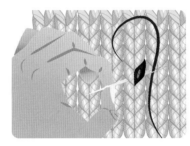

For people who refuse to knit with multiple strands of yarn at one time, but want more color in their finished knits, consider duplicate stitch. You can lay the finished sweater flat and pick exactly which stitch to start your motif with. Amy swears by duplicate stitch.

Take Time for Texture

So far, we've been talking about adding pattern to your knitwear using color. Texture adds pattern *without* changing color. You're creating physical lines when you knit Aran or lace patterns; these lines guide the eyes and create a rhythm in your knitting. Whether it's rumba or rock 'n' roll is up to you.

With heavily textured sweaters, you need to plan differently. More texture means you're creating a thicker and stiffer fabric. So you may want to have more shaping and less ease to make your sweater more flattering.

Ribs, *they* say, don't belong on Big Girls. Say what? Ribs are the ultimate vertical, and an easy way to add shaping. What's not to love?

The key is how you wear your ribs. Focus on fit. (Shut up. We are *not* a broken record.) Ribs can't be tight—on anyone: big, little, square, or round. Skin-tight ribs are ribs pulled out of proportion, changing lines that should be straight into unpredictable waves. Ribs have to skim to stay ribby. Here are some of our best ribbing secrets:

- **The wider the rib, the less it pulls in.** Go and swatch a 1x1 rib. Now swatch a 4x4 rib. See the difference? The 1x1 is a super-sucker, but the 4x4 pulls in gently. Much better.
- **Ribs go with everything.** There's never a reason you can't use ribbing in any knitting pattern wherever it seems right to you. It's the perfect go-with every time.
- **Ribbing can create a waist** without much math. Add a band of ribbing all around your waist. Or just add ribbing at the sides for instant curves—no calculator required.
- **Lace**—it's flirty and feminine. What's not to love? Lace is one of the most versatile textures knitters have in their toolbox.

We love lace as a tool to layer colors. Big openwork lace— shimmery, gently fuzzy, and/or multicolored—works really well. When lace is knitted open and flowy, it lets the color under it show. Shawls are the go-to project for this, but consider the knitter's version of the layered T-shirt look: a long-sleeved, deep-V or scoop-necked pullover in an open-lace pattern, made in a variegated DK or finer yarn, layered over any of the collection of plain, long-sleeved T-shirts in a variety of colors we know you have stashed in your closet. Each shirt color will bring out something different in the lace. Feeling subdued? Go tonal with the undershirt. Feeling like dancing on the bar? Go bright and contrasty.

CABLES AND TWISTS

Cables and twists create gorgeous texture, but they also create direction and volume. Direction is cool—you just need to be happy with what the direction is. Volume, though, takes some clever management. Some cables are deep enough that you can measure their depth with a ruler! A little goes a long way with deeply textured stitch patterns.

Think about cable knitting in terms of curves: sinuous, undulating, sexy curves. If you're not building curves with your cables then you're stacking and twisting stitches over and

A Sincere Ode to Lace

Lace, we love you. Let us count the ways:

- You **lighten the load** visually.

- You are the chameleon of texture stitches. You **work all over**: as an edging, an inset, or a trim. No other type of stitch fits the bill as universally as you do.

- You can be **peek-a-boo or woo-woo**. You can be shy, slutty, or both at the same time. You make us swoon.

- You help knitters **turn disasters into design features**: You can add length to a too-short sweater, turn a misbehaving neckline into a delicate focal point, and make the little bit of yarn we have left for edging be just enough! Like the knitting cavalry, you save the day!

- You are complex, even when you're not. The simplest 4 stitch, 4 row, knit-back repeat looks like it was hard work when done properly. You are **so very satisfying**.

around each other, adding inches and inches, creating—even with all your careful knitting—the most exquisitely cabled shapeless sack.

You can still knit braids. Hell, you can braid like a swiss miss, but keep the stretches between crosses long. Cross every 10 rows, not every 4. It keeps the fabric—and you—smoother.

But what if you love the look of luscious cabled fabric with tons of twists all over? Try these tricks:

Use it in outerwear like jackets and coats. They can be stiffer than next-to-skin garments and still look great. Bonus: You get the long line from shoulder to hip, knee, or calf to make cables. Just promise us you'll wear lean stuff underneath so people don't mistake *you* for everything that's under your coat.

Go as fine-gauge as you can stand. Cables knit from DK-weight yarn are gorgeous.

Mix it up and use ribs and simple knit/purl texture stitches along with your cables. The mix visually lightens while still giving you lots of lush texture.

Knit cables for your couch. How does a gorgeous, chunky, super-bulky Aran-knit throw sound?

KNIT AND PURL

Texture stitches that involve combinations of knit and purl stitches are easy and satisfying. They're like the potato chips of knitting.

Simple all-over knit and purl stitch patterns are easy to follow, memorize, and control. They give substance to the knit fabric, but keep a much lower profile than cables. They can be placed in specific spots or bands, as you'd do with intarsia (without the extra ends to weave in), or you can use them all over.

A quick swatch will tell you if the stitch of your dreams will draw the knitted fabric in or spread it out. Then just mix it with stockinette stitch to high-light your waist or gently flow over happy hips.

While you're swatching your knits and purls, make sure you're not stacking up wide horizontal bands of texture. Even though you're not knitting in bands of color, you could still be knitting wide, unflattering horizontal bands.

On the positive side, knit and purl combos are low-profile ways to add texture. They add less thickness than any other technique we've talked about. They're interesting to knit but not hard in the least, they can be drapey, and there's zero fiddle factor. We love. There is an

infinite variety of combinations of knit/purl stitches to create different patterns. In the first *Treasury of Knitting Patterns* by Barbara Walker, there are 68 knit/purl stitch patterns. Super bonus: With knit/purl combos, you can easily knit vertical bands, stripes, or blocks into your sweaters with no horizontal fallout.

One last surprising tip: Who says sleeves have to match? Your sleeves don't have to match the body of your sweater. No, really, they don't. You can make your sleeves mild or wild. They don't even have to match each other. Add texture and detail on your sleeves, and you can keep your body smooth.

One More ③ indispensable adaptation for big girls

In our first book, we shared the two most indispensable adaptations every Big Girl knitter needs to know—short rows for boobs and waist shaping. Nothing works more body-flattering magic on a knitted rectangle than these two tricks. But they're not the only tricks a knitter should have in her repertoire.

Sometimes taking a different approach is the only way, especially when talking about color and texture on a Big Girl bod. Got your measurement chart filled out? Good! Get your calculator, a little more caffeine, and let's rock a new adaptation!

Get a little on the side!

Side panels add extra width to a garment in the easiest way possible. Simply put, they're pieces you knit separately (usually), and then sew into a sweater's side seams. We love them because you can use them to make a heavily textured or complicated colorwork sweater bigger without messing with texture or color charts for the front and back pieces. They're a great way to customize not only the size of a sweater but also the look—you can do side panels in different colors and textures from the rest of the body. Side panels work in sweaters that already have waist shaping, or you can add waist shaping within the panels to a plain rectangle sweater and make it really fit you!

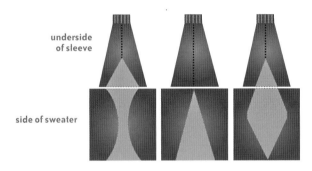

underside of sleeve

side of sweater

The simplest side panels are straight rectangles that add a consistent amount of width to each part of the sweater below the armholes. Or side panels can be worked in a variety of other shapes to add different amounts of width in different areas.

- Hourglass-shaped panels do double duty by offering both extra width and waist shaping, adding more width at the bust and hip than at the waist.
- Triangular panels can be used to add width at the hip but none at the bust, or just the opposite. They can be only a handful of inches in length, adding the critical inches only near the top or bottom of a side seam, or they can taper gradually over the full length of the seam.
- Diamond-shaped panels are useful if more width is needed at the waist than above or below.

To decide what sort of side panel you need, take a look at your sweater pattern. What are the finished measurements at the bust, waist, and hip? Simply calculate your desired sweater measurements—your own bust, waist, and hip

measurements plus the desired amount of ease. The difference between the sweater's finished measurements and what you want them to be—*that's* what defines the size and shape of the side panel! For more information about choosing the right size for you, see "Choose a Size" on page 26 in Chapter 4.

Time for a new pretend Big Girl knitter to help us illustrate our point. Last year, our pretend girl knit herself an intricately cabled sweater. A rectangular thing of beauty! (She hadn't read our book back then.) But in the excitement of starting a new pattern, she completely forgot to check the  dimensions of the finished sweater. In fact, she didn't check the finished measurements for the size she'd knitted until the pieces were done and something seemed not right. She'd thought an XL would fit her. That's the size she wears in all the clothing she buys at retail stores! But XL in this pattern was 6" (12.5cm) too narrow to fit her the way she wanted it to. Bugger.

The knitted pieces have been languishing in a pile of UFOs (unfinished objects.) "What's the point of finishing the sweater," she thinks. But wait, there's hope! Let's teach her how to knit some stockinette side panels.

First, she needs to give us some numbers. Her chart after she filled it in is on page 23.

Sweaters that fit our knitter well have a circumference of about 50" (127cm) at the bust and hips. Her actual bust and hips measure 46" (117cm). Her beautifully knit but too-small sweater pieces are 22" (56 cm) wide, yielding a sweater with a circumference of 44" (112cm).

Step 1: She figures out how much fabric she needs to add with her side panels.

DSW – **ASW** = **SWS** (*Sweater Width Shortfall)*
50" (127cm) – 44" (112cm)= 6" (15cm)

So her side panels will total 6" (15cm) in width, 3" (7.5cm) wide **each** at their widest point. What does that translate to in stitches? 3" (7.5cm) panel x 4 stitches/inch = 12 stitches + 2 selvedge stitches = 14 stitches

So her side panels will be 14 stitches wide at the top and bottom. What are the 2 selvedge stitches for? One stitch is

What is it?	Secret code	Our girlfriend's numbers
body stuff		
BUST	B	46" (117cm)
WAIST	W	42" (106.5cm)
HIPS	H	46" (117cm)
sweater stuff		
STITCHES PER INCH (2.5cm)	S	4
ROWS PER INCH (2.5cm)	R	6
LOWER LENGTH (HEM TO WAIST)	LL	6" (15cm)
UPPER LENGTH (WAIST TO ARMHOLE)	UL	8" (20.5cm)
ACTUAL SWEATER WIDTH	ASW	44" (112cm)
DESIRED SWEATER WIDTH	DSW	50" (127cm)
SW SHORTFALL: DSW - ASW	SWS	6" (15cm)
SHORTFALL PER SIDE: SWS - 2	SPW	3" (7.5cm)
CONVERT SPW TO STITCHES: SPW x S + 2		14
DESIRED SPW AT WAIST:	SPWw	1" (2.5cm)
CONVERT SPWw TO STITCHES: SPW x S + 2		6

needed on each side of the panel so she can sew the panel into the side seam, leaving the 3 full inches (7.5 cm) of the panel to do their job.

She has an hourglass figure (but we like her anyway), which looks great with some waist shaping, so she'll make her side panels hourglass-shaped as well. We don't want to taper the panels down to nothing at the waist because that wouldn't give her enough fabric to sew the sweater together. Let's give the waist portion of her side panel a little less ease than at the bust and hips. That way it'll show off her hourglass figure even more! We'll taper each panel down to 1" (2.5cm) at the waist.

1" (width of panel at waist) x 4 stitches/inch (2.5cm) = 4 stitches + 2 selvedge stitches = 6 stitches

The panel is 14 stitches wide at the top and has to decrease to 6 stitches at the waist. That's 8 stitches to decrease, then increase again. You decrease on both sides of the panel, so 8 total stitches = 4 stitches to decrease from each edge. That's 4 decrease rows.

Step 2: How many rows does she decrease over?

(LL – 1) x R = number of rows over which to work her decreases

(6 – 1) x 6 = 30

So she has 30 rows to spread her decreases over. One Big Girl rule is that we usually set aside 2" (5cm) at the waist—an inch each from the LL and the UL—to work the slimmest part of the piece, whether it's the front of a sweater with waist shaping, or an hourglass-shaped side panel like we're working here.

She'll steal 2 rows from the 2" (5cm) she'd work at the "waist" of the side panel, and add them to the lower section, so she has 32 rows to work her decreases over. This is just to make the math easier.

32 rows ÷ 4 decrease rows = 1 decrease row every 8 rows

See? That's a nice round number. Now she's got to increase back again. It goes like this:

(UL – 1) x R = number of rows over which to work her increases

(8 – 1) x 6 = 42

So she has 42 rows to spread her increases over. She can take 2 rows from this 42 and give them back to the 2" (5cm) of stockinette at the waist, which leaves her with 40 rows. This also makes her math tidier.

40 rows ÷ 4 increase rows = 1 increase row every 10 rows

Using all this information, here's how she would work this panel: Cast on 14 stitches. Work one row in stockinette. (This extra row is worked so the first row and decrease row can both be on the right side of the piece. We'll subtract this row from the rows at the waist section later.) Work 7 more rows in pattern.

Work a decrease row: K1, k2tog, knit to last 3 stitches, ssk, k1. Repeat these 8 rows 3 more times; all 4 decrease rows have been worked. Now work 11 rows in stockinette stitch. This is the 2" (5cm) at the waist, less the one row she added to the bottom of the piece.

Work an increase row: K1, m1 (any increase will work), knit to last stitch, m1, k1. Work 9 rows in stockinette stitch. Repeat these 10 rows 3 more times; all 4 increase rows have been worked, and her side panel is finished!

"But," you ask, "what if she wants to knit a diamond-shaped or triangular panel instead of an hourglass-shaped one?" Good question! She would fill out the chart in exactly the same way, no matter which shape she wanted. In fact, filling out this chart would help her figure out which type of panel would serve her best. If she decided to work a diamond-shaped panel, she would work *increase* rows to reach the desired panel width at the waist, and *decrease* rows to obtain the right width at the underarm. If a triangular panel was in order, she would taper the panel down from the desired width at the hem, to 2 stitches (for the seam allowances) at the bust. Or, if she was making an inverted triangle, she would increase from 2 stitches at the hem to the desired number at the bust. It's that easy.

Of course, changing the width of a sweater under the arm means the sleeve needs to be widened at the underarm as well, or it won't fit into the armhole. Our Big Girl needs to make a triangular sleeve panel to fit into the sleeve seam to widen it. How much does it need to be widened? It needs to start out as wide as the side panel at the underarm, so our Big Girl casts on 14 stitches. The panel needs to narrow gradually until only the 2 selvedge stitches remain. Having 12 stitches to decrease means she needs 6 decrease rows to decrease away all 12 stitches.

The sleeve panel itself should be at least ⅓ to ½ of the sleeve length. Her sleeve is 18" (15.5cm) long, so she wants the panel to be between 6 (15cm) and 9 (23cm) inches long. She decreases every 8 rows:

6 decrease rows worked every 8 rows = 48 rows
48 rows ÷ 6 rows/inch (2.5cm) = 8 inches (20.5cm).

Perfect length! Once her side panels and sleeve panels are sewn into the side and sleeve seams, the sleeves will fit nicely into the armholes.

Our girl has now turned a beautifully textured, too-small rectangle into a curvy, cabled, beautifully textured sweater that fits her perfectly! Now it's your turn. Here's your chart!

What is it?	Secret code	My numbers
body stuff		
BUST	B	
WAIST	W	
HIPS	H	
sweater stuff		
STITCHES PER INCH (2.5cm)	S	
ROWS PER INCH (2.5cm)	R	
LOWER LENGTH (HEM TO WAIST)	LL	
UPPER LENGTH (WAIST TO ARMHOLE)	UL	
ACTUAL SWEATER WIDTH	ASW	
DESIRED SWEATER WIDTH	DSW	
SW SHORTFALL: DSW - ASW	SWS	
SHORTFALL PER SIDE: SWS - 2	SPW	
CONVERT SPW TO STITCHES: SPW x S + 2		
DESIRED SPW AT WAIST:	SPWw	
CONVERT SPWw TO STITCHES: SPW x S + 2		

4

the plain
Vanilla
Customized-
by-You
pullover

Now it's your turn. Allow us to present the Plain Vanilla Customized-by-You Pullover. Just plug in your measurements, do a few super-simple calculations, and you'll have a pattern for a sweater customized to fit exactly the way you want it to, for exactly your curvalicious body and no one else's.

Where's the picture of this sweater? There *is* no picture. We want your Plain Vanilla to be yours, and no two Big Girls will knit the same Plain Vanilla. We want you to imagine *only you* looking gorgeous in this sweater. You're welcome.

Plain Vanilla is a scoop neck, stockinette stitch, hourglass-shaped sweater, designed so you can rock all three Bs. It uses worsted weight yarn for the quickest Big Girl–friendly knit possible and is suitable for yarns wooly, non-wooly, and just about every fiber blend in between.

This sweater takes advantage of the essential adaptations we taught you in *BGK*—boob short rows and waist shaping. To make it easier, we've included a slightly updated version of the short row and waist shaping charts on page 28, tweaked to incorporate feedback from our BGK fitting-class students. We think these charts are even easier to follow than the originals.

The one key thing you need before you can go much further is a set of your current measurements. Remember the measuring chart (page 11) that you groaned over in Chapter 1? If you've had your measuring party and filled it in, all of the numbers you need for this (or any other) pattern will be right at your fingertips. If you didn't fill it out, we'll wait while you call your best knitting girlfriend and get yourself truly measured. There's no point in skipping this step. You want to look fab in your sweaters? You want your sweater to fit? You must measure, period. Bite the bullet, and just do it.

Grab your favorite life preserver (coffee, chocolate, a little salsa music?) and a calculator and jump in the deep end with us.

CHOOSE A SIZE

The first place you should look in any pattern is the finished measurements.

> **If a pattern doesn't list finished measurements, either on their own or on a schematic drawing of the parts of the sweater, pick a different pattern. Guessing isn't fun when you're knitting. It probably means you're wasting your valuable knitting time.**

How do you pick which number to knit? It's easy.

You know your actual bust measurement. Think about how you want this sweater to fit, and add the right amount of ease to get you there. So if your chest (48" [122cm]) plus your favorite ease measurement (4" [10cm], for an average fit) is 52" (132cm), you're gonna knit the size that finishes up at 52" (132cm) around. If you have a hell of a time visualizing stuff like this based on numbers alone, pull out your favorite-fitting sweater and measure its chest. If you do that, you won't need any math—just take the number right off the sweater and try to match it in the finished measurements of the pattern. Sometimes you'll have to pick the closest number to your ideal, because sizes can fall right in between your boobs (ouch!) If you've got to pick between two sizes, choose the smaller one. Hey, knitted fabric stretches.

Don't forget to check the sweater and sleeve length against your measurement chart. It's a snap to shorten and lengthen sweater parts when they're on the needles, but a massive pain in the tush after the sweater is done!

HEM IT!

We have three ways to finish the bottom edge of your sweater. All lay wonderfully flat without sucking in and making sweet unwanted love to your squishy bottom bits. Pick the one you like best!

1. Turned edge | *A totally flat, smooth edge, double thickness.*

Using a needle *one size smaller* than the needle you'll knit the sweater body with, cast on the required number of body stitches using a provisional cast-on, such as the Crochet Chain Cast-on (see page 33). Work in stockinette stitch for 2" (5cm), ending with a wrong-side row. Purl the next row (yes, on the right side) to create a tidy turning row. Work in stockinette stitch for 2" (5cm) more, again ending with a wrong-side row.

Magically attach the hem like this: Remove the waste yarn from your provisional cast-on

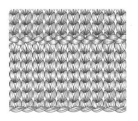

and place the live stitches on a spare needle. Fold the hem along the turning row toward the back of the work, so that the wrong sides of the hem and the facing are touching each other, and the stitches on the spare needle are directly behind the stitches on the working needle. Knit the first stitch from the body together with the first stitch from the cast-on edge. Work across the row in this way, knitting each stitch from the working needle together with the corresponding stitch from the spare needle, until the two rows of stitches have been knit into one single row. Now change to the needle size called for in the pattern and continue knitting upward!

2. Seed stitch edge | *A wonderfully nubby band that lays perfectly flat.*

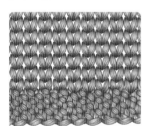

Worked over an odd number of stitches:
Row 1: *K1, p1; repeat from * to last stitch, k1.
Repeat this row for seed stitch.
OR
Worked over an even number of stitches:

Row 1 (RS) *K1, p1; repeat from * to end.
Row 2 (WS) *P1, k1; repeat from * to end.
Repeat these 2 rows for seed stitch.

Seed stitch spreads out, so you need just a little math and a trick or two to make sure your hem doesn't flare. First, use a needle *one size smaller* than the size used for the sweater body. Next, it's the math part, but it's not scary. To counteract the flare, the seed stitch edge is worked on 90 percent of the sweater body stitches. To figure out 90 percent simply multiply the number of stitches you're supposed to cast on for the body by 0.9. If you get a fraction, round down to the closest whole number. When you're finished knitting the edging, but before you can start knitting the sweater body, you need to add the stitches back that you left out when you cast on. How? You just increase evenly across the row.

2. Classic ribbing | *Can't let go of a classic ribbed edging?*

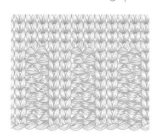

Here's one that won't hang on too tight. No boa constrictors here. Work a 3x3 or 4x4 rib on a needle *one size larger* than the body needle. If you like *flat + nubby* instead of *flat +*

ribbed, try working reverse stockinette ribs in garter stitch instead. To do this, work the right-side rows of your ribbed edge as you normally would, but purl *all* the stitches of the wrong-side rows. Here are directions for a 2x2 *flat + nubby* Garter Rib, worked over a multiple of 4 stitches + 2:

> **Row 1 (RS)** K2, *p2, k2; repeat from * to end.
> **Row 2 (WS)** Purl.
> Repeat these 2 rows for 2x2 *flat + nubby* Garter Rib.

Try swatching different ribbings to see how they look in your yarn. For a cool textured ribbing, check out the stitch pattern for Finagle on page 134!

Worksheets

Before you work through the worksheets on page 28, you need some more information about the dimensions of the sweater you'll be making. As written, the sweater, which begins on page 29, is 25 (25, 25, 25½)" (63.5 [63.5, 63.5, 64.8]cm) long. The underarm is 8½ (9, 9, 9½)" (21.5 [23, 23, 24]cm) deep, and the length from the underarm to the lower edge is 15½ (15, 15, 15)" (39.5 [38, 38, 38]cm). For those of you keeping track, the shoulder shaping makes up the last 1" (2.5cm) of length.

Have a friend measure you. Starting from the midpoint of your shoulder, measure down the side of your back to help determine where the underarm and lower edge of the sweater will sit on you, and where the waist of the sweater will hit compared to your own waist. (You'll need this information when working through the Waist Shaping chart on page 28.) If you want the sweater to be longer or shorter than written, you need to decide now—write this down somewhere—so you can factor these changes into your calculations.

One more important note: The edging of the sweater is 2" (5cm) deep, and you won't begin working waist decreases until after you have completed the edging. To accommodate this, subtract 2" (5cm) from the Lower Length measurement in the Waist Shaping worksheet.

And now for the fun stuff:

Super-Duper Big Girl Knits Bottom-Up Waist Shaping Worksheet

What is it?	Secret code	My numbers
Body stuff		
WAIST *(your actual)*	W	54
EASE *(your favorite ease)*	E	2
IDEAL SWEATER WAIST: **W + E**	ISW	56
Sweater stuff		
STITCH GAUGE PER INCH *(2.5cm)*	SR	5
ROW GAUGE PER INCH *(2.5cm)*	RG	6
LOWER LENGTH *(hem to waist)*	LL	7½
UPPER LENGTH *(waist to armhole)*	UL	7½
LOWER LENGTH−1 *(the −1 accounts for half of the 2" [5cm] straight at the waist —decreases are worked over this measurement)*	LL − 1	6½
UPPER LENGTH−1 *(the −1 accounts for the other half—increases are worked over this measurement)*	UL − 1	6½
SWEATER WAIST *(from the pattern—it's probably the same as the finished Bust measurement)*	SW	56
DIFFERENCE AT WAIST: **SW − ISW**	DW	2
TOTAL DECREASE STITCHES: **DW x S**	TDS	10
NUMBER OF STITCHES TO DECREASE AT EACH EDGE OF FRONT & BACK: **TDS ÷ 4**	TDSe	2
DECREASE AT EACH EDGE OF EVERY____TH ROW: **(LL − 1 x R) ÷ TDSe**	WDR *(waist decrease rows)*	18
INCREASE AT EACH EDGE EVERY____TH ROW: **(UL − 1 x R) ÷ TDSe**	WIR *(waist increase rows)*	18

Super-Duper Big Girl Knits Bottom-Up Short Row Worksheet

What is it?	Secret code	My numbers
body stuff		
FRONT LENGTH *(shoulder to front waist, over your boobs)*	FL	24
BACK LENGTH *(shoulder to back waist)*	BL	20
SIDE LENGTH *(hem to bottom of bra band—1" [2.5cm] or 2" [5cm] below armhole)*	SL	12
NIPPLE DISTANCE *(horizontal distance between nipples)*	ND	13
TASTEFUL NIPPLE DISTANCE *(so short rows don't peak on your nipples):* **ND + 2" (5cm)**	TND	15
sweater stuff		
STITCH GAUGE PER INCH *(2.5cm)*	S	5
ROW GAUGE PER INCH *(2.5cm)*	R	6
SWEATER BUST	SB	56
BUST DART DEPTH: **FL − BL**	BDD	4
BUST DART ROWS: **BDD X R** *This must be an even number! If it is not, round down to the nearest even number.*	BDR	24
FRONT SWEATER WIDTH: **SB ÷ 2**	FSW	28
BUST DART WIDTH: **(FSW − TND) ÷ 2**	BDW	7
BUST DART STITCHES: **BDW X S**	BDS	35
TURNING POINTS FOR EACH SIDE: **BDR ÷ 2**	TP	12
SHORT ROW INCREMENTS: **BDS ÷ TP**	SRI	3

plain vanilla customized-by-you
pullover pattern

DIFFICULTY: 1
BY: JILLIAN MORENO AND MANDY MOORE

16 (17, 17, 18)"

17½ (17½, 18, 18)"

12 (12½, 12½, 13)"

SIZES

L (1X, 2X, 3X)

FINISHED MEASUREMENTS

Chest: 44 (48, 52, 56)" (112 [122, 132, 142]cm)
Length: 25 (25, 25, 25½)" (63.5 [63.5, 63.5, 64.8]cm)

MATERIALS

Aran weight yarn; approximately 1,100 (1,200, 1,250, 1,360) yds (915 [1,006, 1,098, 1,244]m)
1 set US #7 (4.5mm) straight needles
1 US #6 (4mm) circular needle, 16" (40cm) long
Stitch holders
Tapestry needle

GAUGE

18 stitches and 24 rows = 4" (10cm)

ABBREVIATIONS AND TECHNIQUES

See page 32.

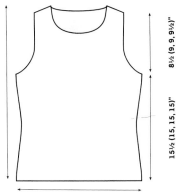

25 (25, 25, 25½)"

8½ (9, 9, 9½)"

15½ (15, 15, 15)"

22 (24, 26, 28)"

BACK

Cast on 100 (108, 118, 126) stitches.

Work your edging of choice (page 26, Hem It!) until the work measures 2" (5cm).

Once the edging is complete, work waist decreases according to the calculations you made in the Waist Shaping worksheet. You will decrease 1 stitch at each edge of the row every __18__ (WDR) rows, __2__ (TDSe) times.

Work decreases on right-side rows as follows:

Decrease Row (RS) K1, k2tog, knit to last 3 stitches, ssk, k1.

To decrease on a wrong-side row, work as follows:

Decrease Row (WS) P1, p2tog tbl, purl to last 3 stitches, p2tog, p1. Decreasing in this way will give you invisible decreases, and will leave your pieces with smooth edges for easy seaming.

After you have worked your last Decrease Row, work 2" (5cm) without further shaping, then begin the waist increases.

Work 1 Increase Row (see below).

Increase 1 stitch at each edge of the row every __18__ (WIR) rows, __1__ (TDSe – 1) times (you will have increased a total of ____ (TDSe) times).

If you're working in stockinette stitch, work increases on right-side rows as follows:

Increase Row (RS) K2, m1, knit to last 2 stitches, m1, k2.

To increase on a wrong-side row, work as follows:

Increase Row (WS) P2, m1p, purl to last 2 stitches, m1p, p2.

Continue in stockinette stitch until the work measures 15½ (15, 15, 15)" (39.5 [38, 38, 38]cm) or desired length to underarm, ending with a wrong-side row.

shape armholes

Bind off 6 (7, 10, 11) stitches at the beginning of the next 2 rows—88 (94, 98, 104) stitches.

Next Row (RS) K1, k2tog, knit to last 3 stitches, ssk, k1.

Purl 1 row.

Repeat these 2 rows 9 (10, 10, 13) times more—68 (72, 76, 76) stitches.

Continue in stockinette stitch until the work measures 23 (23, 23, 23½)" (58.5 [58.5, 58.5, 59.5]cm) and armhole measures 7½ (8, 8, 8½)" (19 [20.5, 20.5, 21.5]cm) inches from initial bind-off, ending with a wrong-side row.

shape back neckline

Next Row (RS) K15 (16, 16, 16) and place these stitches on a stitch holder; bind off next 38 (40, 44, 44) stitches, knit to end—15 (16, 16, 16) stitches.

Purl 1 row.

Next Row (RS) K1, k2tog, knit to end—14 (15, 15, 15) stitches.

Work 3 rows in stockinette stitch, ending with a wrong-side row.

shape left shoulder

K9 (10, 10, 10), W&T. Purl to end.

K5, W&T. Purl to end.

Knit all stitches, picking up wraps and working them together with wrapped stitches.

Purl 1 row. Place all stitches on a stitch holder.

shape right shoulder

Replace the held stitches of the Right Shoulder on the needle with the right side facing, and reattach the yarn.

Next Row (RS) Knit to last 3 stitches, ssk, k1.

Work 4 rows in stockinette stitch, ending with a right-side row.

P10 (10, 10, 10), W&T. Knit to end.

P5, W&T. Knit to end.

Purl all stitches, picking up wraps and working them together with wrapped stitches.

Knit 1 row. Place all stitches on a stitch holder.

FRONT

Cast on and work the edging and waist shaping as for the Back. At the same time, work short-row bust shaping as follows:

Work until the piece measures _____ (SL), ending with a wrong-side row.

Short Row 1 (RS) Knit to last _____ (SRI) stitches, W&T.

Short Row 2 (WS) Purl to last _____ (SRI) stitches, W&T.

Short Row 3 (RS) Knit to last _____ (SRI x 2) stitches, W&T.

Short Row 2 (WS) Purl to last _____ (SRI x 2) stitches, W&T.

Continue in this way, working each short row _____ (SRI) stitches shorter than the last, until you have worked _____ (BDR) short rows. You will end on a wrong side short row.

Next Row (RS) Knit to end, picking up wraps and working them together with wrapped stitches.

Purl 1 row, picking up remaining wraps and working them together with wrapped stitches.

Very Important: *Do not* count the short rows when counting rows between waist shaping rows! Count the rows along or near the edge of the work to be sure you are counting correctly. Likewise, the length of the work must be measured along the edge, because the center of the piece will be longer than the edge.

Continue in stockinette stitch until the work measures 15½ (15, 15, 15)" (39.5 [38, 38, 38]cm) or desired length to underarm, ending with a wrong-side row.

shape armholes

Bind off 6 (7, 10, 11) stitches at the beginning of the next 2 rows—88 (94, 98, 104) stitches.

Next Row (RS) K1, k2tog, knit to last 3 stitches, ssk, k1.

Purl 1 row.

Repeat these 2 rows 9 (10, 10, 13) times more—68 (72, 76, 76) stitches.

Continue in stockinette stitch until the work measures 21 (21, 21, 21½)" (53.5 [53.5, 53.5, 54.6]cm), and armhole measures 5½ (6, 6, 6½)" (14 [15, 15, 16.5]cm) from initial bind-off, ending with a wrong-side row.

shape neckline

Next Row (RS) K21 (26, 27, 27) and place these stitches on stitch holder; bind off the next 20 (20, 22, 22) stitches, knit to end—24 (26, 27, 27) stitches.

Purl 1 row.

Next Row (RS) Bind off 2 stitches, knit to end.

Repeat these 2 rows 2 (3, 3, 3) times more—18 (18, 19, 19) stitches.

Purl 1 row.

Next Row (RS) K1, k2tog, knit to end.

Repeat these 2 rows 3 (2, 3, 3) times more—14 (15, 15, 15) stitches.

Work 3 (3, 1, 1) rows in stockinette stitch, ending with a wrong-side row.

K10 (10, 10, 10), W&T. Purl to end.

K5, W&T. Purl to end.

Knit all stitches, picking up wraps and working them together with wrapped stitches.

Purl 1 row. Place all stitches on a stitch holder.

shape left front neckline and shoulder

Place the held stitches of the Left Front on the needle with the right side facing, and reattach the yarn.

Knit 1 row.

Next Row (WS) Bind off 2 stitches, purl to end.

Repeat these 2 rows 2 (3, 3, 3) times more—18 (18, 19, 19) stitches.

Next Row (RS) Knit to last 3 stitches, ssk, k1.

Purl 1 row.

Repeat these 2 rows 3 (2, 3, 3) times more—14 (15, 15, 15) stitches.

Work 3 (3, 1, 1) rows in stockinette stitch, ending with a right-side row.

P10 (10, 10, 10), W&T. Knit to end.

P5, W&T. Knit to end.

Purl all stitches, picking up wraps and working them together with wrapped stitches.

Knit 1 row. Place all stitches on a stitch holder.

SLEEVES (MAKE 2)

Note: As written, the sleeves are 17½ (17½, 18, 18)" (44.5 [44.5, 45.5, 45.5]cm) long. If you wish to lengthen or shorten the sleeves, you will need to work more or fewer rows in stockinette stitch between the Increase Rows. Our gauge is 6 rows per inch, so for every inch you wish to lengthen or shorten the sleeves, you will need to work 6 rows more or 6 rows less; try to space these rows evenly throughout the sleeve shaping.

Cast on 54 (56, 56, 58) stitches.

Work your edging of choice until the work measures 2" (5cm). Once the edging is complete, continue with Sleeve as follows:

Increase Row (RS) K2, m1, knit to last 2 stitches, m1, k2.

Work 9 rows in stockinette stitch.

Repeat these 10 rows 4 (3, 3, 0) times more—64 (64, 64, 60) stitches.

Work Increase Row.

Work 7 rows in stockinette stitch.

Repeat these 8 rows 3 (5, 5, 9) times more—72 (76, 76, 80) stitches. Continue in stockinette stitch until the work measures 17 (17, 17.5, 17.5, 17.5, 18, 18)" (43 [43, 44.5, 44.5, 44.5, 45.5, 45.5]cm) or desired length to underarm, ending with a wrong-side row.

Bind off 6 (7, 10, 11) stitches at the beginning of the next 2 rows—60 (52, 56, 58) stitches.

Size L Only

Next Row (RS) K1, k2tog, knit to last 3 stitches, ssk, k1.

Next Row (WS) P1, p2tog tbl, purl to last 3 stitches, p2tog, p1—56 stitches.

Sizes 1X, 2X, 3X Only

Work 4 rows in stockinette stitch, ending with a wrong-side row.

Next Row (RS) K1, k2tog, knit to last 3 stitches, ssk, k1.

Work 3 rows in stockinette stitch.

Repeat these 4 rows—(3, 1, 2) times more—(44, 52, 52) stitches.

All Sizes

Next Row (RS) K1, k2tog, knit to last 3 stitches, ssk, k1.

Purl 1 row.

Repeat these 2 rows 16 (9, 13, 12) times more—22 (24, 24, 26) stitches.

Bind off 2 stitches at the beginning of the next 4 rows. Bind off the remaining 14 (16, 16, 18) stitches.

FINISHING

assembly

Join shoulders using the three-needle bind-off (page 33).

Sew sleeves into armholes. Sew sleeve seams and side seams.

neckline

Using the circular needle and beginning at the right shoulder seam, pick up and knit 3 stitches for every 4 rows and 1 stitch in each bound-off stitch around the neckline.

Join to work in the round and work your preferred edging for at least 1" (2.5cm). If you wish to work a Turned Edge for your neckline, see the directions below.

Bind off all stitches loosely.

Weave in all ends and block as desired.

For a Turned Edge, purl 1 round to form a turning ridge.

Knit 3 rounds.

Next Round: *K10, m1; repeat from * until fewer than 10 stitches remain in the round, knit to end.

Knit 3 rounds.

Do not bind off; instead, fold the edge to the inside of the work and sew the live stitches to the inside of the sweater, taking care not to sew too tightly.

the Patterns

The **B3**   **boobs** | **belly** | **butt**

Levels of Difficulty

Each of the patterns in this book is rated according to how much concentration it requires. Just look for these numbers next to the B3 icons, and select a project that's right for you.

1 HALF-CAF (BRAIN NUDGE)
straightforward knitting with shaping

2 ESPRESSO (MODEST AMOUNT OF BRAIN FUEL)
shaping, color work, multiple stitch patterns

3 TRIPLE-SHOT CAFFEINE BOMB WITH WHIPPED CREAM **(ALL BRAIN CELLS ON FULL)**
complex shaping with multiple things happening at the same time

Abbreviations

K: Knit

K2tog: Knit the next 2 stitches together as if they were 1 stitch (forms a right-leaning decrease).

Kfb: Knit into the front and the back of the stitch

LLI (Left Lifted Increase): Use the left needle to pick up the stitch 2 rows below the last stitch on the right needle. Knit into this stitch (1 stitch has been increased).

M1 (Make 1): Insert the left needle, from front to back, under the horizontal strand of yarn which runs between the last stitch on the right needle, and the first stitch on the left needle. Knit into the back of this loop.

M1L (Make 1 Left): Insert the left needle, from front to back, under the horizontal strand which lies between the stitch just knit, and the next stitch. Knit this stitch through its back loop.

M1R (Make 1 Right): Insert the left needle, from back to front, under the horizontal strand which lies between the stitch just knit, and the next stitch. Knit this stitch through its front loop.

M1P (Make 1 Purl): Insert the left needle, from front to back, under the horizontal strand of yarn which runs between the last stitch on the right needle, and the first stitch on the left needle. Purl into the back of this loop.

P: Purl

P2tog: Purl the next 2 stitches together as if they were 1 stitch (forms a right-leaning decrease).

Pfb: Purl in the front and the back of the stitch

RLI (Right Lifted Increase): Insert the right needle into the stitch below the next stitch on the left needle. Pick up this stitch and place it on the left needle, then knit into it—1 stitch has been increased.

SKP (Slip 1, knit 1, pass slipped stitch over): Slip 1, knit the next stitch, pass the slipped stitch over the stitch just knit.

S2KP (Slip 2, Knit 1, Pass slipped stitches over): Slip the next 2 stitches together, knitwise, as if to work a k2tog. Knit the next stitch, then pass both slipped stitches, together, over the stitch just knit. This forms a centered double decrease.

SK2P (Slip 1, knit 2tog, pass slipped stitch over): Slip the next stitch knitwise to the right needle. Knit the next 2 stitches together, then pass the slipped stitch over the stitch just knit. This forms a left-leaning double decrease.

Ssk (Slip, slip, knit): Slip the next 2 stitches knitwise, one at a time, to the right needle. Insert the left needle back into the back of these 2 stitches and knit them together. Forms a left-leaning decrease.

Sssk (Slip, slip, slip, knit): Slip the next 3 stitches knitwise, one at a time, to the right needle. Insert the left needle back into the back of these 3 stitches and knit them together. Forms a left-leaning double decrease.

Tbl: Through back loop(s)

W&T: Wrap and turn; see "Techniques."

YO: Yarn over. Wrap the yarn once around the right needle, so that it goes over the needle from the front to the back. This forms an increase, and will also form a hole in the work.

Techniques

CROCHET CHAIN CAST-ON

Using waste yarn, work a crochet chain several stitches longer than the number of stitches to be cast on. Starting 1 or 2 stitches in from the end of the chain and using the working yarn, pick up and knit 1 stitch in the back loop of each chain stitch until the required number of stitches have been worked. Later, the chain will be unraveled and the resulting live stitches picked up.

THREE-NEEDLE BIND-OFF

Hold both pieces of knitting with right sides together.

Insert needle into first stitch on front needle and first stitch on back needle, and knit them together. Repeat this for the next stitch on the front and back needles. Draw the first stitch worked over the second stitch.

Repeat from * to * until all stitches have been bound off. Break yarn and draw through remaining stitch.

WRAP & TURN (W&T)

Note: *The directions that follow are written for short rows worked in stockinette stitch.*

To wrap and turn on a right-side row, knit to point specified in pattern, bring yarn to front of work between needles, slip next stitch to right-hand needle, bring yarn around this stitch to back of work, slip stitch back to left-hand needle, turn work to begin purling back in the other direction.

To wrap and turn on a wrong-side row, purl to point specified in pattern, bring yarn to back of work between needles, slip next stitch to right-hand needle, bring yarn around this stitch to front of work, slip stitch back to left-hand needle, turn work to begin knitting back in the other direction.

Working Wraps Together with Wrapped Stitches:

When working rows which follow short rows, work the "wraps" at the turning points of the short rows, together with the stitches they wrap, as follows:

When working a right-side row: Knit to wrapped stitch. Slip next stitch from left needle to right needle, use tip of left needle to pick up "wrap" and place it on right needle, insert left needle into both wrap and stitch, and knit them together.

When working a wrong-side row: Purl to wrapped stitch. Slip next stitch from left needle to right needle, use tip of left needle to pick up "wrap" and place it on right needle, slip both wrap and stitch back to left needle, purl together through back loops.

bountiful
bohus

DIFFICULTY: 2
BY: CHRISSY GARDINER

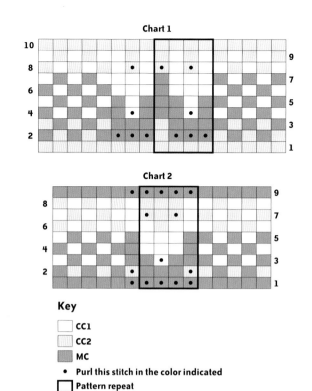

The quintessential yoke sweater, done Big Girl style: cardigan (so you can open or close depending on the level of warmth you're in the mood for), waist shaping (of course!), and a little flaring at the cuff (to modernize). It's knit in the round and steeked, which makes for easy knitting and a cool way to impress your friends: "You *cut* your sweater up the middle?"

For a little online steeky handholding, see this informative article (with pictures!) on Knitty®:
http://www.knitty.com/ISSUEspring03/FEATsteeks.html

SIZES
L (1X, 2X, 3X, 4X, 5X)
Shown in size 1X

FINISHED MEASUREMENTS

Chest: 40 (44, 48, 52, 56, 60)" (101.5 [112, 122, 132, 142, 152.5]cm)
Hips: 47 (51, 55, 59, 63, 67)" (119.5 [129.5, 139.5, 150, 160, 170]cm)
Length: 24 (24, 24, 25, 26, 26)" (61 [61, 61, 63.5, 66, 66]cm)

MATERIALS
Cascade 220; 100% Peruvian Highland wool;
220 yd (201m) per 3½ oz (100g) skein
6 (6, 7, 8, 8, 9) skeins #9412 black/brown (MC)
1 skein #8010 cream (CC1)
1 skein #8021 beige (CC2)
1 US #7 (4.5mm) circular needle, 36" (90cm) long,
or size needed to obtain gauge
1 US #5 (3.75mm) circular needle, 24" (60cm) long
1 set US #7 (4.5mm) double-pointed needles
Note: *If a 36" (90cm) circular needle is unavailable, a 32" (80cm) needle may be substituted for the smaller sizes, or a 40" (100cm) needle for the larger sizes.*

For all sizes, a 12" (30cm) circular needle may be substituted for the double-pointed needles.
Stitch markers
Split ring marker (optional)
Safety pins
Waste yarn
Cable needle
Tapestry needle
Sewing machine
Sewing thread
Sewing needle
6 buttons, 1" (25mm) diameter

GAUGE
20 stitches and 24 rows = 4" (10cm) in stockinette stitch using the larger needle

ABBREVIATIONS AND TECHNIQUES
See page 32.

STITCH PATTERN
C4F Slip the next 2 stitches to a cable needle and hold in the front of the work, k2, k2 from the cable needle.

LOWER BODY

Using the larger circular needle and MC, cast on 236 (256, 276, 296, 316, 336) stitches.

Place marker and join, ensuring that the cast-on edge is not twisted. The stitch marker indicates both the center front of the sweater and the end of the round. This marker will remain in place until the Yoke of the sweater is complete.

The 5 stitches to either side of the center front marker are the steek stitches, and will form a facing once the front of the sweater is sewn and cut.

Round 1 K5, *p2, k2, p2, k4; repeat from * to last 11 stitches, p2, k2, p2, k5.

Round 2 K5, *p2, k2, p2, C4F; repeat from * to last 11 stitches, p2, k2, p2, k5.

Rounds 3–4 Work as for Round 1.

Repeat these 4 rounds until the work measures approximately 3" (7.5cm), ending with Round 4.

Next Round K59 (64, 69, 74, 79, 84), place marker, k118 (128, 138, 148, 158, 168), place marker, knit to end. These markers indicate the locations of the side "seams."

Knit 3 rounds.

Next Round *Knit to 3 stitches before the first marker, k2tog, k2, ssk; repeat from * once more, knit to end.

Repeat the last 4 rounds 8 times more—200 (220, 240, 260, 280, 300) stitches.

Continue in stockinette stitch until the work measures 13 (13, 13, 13, 14, 14)" (33 [33, 33, 33, 35.5, 35.5]cm).

shape bust

Note: The short rows that follow will add 1" (2.5cm) of length to the front of the sweater. If you wish to add more length, more short rows may be worked. You can choose to work the set of given short rows once more for each additional desired inch of length, or you can work a second set of short rows at different increments (i.e., 3-stitch increments instead of 4-stitch increments). Alternatively, you can calculate your own short rows!

Row 1 (RS) K46 (51, 56, 61, 66, 71) (to 4 stitches before side marker), W&T.

Row 2 (WS) P92 (102, 112, 122, 132, 142) (to 4 stitches before side marker), W&T.

Row 3 (RS) K88 (98, 108, 118, 128, 138), W&T.

Row 4 (WS) P84 (94, 104, 114, 124, 134), W&T.

Row 5 (RS) K80 (90, 100, 110, 120, 130), W&T.

Row 6 (WS) P76 (86, 96, 106, 116, 126), W&T.

Knit 1 round, picking up wraps and working them together with wrapped stitches.

Note: From this point, when measuring the length of your work, measure along the side of the work. Do not measure at the front; it is now longer than the rest of the work.

Continue in stockinette stitch until the work measures 16" (40.5cm).

Next Round *Knit to 6 (6, 6, 7, 7, 8) stitches before marker, place the next 12 (12, 12, 14, 14, 16) stitches on hold on a piece of waste yarn, removing marker; repeat from * once, knit to end. Set this piece aside and work the Sleeves. Do not break the yarn; begin working the first Sleeve with a new skein of yarn.

SLEEVES

Using double-pointed needles, cast on 100 (100, 110, 110, 120, 120) stitches. Divide the stitches between the needles and join to begin working in the round, ensuring that the cast-on edge is not twisted. If desired, place a safety pin or split ring marker in the work to indicate the beginning of the round.

Round 1 *P2, k2, p2, k4; repeat from * to end.

Round 2 *P2, k2, p2, C4F; repeat from * to end.

Rounds 3–4 Work as for Round 1.

Repeat these 4 rounds until the work measures approximately 4½" (11.4cm), ending with Round 4.

Size L Only

Next Round K1, *(k2tog) 4 times, k1; repeat from * to end—56 stitches.

Sizes 1X, 2X Only

Next Round *(K2tog) twice, k1; repeat from * to end— -(60, 66, -, -, -) stitches.

Size 3X Only

Next Round *(K2tog, k1) 3 times, k2tog; repeat from * to end—70 stitches.

Size 4X Only

Next Round *(K1, k2tog) 8 times, (k2tog) 3 times; repeat from * to end—76 stitches.

Size 5X Only

Next Round *K1, k2tog; repeat from * to end—80 stitches.

All Sizes

Work in stockinette stitch until the work measures 9" (23cm).

Next Round K1, m1, knit to last stitch, m1, k1.

Knit 3 rounds.

Repeat these 4 rounds 9 times more—76 (80, 86, 90, 96, 100) stitches.

Continue in stockinette stitch until the work measures 17" (43cm) or desired length to underarm, stopping work 6 (6, 6, 7, 7, 8) stitches before the end of the last round. Place the next 12 (12, 12, 14, 14, 16) stitches (last 6 [6, 6, 7, 7, 8] stitches of this round and first 6 [6, 6, 7, 7, 8] stitches of next round) on hold on a piece of waste yarn. Place the remaining 64 (68, 74, 76, 82, 84) stitches on hold on the US #5 (3.75mm) circular needle. Break the yarn, leaving a 12" (30cm) tail.

Make second sleeve in the same way. Place the 12 (12, 12, 14, 14, 16) stitches on hold as for the first sleeve, but do not remove the remaining stitches from the working needles.

YOKE

Pick up the Lower Body and resume working with the attached ball of yarn, working all stitches of the Lower Body and Sleeves onto the long circular needle as follows:

Joining Round Knit the first 44 (49, 54, 58, 63, 67) stitches of the Body (to the first set of held stitches), knit the held stitches of one sleeve, knit the next 88 (98, 108, 116, 126, 134) stitches of the Body, knit the held stitches of the second sleeve, knit the remaining 44 (49, 54, 58, 63, 67) stitches of the Body—304 (332, 364, 384, 416, 436) stitches.

Sizes 1X, 4X, 5X Only:

Knit 1 round, decreasing -(3, -, -, 2, 2) stitches evenly spaced throughout the round. Do not decrease these stitches within the 5 stitches on either side of the center front marker— -(329, -, -, 414, 434) stitches.

All Sizes

Work in stockinette stitch until the work measures 1½ (1½, 1½, 2½, 2½, 3½)" (3.8 [3.8, 3.8, 6.5, 6.5, 9]cm) from the Joining Round.

Decrease Round 1 K7, k2tog, *k3, k2tog; repeat from * to last 5 stitches, k5—245 (265, 293, 309, 333, 349) stitches.

Work all rounds of Chart 1. Work the last round of Chart 1 using CC2.

Decrease Round 2 Continuing with CC2, k6 (8, 6, 6, 10, 10), *k2, k2tog; repeat from * to last 7 (9, 7, 7, 11, 11) stitches, knit to end—187 (203, 223, 235, 255, 267) stitches.

Work all rounds of Chart 2. When Chart 2 is complete, break CC1 and CC2; the rest of the sweater will be worked using MC only.

Decrease Round 3 K5, *k1, k2tog; repeat from * to last 5 (6, 5, 5, 7, 7) stitches, k0 (1, 0, 0, 2, 2). Bind off the last 5 stitches of this round and the first 5 stitches of the next round, removing the marker. From this point, the neckline will be worked back and forth—118 (129, 142, 150, 164, 172) stitches.

shape neckline

Row 1 (RS) K26 (29, 32, 34, 37, 39) (there are 27 [30, 33, 35, 38, 40] stitches on the right needle), place marker, k64 (69, 76, 80, 88, 92), place marker, k22 (25, 28, 30, 33, 35) (to last 5 stitches), W&T.

Row 2 (WS) Purl to last 5 stitches, W&T.

Row 3 (RS) Knit to last 10 stitches, W&T.

Row 4 (WS) Purl to last 10 stitches, W&T.

Row 5 (RS) Knit to last 15 stitches, W&T.

Row 6 (WS) Purl to last 15 stitches, W&T.

Row 7 (RS) Knit to 1 stitch before second marker, W&T.

Row 8 (WS) Purl to 1 stitch before marker, W&T.

Row 9 (RS) Knit to 6 stitches before marker, W&T.

Row 10 (WS) Purl to 6 stitches before marker, W&T.

Row 11 (RS) Knit to 11 stitches before marker, W&T.

Row 12 (WS) Purl to 11 stitches before marker, W&T.

Row 13 (RS) Knit to end of row, picking up wraps and knitting them together with wrapped stitches.

Row 14 (WS) Purl all stitches, removing markers, picking up remaining wraps and purling them together with wrapped stitches.

Size L Only
Row 15 (RS) *K1, k2tog; repeat from * twice more, **k2, k2tog, k1, k2tog; repeat from ** to last 4 stitches, k1, k2tog, k1—84 stitches.

Size 1X Only
Row 15 (RS) K1, (k2tog) 4 times, *k1, k2tog; repeat from * to last 9 stitches, (k2tog) 4 times, k1—84 stitches.

Size 2X Only
Row 15 (RS) K3, *k2tog, k2; repeat from * to last stitch, k1—96 stitches.

Size 3X Only
Row 15 (RS) K1, (k2tog) 7 times, *k1, k2tog; repeat from * to last 15 stitches, (k2tog) 7 times, k1—96 stitches.

Size 4X Only
Row 15 (RS) K1, (k2tog) twice, *k1, (k2tog) twice, k1, k2tog, k1, k2tog; repeat from * to last 5 stitches, (k2tog) twice, k1—104 stitches.

Size 5X Only
Row 15 (RS) K2, *(k2tog) twice, k1; repeat from * to end—104 stitches.

All Sizes
Row 16 (WS) Using US #5 (3.75mm) needle, p3, *k2, p2; repeat from * to last stitch, p1.
Row 17 (RS) K3, *p2, k2; repeat from * to last stitch, k1.
These 2 rows set the rib pattern for the neckband. Continue in pattern until the neckband measures 1" (2.5mm).
Loosely bind off all stitches in pattern.

FINISHING

grafting
Graft the held stitches of the Body and Sleeves together at the underarms.

steeking
Sew a line of running stitch using waste yarn in a contrasting color down the center of the work, between the two central columns of stitches. This will form a guide for sewing and cutting. Sew two more lines of running stitch, each five columns of stitches away from the first line of stitching at the center of the work. These delineate the front edges of the cardigan, and will form guides for picking up stitches for the button and buttonhole bands.
Machine stitch up the first and last columns of stitches of the round (the two center front stitches), stretching the fabric slightly while sewing to maintain elasticity. Run a second line of stitching down the columns of stitches next to the central stitches.
Cut the steek down the center of the work, along the central line of running stitch.
Try the cardigan on to determine the best placement for the 6 buttons. Use safety pins to mark these points along the right side of the cardigan, close to the right front edge (defined by the line of running stitch 5 stitches away from the cut edge).

buttonhole band
With the right side facing, beginning at the lower right front edge, using the US #5 (3.75mm) circular needle and MC and using the line of running stitch as a guide, pick up and knit 3 stitches for every 4 rows along the right front edge of the cardigan and along the edge of the Neckband.
Count the number of stitches on the needle. When working the first row, increase or decrease 1 or 2 stitches to obtain a multiple of 4 stitches + 2.
Row 1 (WS) P2, *k2, p2; repeat from * to end.
Row 2 (RS) K2, *p2, k2; repeat from * to end.
Rows 3–6 Work as for Rows 1–2.
Row 7 (WS) *Work in pattern to 2 stitches before the marked position of a button, bind off 4 stitches; repeat from * to end.
Row 8 (RS) Work all stitches in pattern, casting on 4 stitches over each set of bound-off stitches.
Work 5 more rows in pattern.
Bind off all stitches.

button band
Pick up stitches along the left front edge of the cardigan and work as for the Buttonhole Band, omitting buttonholes.

assembly
Fold the front facings to the inside of the sweater and lightly steam block. Sew the edges of the facings loosely in place, sewing carefully so that the stitches are not visible from the right side of the work.
Weave in all ends and block the sweater as desired.
Sew the buttons to the Button Band, opposite the buttonholes.

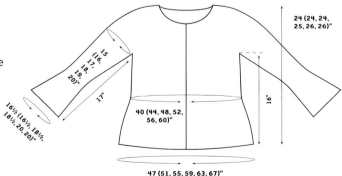

susie
hoodie

DIFFICULTY: 2
BY: MANDY MOORE

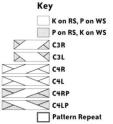

Key

	K on RS, P on WS
	P on RS, K on WS
	C3R
	C3L
	C4R
	C4L
	C4RP
	C4LP
	Pattern Repeat

You've seen lushly cabled sweaters you long to knit, but are they too much of a good thing? Susie is just right. A vertical band of the most complex-looking (but not difficult to knit) cabling is all this hoodie needs to catch the eye and satisfy your cable needle. Don't miss the hem detailing—this sweater has you looking great coming *and* going.

CABLE CHART

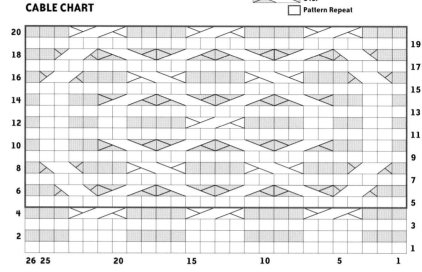

SIZES
L (1X, 2X, 3X, 4X)
Shown in size 1X

FINISHED MEASUREMENTS
Bust: 44 (48, 52, 56, 60)" (112 [122, 132, 142, 152.5]cm), with front bands overlapped
Length: 32" (81cm)

MATERIALS

10 (10, 11, 12, 13) skeins Tahki Donegal Tweed Homespun; 100% wool; 183 yd (167m) per 3½ oz (100g) skein; #863 (red)
1 US #7 (4.5mm) circular needle, 32" (80cm) long or longer
1 US #8 (5mm) circular needle, 32" (80cm) long or longer, *or size needed to obtain gauge*
1 set US #8 (5mm) double-pointed needles
1 spare circular needle or set of double-pointed needles, US #8 (5mm) or smaller
7 stitch markers
Cable needle
Waste yarn
Tapestry needle

GAUGE
17 stitches and 25 rows = 4" (10cm) in stockinette stitch on larger needles

ABBREVIATIONS AND TECHNIQUES
See page 32.

STITCH PATTERNS
C3LP (Cable 3 Left Purl) Slip next 2 stitches to cable needle and hold to front of work, p1, k2 from cable needle.
C3RP (Cable 3 Right Purl) Slip next stitch to cable needle and hold to back of work, k2, p1 from cable needle.
C4L (Cable 4 Left) Slip next 2 stitches to cable needle and hold to front of work, k2, k2 from cable needle.
C4R (Cable 4 Right) Slip next stitch to cable needle and hold to back of work, k2, k2 from cable needle.
C4LP (Cable 4 Left Purl) Slip next 2 stitches to cable needle and hold to front of work, p2, k2 from cable needle.
C4RP (Cable 4 Right Purl) Slip next stitch to cable needle and hold to back of work, k2, p2 from cable needle.

PATTERN NOTES
When working from Cable Chart, work Rows 1–20 once, then repeat Rows 5–20.

LOWER BODY

Using smaller circular needle, cast on 235 (251, 267, 287, 303) stitches. Do not join; body is worked back and forth in rows.

Row 1 (WS) Slip 1, p27, place marker, k39 (43, 47, 52, 56), place marker, k51 (55, 59, 64, 68), place marker, k50 (54, 58, 63, 67), place marker, k39 (43, 47, 52, 56), place marker, p28.

This row takes the place of Row 1 of the Cable Chart. The 28 stitches at each end of the work will form the cabled front panels; the first and last markers mark the edges of these panels. The remaining markers indicate the locations of the side "seam" placement and center back of the garment.

Row 2 (RS) Slip 1, k1, work Row 2 of Cable Chart, knit to last marker, work Row 2 of Cable Chart, k2.

Rows 3 and 5 (WS) Slip 1, purl to first marker (next row of Cable Chart), knit to last marker, purl to end.

Row 4 (Bias Shaping Row) (RS) Slip 1, k1, work next row of Cable Chart, k2tog, knit to 2 stitches before second marker, kfb, k1, kfb, knit to 2 stitches before third marker, ssk, k1, k2tog, knit to 2 stitches before fourth marker, kfb, k1, kfb, knit to 2 stitches before last marker, ssk, work next row of Cable Chart, k2.

Repeat Rows 2–5 twice more, then work Rows 2 and 3 once—15 rows of garter st have been worked.

Using larger circular needle, proceed as follows:

Bias Shaping Row (RS) Slip 1, k1, work next row of Cable Chart, k2tog, knit to 2 stitches before second marker, kfb, k1, kfb, knit to 2 stitches before third marker, ssk, k1, k2tog, knit to 2 stitches before fourth marker, kfb, k1, kfb, knit to 2 stitches before last marker, ssk, work next row of Cable Chart, k2.

Note: Bias Shaping Row is worked every fourth row throughout Body, unless otherwise noted.

Work 3 rows in pattern as set, working cable panels before the first marker and after the last marker, and working all other stitches in stockinette stitch.

Repeat the last 4 rows 4 times more.

waist decrease

Note: All waist shaping is worked on rows that are *not* Bias Shaping Rows.

Work Bias Shaping Row.

Work 1 row in pattern.

First Waist Decrease Row (RS) Slip 1, k1, work next row of Cable Chart, k19 (21, 23, 25, 27), ssk, knit to second marker, k15 (16, 18, 20, 21), k2tog, k15 (16, 18, 20, 21), k2tog, knit to third marker, k17 (19, 19, 20, 22), ssk, k15 (16, 18, 20, 21), ssk, k33 (36, 40, 45, 48), k2tog, work in pattern to end—229 (245, 261, 281, 297) stitches.

Work 11 rows in pattern, working Bias Shaping Row every fourth row as set.

Second Waist Decrease Row (RS) Slip 1, k1, work next row of Cable Chart, k19 (21, 23, 25, 27), ssk, knit to second marker, k14 (15, 17, 19, 20), k2tog, k14 (15, 17, 19, 20), k2tog, knit to third marker, k17 (19, 19, 20, 22), ssk, k14 (15, 17, 19, 20), ssk, k31 (34,

38, 43, 46), k2tog, work in pattern to end—223 (239, 255, 275, 291) stitches.

Work 11 rows in pattern, working Bias Shaping Row every fourth row as set.

Third Waist Decrease Row (RS) Slip 1, k1, work next row of Cable Chart, k19 (21, 23, 25, 27), ssk, knit to second marker, k13 (14, 16, 18, 19), k2tog, k13 (14, 16, 18, 19), k2tog, knit to third marker, k17 (19, 19, 20, 22), ssk, k13 (14, 16, 18, 19), ssk, k29 (32, 36, 41, 44), k2tog, work in pattern to end—217 (233, 249, 269, 285) stitches.

Work 11 rows in pattern, working Bias Shaping Row every fourth row as set.

Fourth Waist Decrease Row (RS) Slip 1, k1, work next row of Cable Chart, k19 (21, 23, 25, 27), ssk, knit to second marker, k12 (13, 15, 17, 18), k2tog, k12 (13, 15, 17, 18), k2tog, knit to third marker, k17 (19, 19, 20, 22), ssk, k12 (13, 15, 17, 18), ssk, k27 (30, 34, 39, 42), k2tog, work in pattern to end—211 (227, 243, 263, 279) stitches.

Work 11 rows in pattern, working Bias Shaping Row every fourth row as set.

Fifth Waist Decrease Row (RS) Slip 1, k1, work next row of Cable Chart, k19 (21, 23, 25, 27), ssk, knit to second marker, k11 (12, 14, 16, 17), k2tog, k11 (12, 14, 16, 17), k2tog, knit to third marker, k17 (19, 19, 20, 22), ssk, k11 (12, 14, 16, 17), ssk, k25 (28, 32, 37, 40), k2tog, work in pattern to end—205 (221, 237, 257, 273) stitches.

Work 11 rows in pattern, working Bias Shaping Row every fourth row as set.

waist increase

First Waist Increase Row (RS) Slip 1, k1, work next row of Cable Chart, k20 (22, 24, 26, 28), m1, knit to second marker, k12 (13, 15,

The Lower Body is now complete; work measures 22¼" (56.5cm). Each Front has 65 (69, 73, 78, 82) stitches (including cable panels), and the Back has 93 (101, 109, 119, 127) stitches. Set aside to work the Sleeves; do not break the yarn.

SLEEVES

cuff

Using smaller double-pointed needles, cast on 30 stitches.
Row 1 (RS) Slip 1, k1, work first row of Cable Chart, k2.
Row 2 (WS) Slip 1, purl to end.
Working edge stitches in stockinette stitch as set and slipping first stitch of each row, work Rows 1–20 once, then work Rows 5–20, 5 times. Bind off all stitches purlwise; do not break the yarn. Slip the last stitch to larger double-pointed needle.

arm

With wrong side facing, pick up and p1 in each slipped stitch along the cuff edge and 1 stitch in the edge of the cast-on row— 52 stitches.
Knit 1 row. Distribute the stitches evenly among the double-pointed needles and join to begin working in the round. If desired, once the work has progressed several inches, place a safety pin or split ring marker in the work to indicate the beginning of the round.
Knit 6 (6, 5, 5, 4) rounds.
Increase Round K1, kfb, knit to last 3 stitches of round, kfb, k2.
Repeat these 7 (7, 6, 6, 5) rounds 9 (9, 11, 11, 13) times more—72 (72, 76, 76, 80) stitches.
Continue in stockinette stitch until the work measures 18" (45.5cm), or desired length to underarm.
Next Round Knit to last 2 stitches of round, place next 4 stitches (last 2 stitches of round and first 2 stitches of next round) on hold on waste yarn; place all other stitches on hold on spare circular or double-pointed needle(s). Break the yarn, leaving a 12" (30cm) tail.
Make second sleeve in the same way. Place 4 stitches on waste yarn and break the yarn as for the first sleeve, but do not remove this sleeve from the working needles.

YOKE

Joining Row (RS) Using the ball of yarn attached to the Right Front, work in pattern to 2 stitches before second marker, place next 4 stitches on waste yarn, removing side marker; place marker on needle, knit all stitches of one Sleeve, place marker, knit to 2 stitches before fourth body marker (at left side "seam"), place next 4 stitches on waste yarn, removing side marker; place marker, knit all stitches of second Sleeve, place marker, work in pattern to end—351 (367, 391, 411, 435) stitches; 7 markers on needle.
Next Row (WS) Slip 1, purl to end.

17, 18), m1, k12 (13, 15, 17, 18), m1, knit to third marker, k17 (19, 19, 20, 22), m1, k12 (13, 15, 17, 18), m1, k26 (29, 33, 38, 41), m1, work in pattern to end—211 (227, 243, 263, 279) stitches.
Work 15 rows in pattern, working Bias Shaping Row every fourth row as set.
Second Waist Increase Row (RS) Slip 1, k1, work next row of Cable Chart, k20 (22, 24, 26, 28), m1, knit to second marker, k13 (14, 16, 18, 19), m1, k13 (14, 16, 18, 19), m1, knit to third marker, k17 (19, 19, 20, 22), m1, k13 (14, 16, 18, 19), m1, k28 (31, 33, 40, 43), m1, work in pattern to end—217 (233, 249, 269, 285) stitches.
Work 15 rows in pattern, working Bias Shaping Row every fourth row as set.
Third Waist Increase Row (RS) Slip 1, k1, work next row of Cable Chart, k20 (22, 24, 26, 28), m1, knit to second marker, k14 (15, 17, 19, 20), m1, k14 (15, 17, 19, 20), m1, knit to third marker, k17 (19, 19, 20, 22), m1, k14 (15, 17, 19, 20), m1, k30 (33, 37, 42, 45), m1, work in pattern to end—223 (239, 255, 275, 291) stitches.
Work 15 rows in pattern, working Bias Shaping Row every fourth row as set.

Sizes 1X, 2X, 3X, 4X Only

Row 1 (RS) Slip 1, k1, work next row of Cable Chart, k2tog, knit to 3 stitches before second marker, ssk, k1, k2tog, knit to 2 stitches before third marker, ssk, k1, k2tog, knit to 2 stitches before fourth marker, ssk, k1, k2tog, knit to 3 stitches before fifth marker, ssk, k1, k2tog, knit to 2 stitches before sixth marker, ssk, k1, k2tog, knit to 2 stitches before seventh marker, ssk, work cable panel to end—12 stitches decreased.

Rows 2 and 4 (WS) Slip 1, purl to end.

Row 3 (RS) Slip 1, k1, work next row of Cable Chart, knit to 3 stitches before second marker, ssk, k1, k2tog, knit to 2 stitches before third marker, ssk, k1, k2tog, knit to 3 stitches before fifth marker, ssk, k1, k2tog, knit to 2 stitches before sixth marker, ssk, k1, k2tog, knit to seventh marker, work cable panel to end—8 stitches decreased.

Repeat these 4 rows -(3, 7, 11, 14) times more— -(287, 231, 171, 135) stitches.

Sizes L, 1X, 2X, 3X Only

Row 1 (RS) Slip 1, k1, work next row of Cable Chart, k2tog, knit to second marker, k2tog, knit to 2 stitches before third marker, ssk, knit to 2 stitches before fourth marker, ssk, k1, k2tog, knit to fifth marker, k2tog, knit to 2 stitches before sixth marker, ssk, knit to 2 stitches before seventh marker, ssk, work cable panel to end—8 stitches decreased.

Rows 2 and 4 (WS) Slip 1, purl to end.

Row 3 (RS) Slip 1, k1, work next row of Cable Chart, knit to 3 stitches before second marker, ssk, k1, k2tog, knit to 2 stitches before third marker, ssk, k1, k2tog, knit to 3 stitches before fifth marker, ssk, k1, k2tog, knit to 2 stitches before sixth marker, ssk, k1, k2tog, knit to seventh marker, work cable panel to end—8 stitches decreased.

Repeat these 4 rows 14 (10, 6, 2, -) times more—111 (111, 119, 123, -) stitches.

All Sizes

Each Front has 33 (33, 33, 34, 35) stitches, each Sleeve has 8 (8, 12, 12, 16) stitches, and the Back has 29 (29, 29, 31, 33) stitches.

HOOD

Next Row (RS) Slip 1, k1, work next row of Cable Chart, knit to last marker, removing second, fourth, and sixth markers; work in pattern to end.

The markers at the edges of the cable panels and the markers at the back raglan shaping lines remain.

Note: Do not work Bias Shaping Rows while working the hood; bias shaping is complete.

Work 5 rows in pattern, working cable panels as set, and working all other stitches in stockinette stitch.

Hood Increase Row (RS) Slip 1, k1, work next row of Cable Chart, kfb, knit to second marker, kfb, knit to 2 stitches before next marker, kfb, knit to 2 stitches before next marker, kfb, work in pattern to end.

Repeat these 6 rows 4 times more—131 (131, 139, 143, 155) stitches; 39 (39, 39, 41, 43) stitches between second and third markers.

Work in pattern as set until hood measures approximately 10 (10, 10, 9½, 9¼)" (25.5 [25.5, 25.5, 24, 23.5]cm), ending with row 15 (15, 15, 13, 11) of Cable Chart.

Note: It is more important to end this section on the correct row of the Cable Chart than it is to achieve the exact length given.

Hood Decrease Row (RS) Slip 1, k1, work next row of Cable Chart, knit to second marker, k2tog, knit to 2 stitches before third marker, ssk, work in pattern to end.

Work 1 row in pattern.

Repeat these 2 rows 17 (17, 17, 18, 19) times more—95 (95, 103, 105, 115) sts; 3 stitches between second and third markers. You should have just completed Row 19 of Cable Chart.

Next Row (RS) Slip 1, k1, work next row of Cable Chart, knit to second marker, remove marker, k2tog. Do not work to the end of this row. Slip the remaining half of the stitches to a spare circular needle, removing marker. Graft the two halves of the hood together.

FINISHING

Graft the Sleeves to the Body at underarms.

Sew the ends of the cuffs together.

Weave in all ends and block as desired.

15½"

17 (17, 18, 18, 18¾)"

18"

Bust: 44 (48, 52, 56, 60)"

32¼"

22¼"

Waist: 38 (42, 46, 52, 56)"

Lower Edge: 47½ (51¼, 55, 59¾, 63½)"

modular spiral
jacket

This modular-knit jacket can make you look curvy even if you aren't. Carefully shaped color blocks create visual curves where they should be, and the flared sleeves balance heavy upper arms, if you've got 'em. The neckline? Low and lovely. And don't balk at the wee bit of intarsia . . . it's just a little. It won't hurt.

SIZE
L (1X, 2X, 3X)
Shown in size 1X

FINISHED MEASUREMENTS
Chest: 42 (46, 50, 54)" (106.5 [117, 127, 137]cm)
Length: 23" (58.5cm)

MATERIALS

Jo Sharp Classic DK Wool; 100% wool; 107 yd (98m) per 1¾ oz (50g) skein

11 (12, 14, 16) skeins #312 Renaissance (deep blue, MC)
7 skeins #347 Orient (silver, CC)
1 set US #6 (4mm) straight needles *or size needed to obtain gauge*
1 set US #6 (4mm) double-point needles (for applied I-Cord)
Waste yarn
Stitch holder
Tapestry needle
7 buttons, ⅞" (22mm) diameter

GAUGE
22 stitches and 28 rows = 4" (10cm) in stockinette stitch

ABBREVIATIONS AND TECHNIQUES
See page 32.

PATTERN NOTES
Applied I-Cord Using a double-pointed needle, cast on 5 stitches.
Next Row Using a second double-pointed needle, k4, (ssk) the last stitch of the I-Cord together with the first stitch from the straight needle, which holds the work.
Slide the 5 stitches just worked to other end of the double-point needle and bring the yarn around the back of the work, ready to begin working the next row. The right side of the work is always facing.
Repeat this row until all of the stitches from the straight needle have been worked. Bind off the 5 I-Cord stitches.
Note: *Label each panel as it is completed to be sure you don't mix the panels up!*

Spiral Jacket

Chart A

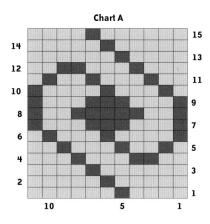

Chart B

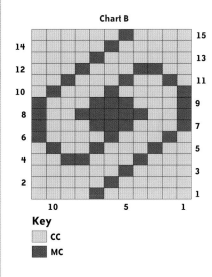

Key
CC
MC

RIGHT FRONT PANEL

Using CC and straight needles, cast on 33 stitches.
Row 1 (WS) P11, place marker, p11, place marker, purl to end.
Rows 2 and 3 Work 2 more rows in stockinette stitch.
Row 4 (RS) Knit to marker, work Row 1 of Chart A to next marker, knit to end.

From this point, continue working Rows 1–15 of Chart A between markers. Chart will be worked a total of 10 times.
Rows 5–7 Work in stockinette stitch.
Row 8 (RS) K1, ssk, knit to last 3 stitches, k2tog, k1.
Rows 9–20 Work as for Rows 5–8, 3 times more—25 stitches.
Rows 21–25 Work in stockinette stitch.

Rows 103–107 Work in stockinette stitch.
Row 108 (RS) K1, ssk, knit to last 3 stitches, k2tog, k1.
Rows 109–113 Work in stockinette stitch.
Rows 114–137 Work as for Rows 102–113, twice more—24 stitches.
Row 138 (RS) Work as for Row 108.
Rows 139–143 Work in stockinette stitch.
Rows 144–149 Work as for Rows 138–143, once more—20 stitches.
Row 150 (RS) K1, ssk, knit to end, k2tog, k1—19 stitches.
Rows 151–153 Work last 3 rows of Chart A. Break MC.
Rows 154 and 155 Work in stockinette stitch using CC only.
Row 156 (RS) Bind off 6 stitches, knit to end.
Row 157 (WS) Purl all stitches.
Rows 158 and 159 Work as for Rows 156 and 157.
Bind off remaining 7 stitches.

RIGHT BACK PANEL

Using CC, cast on 37 stitches.
Row 1 (WS) P13, place marker, p11, place marker, purl to end.
Rows 2 and 3 Work 2 more rows in stockinette stitch.
Row 4 (RS) Knit to marker, work Row 1 of Chart A to next marker, knit to end.
From this point, continue working Rows 1–15 of Chart A between markers.
Rows 5–7 Work in stockinette stitch.
Row 8 (RS) K1, ssk, knit to last 3 stitches, k2tog, k1.
Rows 9–20 Work as for Rows 5–8, 3 times more—29 stitches.
Rows 21–25 Work in stockinette stitch.
Row 26 (RS) Work as for Row 8.
Rows 27–38 Work as for Rows 21–26, twice more—23 stitches.
Rows 39–67 Work in stockinette stitch (29 rows).
Row 68 (RS) K1, m1, knit to last stitch, m1, k1.
Rows 69–73 Work in stockinette stitch.
Rows 74–97 Work as for Rows 68–73, 4 times more—33 stitches.
Rows 98–103 Work in stockinette stitch.
Row 104 (RS) K1, ssk, knit to end—32 stitches.
Rows 105–115 Work in stockinette stitch.
Row 116 (RS) Work as for Row 104.
Rows 117–140 Work as for Rows 105–116, twice more—29 stitches.
Rows 141–145 Work in stockinette stitch.
Row 146 Work as for Row 104.
Rows 147–152 Work as for Rows 141–146—27 stitches.
Row 153 (WS) Bind off 7 stitches, purl to end—20 stitches.
The last row of Chart A has just been completed; break MC.
Continue in stockinette stitch using CC only.
Row 154 (RS) Knit all stitches.
Row 155 (WS) Bind off 1 stitch, purl to end.
Row 156 (RS) Bind off 6 stitches, knit to end.

Row 26 (RS) Work as for Row 8.
Rows 27–38 Work as for Rows 21–26, twice more—19 stitches.
Rows 39–67 Work in stockinette stitch (29 rows).
Row 68 (RS) K1, m1, knit to last stitch, m1, k1.
Rows 69–71 Work in stockinette stitch.
Rows 72–83 Work as for Rows 68–71, 3 times more—27 stitches.
Row 84 (RS) Work as for Row 68.
Rows 85–89 Work in stockinette stitch.
Rows 90–101 Work as for Rows 84–89, twice more—33 stitches.
Row 102 (RS) K1, ssk, knit to end.
Rows 103–107 Work in stockinette stitch.
Row 108 (RS) K1, ssk, knit to last 3 stitches, k2tog, k1.
Rows 109–113 Work in stockinette stitch.
Rows 114–137 Work as for Rows 102–113, twice more—24 stitches.
Row 138 (RS) Work as for Row 108.
Rows 139–143 Work in stockinette stitch.
Rows 144–149 Work as for Rows 138–143, once more—20 stitches.
Row 150 (RS) Knit to last 3 stitches, k2tog, k1—19 stitches.
Rows 151–153 Work last 3 rows of Chart A. Break MC.
Rows 154–156 Work in stockinette stitch using CC only.
Row 157 (WS) Bind off 6 stitches, purl to end.
Row 158 (RS) Knit all stitches.
Rows 159 and 160 Work as for Rows 157 and 158.
Bind off remaining 7 stitches.

LEFT FRONT PANEL

Work as for Right Front Panel through Row 101, EXCEPT work from Chart B instead of Chart A.
Row 102 (RS) Knit to last 3 stitches, k2tog, k1.

Row 157 (WS) Purl all stitches.
Rows 158 and 159 Work as for Rows 156 and 157.
Bind off remaining 7 stitches.

LEFT BACK PANEL

Work as for Right Back Panel through Row 103, EXCEPT work from Chart B instead of Chart A.
Row 104 (RS) Knit to last 3 stitches, k2tog, k1—32 stitches.
Rows 105–115 Work in stockinette stitch.
Row 116 (RS) Work as for Row 104.
Rows 117–140 Work as for Rows 105–116, twice more—29 stitches.
Rows 141–145 Work in stockinette stitch.
Row 146 Work as for Row 104.
Rows 147–152 Work as for Rows 141–146—27 stitches.
Row 153 (WS) Purl all stitches.
The last row of Chart A has just been completed; break MC. Continue in stockinette stitch using CC only.
Row 154 (RS) Bind off 7 stitches, knit to end—20 stitches.
Row 155 (WS) Purl all stitches.
Row 156 (RS) Bind off 1 stitch, knit to end.
Row 157 (WS) Bind off 6 stitches, purl to end.
Row 158 (RS) Knit all stitches.
Rows 159 and 160 Work as for Rows 157 and 158.
Bind off remaining 7 stitches.

RIGHT SLEEVE PANEL

Note: The wider cast-on edge of the Sleeve Panel is the lower edge.
Using CC, cast on 45 stitches.
Set-Up Row (WS) P17, place marker, p11, place marker, purl to end.
Work 2 (4, 6, 8) rows in stockinette stitch.
Decrease Row (RS) K1, ssk, knit to marker, work Row 1 of Chart A to next marker, knit to last 3 stitches, k2tog, k1—43 stitches.
From this point, continue working Rows 1–15 of Chart A between markers while working as follows. Chart will be worked 9 times.
Work 3 rows in stockinette stitch.
Work Decrease Row.
Repeat these 4 rows 7 times more—27 stitches.
Continue in stockinette stitch until all rows of Chart A have been worked 9 times.
Break MC and work 3 (5, 7, 9) rows using CC only.
Bind off all stitches.

LEFT SLEEVE PANEL

Work as for Right Sleeve Panel, EXCEPT work from Chart B instead of Chart A.

RIGHT SIDE FRONT PANEL

Using MC and with the right side facing, beginning 5" (12.5cm) from the upper edge, pick up and knit 3 stitches for every 4 rows along the left edge of the Right Front Panel. Make a note of the number of stitches you have picked up. The section of the panel edge without picked-up stitches will form part of the armhole edge; the decreases worked at one edge of this panel will shape the armhole.
Next Row (WS) Knit to last 3 stitches, k2tog, k1.
Next Row (RS) K1, ssk, knit to end.
Repeat these 2 rows 5 (3, 2, 1) times more—12 (8, 6, 4) stitches have been decreased.
Knit 1 row.
Next Row (RS) K1, ssk, knit to end.
Repeat these 2 rows 4 (10, 15, 20) times more—17 (19, 22, 25) stitches have been decreased.
Knit 2 rows.
Loosely bind off all stitches.

LEFT SIDE FRONT PANEL

Using MC and with the right side facing, beginning at the lower right corner, pick up and knit 3 stitches for every 4 rows along the right edge of the Left Front Panel, ending 5" (12.5cm) from the upper edge. Be sure that you have picked up the same number of stitches on this panel as you did on the Right Front Panel.
Next Row (WS) K1, ssk, knit to end.
Next Row (RS) Knit to last 3 stitches, k2tog, k1.
Repeat these 2 rows 5 (3, 2, 1) times more—12 (8, 6, 4) stitches have been decreased.
Knit 1 row.
Next Row (RS) Knit to last 3 stitches, k2tog, k1.
Repeat these 2 rows 4 (10, 15, 20) times more—17 (19, 22, 25) stitches have been decreased.
Knit 2 rows.
Loosely bind off all stitches.

RIGHT SIDE BACK PANEL

Work as for Left Side Front Panel.

LEFT SIDE BACK PANEL

Work as for Right Side Front Panel.

SIDE PANELS (MAKE 2)

Using MC, cast on 9 stitches.
Rows 1–14 Work in stockinette stitch, beginning with a right-side row.
Row 15 (RS) K4, k2tog, k3.
Rows 16–20 Work in stockinette stitch.
Row 21 (RS) K3, k2tog, k3.

Rows 22–26 Work in stockinette stitch.
Row 27 (RS) K3, k2tog, k2.
Rows 28–32 Work in stockinette stitch.
Row 33 (RS) K2, k2tog, k2.
Rows 34–38 Work in stockinette stitch.
Row 39 (RS) K2, k2tog, k1—4 stitches.
Rows 40–68 Work in stockinette stitch.
Row 69 (RS) K2, m1, k2.
Rows 70–78 Work in stockinette stitch.
Row 79 (RS) K3, m1, k2.
Rows 80–88 Work in stockinette stitch.
Row 89 (RS) K3, m1, k3—7 stitches.
Continue in stockinette stitch until the work measures 15 (14½, 14, 13½)" (38 [37, 35.5, 34.5]cm).
Bind off all stitches.

SLEEVES (MAKE 2)

Both sleeves are worked in the same way.
Using MC, beginning at the upper left corner of one sleeve panel with the right side facing, pick up and knit 3 stitches for every 4 rows along the left side of the panel.
Row 1 (WS) Knit to last stitch, p1.
Row 2 (RS) Slip 1, ssk, knit to end.
Repeat these 2 rows 16 (18, 21, 23) times more—17 (19, 22, 24) stitches have been decreased.
The short rows worked in the next section of sleeve shaping will help prevent the lower edge of the sleeve from flaring too widely.
Odd-Numbered Rows 1–11 (WS) Knit to last stitch, p1.
Row 2 (RS) Slip 1, ssk, knit to last 8 stitches, W&T.
Row 4 (RS) Slip 1, ssk, knit to last 16 stitches, W&T.
Row 6 (RS) Slip 1, ssk, knit to last 24 stitches, W&T.
Row 8 (RS) Slip 1, ssk, knit to last 32 stitches, W&T.
Row 10 (RS) Slip 1, ssk, knit to last 40 stitches, W&T.
Row 12 (RS) Slip 1, ssk, knit to last 48 stitches, W&T.
Row 13 (WS) Knit to last stitch, p1—23 (25, 28, 30) stitches have been decreased.
When working the next row, pick up all wraps and work them together with the wrapped stitches.
Next Row (RS) Slip 1, knit to end.
Next Row (WS) Knit to last stitch, p1.
Repeat these 2 rows 3 times more. Place all stitches on a stitch holder.
Using MC, beginning at the lower right corner of the sleeve panel with the right side facing, pick up and knit 3 stitches for every 4 rows along the right side of the panel.
Row 1 (WS) Slip 1, knit to end.
Row 2 (RS) Knit to last 3 stitches, k2tog, k1.
Repeat these 2 rows 16 (18, 21, 23) times more—17 (19, 22, 24) stitches have been decreased.
The short rows worked in the next section of sleeve shaping will

help prevent the lower edge of the sleeve from flaring too widely.
Row 1 (WS) Slip 1, knit to last 8 stitches, W&T.
Even-Numbered Rows 2–10 (RS) Knit to last 3 stitches, k2tog, k1.
Row 3 (WS) Slip 1, knit to last 16 stitches, W&T.
Row 5 (WS) Slip 1, knit to last 24 stitches, W&T.
Row 7 (WS) Slip 1, knit to last 32 stitches, W&T.
Row 9 (WS) Slip 1, knit to last 40 stitches, W&T.
Row 11 (WS) Slip 1, knit to last 48 stitches, W&T.
Row 12 (RS) Knit to last 3 stitches, k2tog, k1—23 (25, 28, 30) stitches have been decreased.
When working the next row, pick up all wraps and work them together with the wrapped stitches.
Next Row (WS) Knit to last stitch, p1.
Next Row (RS) Slip 1, knit to end.
Repeat these 2 rows 3 times more.
Replace the held stitches from the first side of the sleeve on one needle, and graft them together with the stitches from the second side of the sleeve.

CENTER BACK PANEL

Using MC, with the right side facing and beginning at the bound-off back neckline edge of the Right Back Panel, pick up and knit 3 stitches for every 4 rows along the left side of the panel.
Beginning with a wrong-side row, knit 41 (47, 53, 57) rows. Break the yarn and leave the stitches on the needle.
Using the other needle and MC, with the right side facing and beginning at the lower edge, pick up and knit the same number of stitches along the right edge of the Left Back Panel as you picked up from the Right Back Panel. Graft these stitches to the stitches on the other needle.

LEFT CENTER FRONT PANEL

Using MC, with the right side facing and beginning 8" (20.5cm) below the upper edge, pick up and knit 3 stitches for every 4 rows along the left side of the Left Front Panel.
Knit 3 (3, 5, 5) rows.
Next Row (RS) Bind off 1 stitch, knit to end.
Repeat these 4 (4, 6, 6) rows 3 times more—4 stitches have been bound off.
Knit 9 (11, 7, 9) rows. Break MC.
Using CC, work Applied I-Cord (see directions in Pattern Notes).

RIGHT CENTER FRONT PANEL

Using MC, with the right side facing and beginning at the lower edge, pick up and knit the same number of stitches along the right edge of the Right Front Panel as you picked up from the Left Front Panel.
Knit 4 (4, 6, 6) rows.
Next Row (WS) Bind off 1 stitch, knit to end.

FINISHING

assembly

Sew the Fronts to the Back at the shoulders.
Sew the stockinette stitch side panels to the bound-off stitches of the Side Front and Side Back panels.
Sew the Sleeves into the armholes.

neckline edging

Using CC, with right side facing and beginning at right front edge, pick up and knit 1 stitch in every bound-off stitch, 1 stitch in every garter stitch ridge, and 3 stitches for every 4 rows around the neckline edge.
Work 3 rows in stockinette stitch.
Bind off all stitches.

Weave in all ends.
Block as desired.
Sew the buttons to the left front opposite the buttonholes.

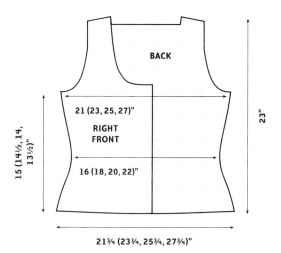

BACK

21 (23, 25, 27)"

15 (14½, 14, 13½)"

RIGHT
FRONT

16 (18, 20, 22)"

23"

21¾ (23¾, 25¾, 27¾)"

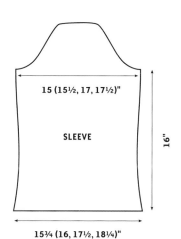

15 (15½, 17, 17½)"

SLEEVE

16"

15¾ (16, 17½, 18¼)"

Knit 3 (3, 5, 5) rows.
Repeat these 4 (4, 6, 6) rows 3 times more.
Bind off 1 stitch at the beginning of the next row—5 stitches have been bound off.
Knit 4 (6, 2, 4) rows.
On the next row, a right-side row, 7 buttonholes will be worked. To determine the spacing of your buttonholes, count the number of stitches on the needle. Subtract 21 from this number (each buttonhole is 3 stitches wide), and divide the remaining number by 7. The number you've ended up will be called S, and represents the number of stitches between buttonholes.
At the beginning and end of the row, before the first buttonhole and after the last, you will work half of S stitches. If S is an odd number, work 1 stitch less before the first buttonhole than you work after the last buttonhole.
Next Row (RS) Knit half of S stitches, bind off 3 stitches, *knit until there are S stitches on your right needles after the last set of bound-off stitches, bind off 3 stitches; repeat from * 5 times more, knit the remaining (half of S) stitches.
Next Row (WS) *Knit to the first set of bound-off stitches, cast on 3 stitches; repeat from * 6 times more, knit to end.
Knit 2 rows.
Using CC, work Applied I-Cord.

boo, too

DIFFICULTY: 2
BY: JILLIAN MORENO FOR ACME KNITTING COMPANY

Life is too short to knit boring sweaters, so Jillian designed a crazy ruffled-bottom sweater for her daughter (she's the "Boo"). When grown-up girlies saw it, they wanted one for themselves. Ms. J was glad to oblige with Boo, Too.

Two colors of Noro Silk Garden and a 2x2 slip stitch transform chunks of horizontal color into an intriguing vertical pattern. The ruffles frame the Bs you want to show off, and the curvy shape works great with your curvy shape.

SIZES

L (1X, 2X, 3X)

Shown in size 1X

FINISHED MEASUREMENTS

Chest: 43 (47, 51, 55)" (109 [119.4, 129.5]cm)

Length: 22½ (23½, 24½, 25½)" (58.5 [61, 63.5]cm)

MATERIALS

Noro Silk Garden; 45% silk, 45% kid mohair, 10% lamb's wool; 110 yd (100m) per 1¾ oz (50g) ball

6 (6, 7, 8) balls #084 (reds and pinks, MC)

6 (6, 7, 8) balls #065 (grays and blues, CC1)

Noro Cash Iroha; 40% silk, 30% lamb's wool, 20% cashmere, 10% nylon; 100 yd (91m) per 1½ oz (40g) ball

4 (4, 5, 5) balls #100 (green, CC2)

3 (3, 4, 4) balls #103 (purple, CC3)

1 US #8 (5mm) circular needle, 24" (60cm) long, *or size needed to obtain gauge*

1 US #7 (4.5mm) circular needle, 32" (80cm) long

3 buttons, ¾" (2cm) diameter

Tapestry needle

GAUGE

22 stitches and 36 rows = 4" (10cm) in Corrugated Slip Stitch pattern using the larger needle

ABBREVIATIONS AND TECHNIQUES

See page 32.

STITCH PATTERNS

Corrugated Slip Stitch

(Worked over a multiple of 4 stitches)

Note: *Slip all slipped stitches purlwise with yarn held to WS of work.*

Row 1 (RS) Using MC, k1, *slip 2, k2, repeat from * to last 3 stitches, slip 2, k1.

Row 2 (WS) Using MC, k1, *slip 2, p2, repeat from * to last 3 stitches, slip 2, k1.

Row 3 (RS) Using CC1, k1, *k2, slip 2, repeat from * to last 3 stitches, k3.

Row 4 (WS) Using CC1, k1, *p2, slip 2, repeat from * to last 3 stitches, p2, k1.

These 4 rows form Corrugated Slip Stitch.

Seed Stitch

(Worked over an odd number of stitches)

Row 1 *K1, p1, repeat from * to last stitch, k1.

Repeat row 1 for Seed Stitch.

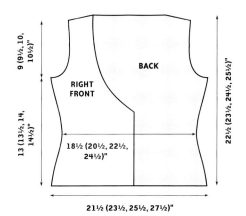

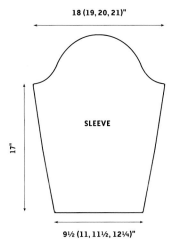

BACK

Using the larger needle and CC1, cast on 120 (132, 140, 152) stitches.

Purl 1 row (wrong side). Join MC.

Work 4 (6, 8, 10) rows in Corrugated Slip Stitch.

waist shaping

Decrease Row (RS) Ssk, work in pattern to last 2 stitches, k2tog.

Work 5 rows in pattern.

Repeat these 6 rows 7 times more—104 (116, 124, 136) stitches.

Work 12 rows in pattern (18 rows after last decrease row).

Increase Row (RS) K1, m1, work in pattern to last stitch, m1, k1.

Work 5 rows in pattern.

Repeat these 6 rows 7 times more—120 (132, 140, 152) stitches.

Continue in pattern until the work measures 13 (13½, 14, 14½)" (33 [34.5, 35.5, 37]cm) or desired length to underarm, ending with a wrong-side row.

armhole shaping

Bind off 10 (10, 11, 12) stitches at the beginning of the next 2 rows—100 (112, 118, 128) stitches.

Decrease Row (RS) Ssk, work in pattern to last 2 stitches, k2tog.

Work 1 row in pattern.

Repeat these 2 rows 8 (11, 10, 13) times more—82 (88, 96, 100) stitches.

Continue in pattern until the work measures 22 (23, 24, 25)" (56 [58.5, 61, 63.5]cm), ending with a wrong-side row. Armhole measures 9 (9½, 10, 10½)" (23 [24, 25.5, 26.5]cm) from initial bind-off.

shape shoulders

Bind off 7 (7, 8, 9) stitches at the beginning of the next 2 rows.

Bind off 7 (8, 8, 9) stitches at the beginning of the next 2 rows.

Bind off 8 (8, 10, 10) stitches at the beginning of the next 2 rows.

Bind off remaining 38 (42, 44, 44) stitches.

LEFT FRONT

Note: Read ahead! Waist, neckline, and armhole shaping directions are worked simultaneously.

Using the larger needle and CC1, cast on 56 (64, 68, 72) stitches.

Purl 1 row (wrong side). Join MC.

Work 4 (6, 8, 10) rows in Corrugated Slip Stitch.

waist shaping

Decrease Row (RS) Ssk, work in pattern to end.

Work 5 rows in pattern.

Repeat these 6 rows 7 times more—48 (56, 60, 64) stitches.

Work 12 rows in pattern (18 rows after last decrease row).

Increase Row (RS) K1, m1, work in pattern to end.

Work 5 rows in pattern.

Repeat these 6 rows 7 times more—56 (64, 68, 72) stitches.

AT THE SAME TIME, when the work measures 8 (9, 10, 10½)" (20.5 [23, 25.5, 26.5]cm), or 5 (4½, 4, 4)" (12.5 [11, 10, 10]cm) less than the desired length to underarm, begin working neckline shaping as follows.

neckline shaping

Neckline Decrease Row (RS) Work in pattern to last 2 stitches, k2tog.

Work 3 rows in pattern.

Repeat these 4 rows 5 (6, 6, 5) times more.

Work Neckline Decrease Row.

Work 5 rows in pattern.

Repeat these 6 rows 4 (5, 6, 5) times more.

Work Neckline Decrease Row.

Work 7 rows in pattern.

Repeat these 8 rows 3 (5, 5, 5) times more—15 (19, 20, 18) stitches have been decreased at neckline edge.

AT THE SAME TIME, when the work measures 13 (13½, 14, 14½)" (33 [34.5, 35.5, 37]cm) or desired length to underarm, ending with a wrong-side row, begin working armhole shaping as follows.

armhole shaping

Next Row (RS) Bind off 10 (10, 11, 12) stitches, work in pattern to end.

Work 1 row in pattern.

Decrease Row (RS) Ssk, work in pattern to end.

Repeat these 2 rows 8 (11, 10, 13) times more.

When all neckline and armhole shaping is complete, 22 (23, 26, 28) stitches remain.

Continue in pattern until the work measures 22 (23, 24, 25)" (56 [58.5, 61, 63.5]cm), ending with a wrong-side row. Armhole measures 9 (9½, 10, 10½)" (23 [24, 25.5, 26.5]cm) from initial bind-off.

shape shoulder

Row 1 (RS) Bind off 7 (7, 8, 9) stitches, work in pattern to end.

Row 2 (WS) Work all stitches in pattern.

Row 3 (RS) Bind off 7 (8, 8, 9) stitches, work in pattern to end.

Row 4 (WS) Work all stitches in pattern.

Bind off remaining 8 (8, 10, 10) stitches.

RIGHT FRONT

Note: Read ahead! Waist, neckline, and armhole shaping directions are worked simultaneously.

Using the larger needle and CC1, cast on 56 (64, 68, 72) stitches.

Purl 1 row (wrong side). Join MC.

Work 4 (6, 8, 10) rows in Corrugated Slip Stitch.

shape waist

Decrease Row (RS) Work in pattern to last 2 stitches, k2tog.

Work 5 rows in pattern.

Repeat these 6 rows 7 times more—48 (56, 60, 64) stitches.

Work 12 rows in pattern (18 rows after last decrease row).

Increase Row (RS) Work in pattern to last stitch, m1, k1.

Work 5 rows in pattern.

Repeat these 6 rows 7 times more—56 (64, 68, 72) stitches.

AT THE SAME TIME, when the work measures 8 (9, 10, 10½)" (20.5 [23, 25.5, 26.5]cm), or 5 (4½, 4, 4)" (12.5 [11, 10, 10]cm) less than the desired length to underarm, begin working neckline shaping as follows.

shape neckline

Neckline Decrease Row (RS) Ssk, work in pattern to end.

Work 3 rows in pattern.

Repeat these 4 rows 5 (6, 6, 5) times more.

Work Neckline Decrease Row.

Work 5 rows in pattern.

Repeat these 6 rows 4 (5, 6, 5) times more.

Work Neckline Decrease Row.

Work 7 rows in pattern.

Repeat these 8 rows 3 (5, 5, 5) times more—15 (19, 20, 18) stitches have been decreased at the neckline edge.

AT THE SAME TIME, when the work measures 13 (13½, 14, 14½)" (33 [34.5, 35.5, 37]cm) or the desired length to the underarm, ending with a right-side row, begin working armhole shaping as follows.

shape armhole

Next Row (WS) Bind off 10 (10, 11, 12) stitches, work in pattern to end.

Decrease Row (RS) Work in pattern to last 2 stitches, k2tog.

Work 1 row in pattern.

Repeat these 2 rows 8 (11, 10, 13) times more.

Once the neckline and armhole shaping is complete, 22 (23, 26, 28) stitches remain.

Continue in pattern until the work measures 22 (23, 24, 25)" (56 [58.5, 61, 63.5]cm), ending with a right-side row. Armhole measures 9 (9½, 10, 10½)" (23 [24, 25.5, 26.5]cm) from initial bind-off.

shape shoulder

Row 1 (WS) Bind off 7 (7, 8, 9) stitches, work in pattern to end.

Row 2 (RS) Work all stitches in pattern.

Row 3 (WS) Bind off 7 (8, 8, 9) stitches, work in pattern to end.

Row 4 (RS) Work all stitches in pattern.

Bind off remaining 8 (8, 10, 10) stitches.

SLEEVES (MAKE 2)

Using the larger needle and CC1, cast on 52 (60, 64, 72) stitches.

Purl 1 row (wrong side).

Work 4 (8, 6, 4) rows in Corrugated Slip Stitch.

Increase Row (RS) K1, m1, work in pattern to last stitch, m1, k1.

Work 5 rows in pattern.

Repeat these 6 rows 23 (21, 22, 23) times more—100 (104, 110, 120) stitches.

Continue in pattern until the work measures 17" (43cm) or the desired length to underarm, ending with a wrong-side row.

sleeve cap shaping

Bind off 10 (10, 11, 12) stitches at the beginning of the next 2 rows—80 (84, 88, 96) stitches.

Decrease Row (RS) Ssk, work in pattern to last 2 stitches, k2tog.

Work 1 row in pattern.

Repeat these 2 rows 10 (9, 10, 11) times more—58 (64, 66, 72) stitches.

Work Decrease Row.

Work 3 rows in pattern.

Repeat these 4 rows 2 (3, 3, 4) times more—52 (56, 58, 62) stitches.

Work Decrease Row. Work 1 row in pattern.

Repeat these 2 rows 9 times more.

Bind off remaining 32 (36, 38, 42) stitches.

FINISHING

assembly

Sew the shoulder seams.

Sew the Sleeves into the armholes.

Sew the sleeve seams and side seams.

button band

With the right side facing, using the smaller needle and CC2, pick up and knit 2 stitches for every 3 rows along the edge of the Right Front, between the bottom edge and the first neckline decrease. Work 7 rows in Seed Stitch.

Bind off all stitches.

buttonhole band

With the right side facing, using the smaller needle and CC2, pick up and knit 2 stitches for every 3 rows along the edge of the Left Front, between the first neckline decrease and the bottom edge. Work 3 rows in Seed Stitch. Work buttonholes as follows:

Buttonhole Row 1 (RS) Work 7 (8, 9, 10) stitches in Seed Stitch, bind off 2 stitches, *work 5 (6, 7, 8) stitches in Seed Stitch, bind off 2 stitches, repeat from * once more, work remaining stitches in Seed Stitch.

Row 2 (WS) Work in Seed stitch, casting on 2 stitches over each pair of bound-off stitches.

Work 2 more rows in Seed Stitch. Bind off all stitches.

Lightly steam block the sweater.

Sew on the buttons.

double ruffle edge

Ruffle A Using the smaller needle and CC3, with the right side facing, pick up and knit 1 stitch in each cast-on stitch along the lower edge of the sweater.

Rows 1 and 2 Knit.

Rows 3–6 Work in stockinette stitch.

Rows 7 and 8 Kfb into each stitch, doubling the number of stitches in each row. When row 8 is complete, there will be 4 times the original number of stitches on the needle.

Bind off all stitches loosely.

Ruffle B Using the smaller needle and CC2, with the wrong side facing, pick up and knit 1 stitch in each garter stitch bump at the base of the ruffle.

Purl 1 row.

Work rows 3–8 as for Ruffle A.

Bind off all stitches.

Work ruffles as above around the lower edge of each Sleeve, using the smaller needle and picking up and knitting 1 stitch in each cast-on stitch.

Using the smaller needle and CC2, pick up 2 stitches for every 3 rows along the shaped front edges of the neckline and 4 stitches for every 5 bound-off stitches along the back neckline. Work ruffles as above around the neckline, except work Ruffle A with CC2 and Ruffle B with CC3.

Weave in all ends.

hot cocoa
jacket

Warm as a cup of the good stuff, this gorgeous double-breasted cardigan will do double duty. Wear it on weekends with a turtleneck, jeans, and boots, or dress it up for workdays. The combination of directional knit/purl stitches helps create visual panels that shape the body in the most flattering way. It looks harder to knit than it is, which is always good for impressing your friends.

SIZE

L (1X, 2X, 3X)
Shown in size 1X

FINISHED MEASUREMENTS

Chest: 44½ (49, 53½, 58)" (113 [124.5, 136, 147.3]cm)
Length: 24 (25½, 26, 26)" (61 [64.8, 66, 66]cm)

MATERIALS

14 (15, 16, 17) skeins RYC Cashsoft DK; 57% extra fine merino, 33% microfibre, 10% cashmere; 142 yd (130m) per 1¾ oz (50g) skein; #517 Donkey (deep taupe)
1 US #6 (4mm) circular needle, 32" (80cm) long, *or size needed to obtain gauge*
Stitch markers
3 buttons, 1¼" (3cm) diameter
Tapestry needle
Sewing thread
Sewing needle

GAUGE

22 stitches and 30 rows = 4" (10cm) over all stitch patterns

ABBREVIATIONS AND TECHNIQUES

See page 32.

STITCH PATTERNS

K1 tbl Knit the next stitch through the back loop, wrapping the yarn counter-clockwise around the right needle.

Kc tbl (Knit crossed through back loop) Knit the next stitch through the back loop, but wrap the yarn clockwise around the right needle (instead of counter-clockwise as usual). The orientation of the new stitch on the right needle will be reversed.

Rice Stitch (Worked over an odd number of stitches)
Row 1 (RS) P1, *k1 tbl, p1, repeat from * to end.
Row 2 (WS) Knit all stitches.
Repeat these 2 rows for Rice Stitch.

Left Slant Stitch (Worked over a multiple of 3 stitches)
Row 1 (RS) *P1, (k1 tbl) twice, repeat from * to end.
Even-Numbered Rows 2, 4, and 6 (WS) Knit all stitches.

Row 3 (RS) *K1 tbl, p1, k1 tbl, repeat from * to end.
Row 5 (RS) *K2 tbl, p1, repeat from * to end.
Repeat Rows 1–6 for Left Slant Stitch.

Right Slant Stitch (Worked over a multiple of 3 stitches)
Note: *After working each wrong-side row, the stitches will be twisted. Do not untwist them when working right-side rows.*
Row 1 (RS) *K2, p1 tbl, repeat from * to end.
Even-Numbered Rows 2, 4, and 6 (WS) (Kc tbl) to end.
Row 3 (RS) *K1, p1 tbl, k1, repeat from * to end.
Row 5 (RS) *P1 tbl, k2, repeat from * to end.

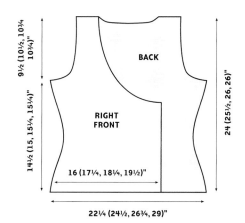

9½ (10½, 10¾ 10¾)"

BACK

14½ (15, 15¼, 15¼)"

RIGHT FRONT

24 (25½, 26, 26)"

16 (17¼, 18¼, 19½)"

22¼ (24½, 26¾, 29)"

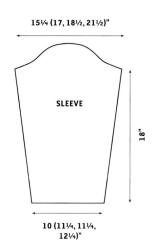

15¼ (17, 18½, 21½)"

SLEEVE

18"

10 (11¼, 11¼, 12¼)"

BACK

Cast on 123 (135, 147, 159) stitches.

Set-Up Row (RS) K1, work 33 (39, 45, 51) stitches in Left Slant Stitch, place marker, work 55 stitches in Rice Stitch, place marker, work 33 (39, 45, 51) stitches in Right Slant Stitch, k1. Work 3 rows in pattern as set, working edge stitches in stockinette stitch.

waist shaping

Decrease Row (RS) K1, k2tog, work in pattern to last 3 stitches, ssk, k1.

Work 5 rows in pattern.

Repeat these 6 rows 7 times more, then work Decrease Row once more—105 (117, 129, 141) stitches.

Work 2 rows in pattern. Work measures 7¼" (18.5cm).

Next Row (WS) P1, knit to second marker, (kc tbl) to last stitch, p1.

Next Row (RS) K1, work in Right Slant Stitch to first marker, work in Rice Stitch to second marker, work in Left Slant Stitch to last stitch, k1.

Continue working in these stitch patterns as set until Back is completed.

Work 3 rows in pattern.

Increase Row (RS) K1, m1, work in pattern to last stitch, m1, k1.

Work 5 rows in pattern.

Repeat these 6 rows 7 times more, then work Increase Row once more—123 (135, 147, 159) stitches.

Continue in pattern until the work measures 14½ (15, 15¼, 15¼)" (37 [38, 38.5, 38.5]cm), ending with a wrong-side row.

shape armholes

Bind off 4 (4, 6, 8) stitches at the beginning of the next 2 rows.

Bind off 3 stitches at the beginning of the next 2 rows.

Bind off 2 stitches at the beginning of the next 2 rows—105 (117, 125, 133) stitches.

Decrease Row (RS) K1, k2tog, work in pattern to last 3 stitches, ssk, k1.

Work 1 row in pattern.

Repeat these 2 rows 2 (4, 4, 8) times more, then work Decrease Row once more—97 (105, 113, 113) stitches.

Work 3 rows in pattern.

Work Decrease Row.

Repeat these 4 rows 3 (2, 3, 1) times more—89 (99, 105, 109) stitches.

Continue in pattern until the work measures 23½ (25, 25½, 25½)" (59.5 [63.5, 64.7, 64.7]cm), and armholes measure 9 (10, 10¼, 10¼)" (23 [25.5, 26, 26]cm), ending with a wrong-side row.

shape back neckline

Next Row (RS) Work 37 (35, 38, 39) stitches in pattern, bind off 15 (29, 29, 31) stitches, work in pattern to end.

Work in pattern to the end of the first set of stitches on the needle. Turn work.

Next Row (RS) Bind off 8 (6, 6, 6) stitches, work in pattern to end—29 (29, 32, 33) stitches.

Work in pattern to the end of the first set of stitches on the needle. Turn work.

Next Row (RS) Bind off 3 (3, 4, 3) stitches, work in pattern to end.

Bind off remaining 26 (26, 28, 30) stitches.

Rejoin yarn to the remaining stitches with the wrong side facing.

Next Row (WS) Bind off 8 (6, 6, 6) stitches, work in pattern to end—29 (29, 32, 33) stitches.

Work 1 row in pattern.

Next Row (RS) Bind off 3 (3, 4, 3) stitches, work in pattern to end.

Work 1 row in pattern.

Bind off the remaining 26 (26, 28, 30) stitches.

LEFT FRONT

Cast on 89 (95, 101, 107) stitches.

Set-Up Row (RS) K1, work 33 (39, 45, 51) stitches in Left Slant Stitch, place marker, work 55 stitches in Rice Stitch.

Work 3 rows in pattern as set.

Decrease Row (RS) K1, k2tog, work in pattern to end.

Work 5 rows in pattern.

Repeat these 6 rows 7 times more, then work Decrease Row once more—80 (86, 92, 98) stitches.

Work 2 rows in pattern. The work measures 7¼" (18.5cm).

Next Row (WS) Knit to marker, (kc tbl) to last stitch, p1.

Next Row (RS) K1, work in Right Slant Stitch to marker, work in Rice Stitch to end.

Continue working in these stitch patterns as set until the Left Front is completed.

Work 3 rows in pattern.

Note: Read ahead! Waist, neckline, and armhole shaping directions are worked simultaneously.

Increase Row (RS) K1, m1, work in pattern to end.

Work 5 rows in pattern.

Repeat these 6 rows 7 times more, then work Increase Row once more.

Continue in pattern until the work measures 14½ (15, 15¼, 15¼)" (37 [38, 38.5, 38.5]cm), ending with a wrong-side row, then proceed to armhole shaping.

AT THE SAME TIME, when the work measures 10 (11½, 12, 12)" (28 [29.2, 30.5, 30.5]cm), ending with a wrong-side row, work a buttonhole as follows:

Next Row (RS) Work in pattern to last 11 stitches, bind off 3 stitches, work in pattern to end.

Work next row in pattern, casting on 3 stitches over bound-off stitches.

Work 1 more row in pattern.

shape neckline

Next Row (WS) Bind off 3 stitches, work in pattern to end.

Work 1 row in pattern.

Repeat these 2 rows 5 (9, 6, 7) times more—37 (25, 34, 31) stitches remain in the Rice Stitch panel.

Next Row (WS) Bind off 2 stitches, work in pattern to end.

Work 1 row in pattern.

Repeat these 2 rows 4 (0, 4, 3) times more, then work the first of these 2 rows again—25 (21, 22, 21) stitches remain in Rice Stitch panel.

Next Row (RS) Work in pattern to last 3 stitches, ssk, k1.

Work 1 row in pattern.

Repeat these 2 rows 9 (9, 9, 7) times more—15 (11, 12, 13) stitches remain in the Rice Stitch panel.

Work 2 rows in pattern.

Next Row (RS) Work in pattern to last 3 stitches, ssk, k1.

Work 3 rows in pattern.

Repeat these 4 rows 5 (6, 8, 9) times more—9 (4, 3, 3) stitches remain in the Rice Stitch panel. Neckline shaping is complete.

AT THE SAME TIME, when the work measures 14½ (15, 15¼, 15¼)" (37 [38, 38.5, 38.5]cm), ending with a wrong-side row, shape the armhole as follows:

shape armholes

Next Row (RS) Bind off 4 (4, 6, 8) stitches, work in pattern to end.

Work 1 row in pattern.

Next Row (RS) Bind off 3 stitches, work in pattern to end.

Work 1 row in pattern.

Next Row (RS) Bind off 2 stitches, work in pattern to end.

Work 1 row in pattern.

Decrease Row (RS) K1, k2tog, work in pattern to end.

Work 1 row in pattern.

Repeat these 2 rows 2 (4, 4, 8) times more, then work Decrease Row once more.

Work 3 rows in pattern.

Work Decrease Row.

Repeat these 4 rows 3 (2, 3, 1) times more.

When all neckline and armhole shaping has been completed, 26 (26, 28, 30) stitches remain.

Continue in pattern until the work measures 24 (25½, 26, 26)" (61 [64.8, 66, 66]cm), and armholes measure 9½ (10½, 10¾, 10¾)" (24 [26.5, 27.3, 27.3]cm).

Bind off all stitches.

RIGHT FRONT

Cast on 89 (95, 101, 107) stitches.

Set-Up Row (RS) Work 55 stitches in Rice Stitch, place marker, work 33 (39, 45, 51) stitches in Right Slant Stitch, k1.

Work 3 rows in pattern as set.

Decrease Row (RS) Work in pattern to last 3 stitches, ssk, k1.

Work 5 rows in pattern.

Repeat these 6 rows 7 times more, then work Decrease Row once more—80 (86, 92, 98) stitches.

Work 2 rows in pattern. Work measures 7¼" (18.5cm).

Next Row (WS) P1, knit to last stitch.

Next Row (RS) Work in Rice Stitch to marker, work in Left Slant Stitch to last stitch, p1.

Continue working in these stitch patterns as set until the Right Front is completed.

Work 3 rows in pattern.

Note: Read ahead! Multiple sets of shaping instructions are worked at the same time.

Increase Row (RS) Work in pattern to last stitch, m1, k1.

Work 5 rows in pattern.

Repeat these 6 rows 7 times more, then work Increase Row once more.

Continue in pattern until the work measures 14½ (15, 15¼, 15¼)" (37 [38, 38.5, 38.5]cm), ending with a wrong-side row, then proceed to armhole shaping.

AT THE SAME TIME, when the work measures 10 (11½, 12, 12)" (28 [29.2, 30.5, 30.5]cm), ending with a wrong-side row, work a buttonhole as follows:

Next Row (RS) Work 8 stitches in pattern, bind off 3 stitches, work in pattern to end.

Work next row in pattern, casting on 3 stitches over bound-off stitches.

Work 2 more rows in pattern.

shape neckline

Next Row (RS) Bind off 3 stitches, work in pattern to end.

Work 1 row in pattern.

Repeat these 2 rows 5 (9, 6, 7) times more—37 (25, 34, 31) stitches remain in the Rice Stitch panel.

Next Row (WS) Bind off 2 stitches, work in pattern to end.

Work 1 row in pattern.

Repeat these 2 rows 5 (1, 5, 4) times more—25 (21, 22, 21) stitches remain in the Rice Stitch panel.

Next Row (RS) K1, k2tog, work in pattern to end.

Work 1 row in pattern.

Repeat these 2 rows 9 (9, 9, 7) times more—15 (11, 12, 13) stitches remain in the Rice Stitch panel.

Work 2 rows in pattern.

Next Row (RS) K1, k2tog, work in pattern to end.

Work 3 rows in pattern.

Repeat these 4 rows 5 (6, 8, 9) times more—9 (4, 3, 3) stitches remain in the Rice Stitch panel. Neckline shaping is complete.

AT THE SAME TIME, when the work measures 14½ (15, 15¼, 15¼)" (37 [38, 38.5, 38.5]cm), ending with a right-side row, shape the armhole as follows.

Continue working in these stitch patterns as set until Sleeve is completed.

Work 1 row in pattern.

Increase Row (RS) K1, m1, work in pattern to last stitch, m1, k1.

Work 9 (7, 5, 5) rows in pattern.

Repeat these 10 (8, 6, 6) rows 7 (15, 19, 13) times more—72 (94, 102, 96) stitches.

Sizes L, 3X Only

Work Increase Row as above.

Work 7 (-, -, 3) rows in pattern.

Repeat these 8 (-, -, 4) rows 5 (-, -, 10) times more—84 (-, -, 118) stitches.

All Sizes

Continue in pattern until the work measures 18" (45.5cm), ending with a wrong-side row.

shape sleeve cap

Bind off 5 (3, 4, 3) stitches at the beginning of the next 2 (4, 2, 6) rows—74 (82, 94, 100) stitches.

Bind off 2 stitches at the beginning of the next 8 (6, 12, 8) rows—58 (70, 70, 84) stitches.

Next Row (RS) K1, k2tog, work in pattern to last 3 stitches, ssk, k1.

Work 1 row in pattern.

Repeat these 2 rows 11 (14, 14, 16) times more—34 (40, 40, 50) stitches.

Bind off 2 (2, 2, 3) stitches at the beginning of the next 2 (4, 4, 4) rows—30 (32, 32, 38) stitches.

Bind off 3 (4, 4, 4) stitches at the beginning of the next 2 rows.

Bind off the remaining 24 (24, 24, 30) stitches.

FINISHING

Sew shoulder seams.

front edges

Three stitches from the front edge of each Front piece; fold the work to the inside and sew in place. Be sure not to sew too tightly.

collar

With wrong side facing, beginning at left front edge, pick up and knit 1 stitch in each bound-off stitch and 3 stitches for every 4 rows along the neckline edge, placing a stitch marker at each shoulder seam and ending at the right front edge.

Work 2 rows in Rice Stitch, beginning with a wrong-side row.

Note: When working the collar, when the wrong side of the jacket is facing, the right side of the collar will be facing. This is so that when the jacket is worn and the collar is folded back, the right side of the collar will be facing. From this point, rows labeled right or wrong-side rows will refer to the right or wrong side of the *collar*, not the jacket. The stitch markers at the right

shape armholes

Next Row (WS) Bind off 4 (4, 6, 8) stitches, work in pattern to end.

Work 1 row in pattern.

Next Row (WS) Bind off 3 stitches, work in pattern to end.

Work 1 row in pattern.

Next Row (WS) Bind off 2 stitches, work in pattern to end.

Decrease Row (RS) Work in pattern to last 3 stitches, ssk, k1.

Work 1 row in pattern.

Repeat these 2 rows 2 (4, 4, 8) times more, then work Decrease Row once more.

Work 3 rows in pattern.

Work Decrease Row.

Repeat these 4 rows 3 (2, 3, 1) times more.

When all neckline and armhole shaping has been completed, 26 (26, 28, 30) stitches remain.

Continue in pattern until the work measures 24 (25½, 26, 26)" (61 [64.8, 66, 66]cm), and armholes measure 9½ (10½, 10¾, 10¾)" (24 [26.5, 27.3, 27.3]cm).

Bind off all stitches.

SLEEVES (MAKE 2)

Cast on 56 (62, 62, 68) stitches.

Set-Up Row (RS) K1, work 27 (30, 30, 33) stitches in Right Slant Stitch, place marker, work 27 (30, 30, 33) stitches in Left Slant Stitch, k1.

and left shoulder seams will be referred to as the right and left markers, respectively.

As you work the short rows that shape the collar, when you encounter a wrapped stitch from a previous short row, pick up the wrap and work it together with the stitch it had wrapped.

Beginning with a wrong-side row (starting at the right front edge of the jacket), work short rows as follows:

Work to 7 stitches past left marker, W&T. Work to 7 stitches past right marker, W&T.

Work to 14 stitches past left marker, W&T. Work to 14 stitches past right marker, W&T.

Work to 21 stitches past left marker, W&T. Work to 21 stitches past right marker, W&T.

Work to 28 stitches past left marker, W&T. Work to 28 stitches past right marker, W&T.

Work to 35 stitches past left marker, W&T. Work to 35 stitches past right marker, W&T.

Work to 42 stitches past left marker, W&T. Work to 42 stitches past right marker, W&T.

Work to 49 stitches past left marker, W&T. Work to 49 stitches past right marker, W&T.

Work to 56 stitches past left marker, W&T. Work to 56 stitches past right marker, W&T.

Work to 63 stitches past left marker, W&T. Work to 63 stitches past right marker, W&T.

Work to 70 stitches past left marker, W&T. Work to 70 stitches past right marker, W&T.

Work to 77 stitches past left marker, W&T. Work to 77 stitches past right marker, W&T.

Work to 84 stitches past left marker, W&T. Work to 84 stitches past right marker, W&T.

Work to end.

Continue working in Rice Stitch across the full collar until the collar is 5¼" (13.3cm) deep at center back.

Loosely bind off all stitches.

assembly

Sew sleeves into armholes.

Sew the side seams and sleeve seams.

Weave in all ends and block the jacket as desired.

Try the jacket on to determine the best locations for the buttons. One button should be on the left front, and the other should be on the inside of the right front.

Sew buttons in place.

peapod aran
jacket

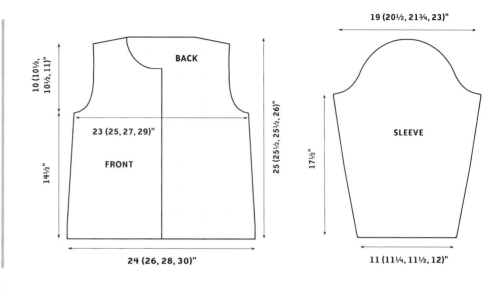

This is about as crazy as we get . . . crazy in love. There is a lot going on with this jacket, and it all follows the rules. All the texture creates verticals, and notice it's not piled on top of itself, but spaced out with smoothness in between, so each vertical can do its job. The collar is a riot of bobbles to balance girls who've got more on the bottom. Crazy in love, yup.

SIZES

L (1X, 2X, 3X)
Shown in size 1X

FINISHED MEASUREMENTS

Bust: 46 (50, 54, 58)" (117 [127, 137, 147.3]cm)
Length: 25 (25½, 25½, 26)" (63.5 [64.8, 64.8, 66]cm)

MATERIALS

29 (32, 35, 39) skeins Cleckheaton Country 8-ply; 100% wool; 104 yd (95m) per 1¾ oz. (50g) skein; #2250 lime green
1 set US #6 (4mm) straight needles, *or size needed to obtain gauge*
1 set US #3 (3.25mm) straight needles
Stitch markers
2 cable needles
Tapestry needle
5 buttons (buy buttons after sweater is complete to ensure a proper fit for the buttonholes.)

GAUGE

22 stitches and 30 rows = 4" (10cm) in stockinette stitch on larger needles.
61 stitches of Cable Chart measure 8¾" (22.2 cm).

ABBREVIATIONS AND TECHNIQUES

See page 32.

STITCH PATTERNS

C3L (Cable 3 Left) Slip next 2 stitches to cable needle and hold to front of work, p1, k2 from cable needle.

C3R (Cable 3 Right) Slip next stitch to cable needle and hold to back of work, k2, p1 from cable needle.

RT (Right Twist) Knit into front of second stitch on left needle, but do not drop from left needle; knit into first stitch on left needle and drop both stitches from left needle.

MB (Make Bobble) (K1, p1, k1, p1, k1) into next stitch (1 stitch increased to 5 stitches), turn work; p5, turn work; k5, turn work; p5, turn work; k5, turn work; p5, turn work; slip 3, k2tog, pass 3 slipped stitches over stitch just knit (5 stitches decreased to 1 stitch).

CCA (Center Cable A) Slip next 3 stitches to first cable needle and hold to back of work, slip next 3 stitches to second cable needle and hold to front of work, k3, k3 from second cable needle, k3 from first cable needle.

CCB (Center Cable B) Slip next 3 stitches to first cable needle and hold to back of work, slip next 3 stitches to second cable needle and also hold to back of work, k3, k3 from second cable needle, k3 from first cable needle.

Continue working with the larger needles.

Next Row (WS) P2, *k1, p1, repeat from * 3 times more, knit to marker, work row 2 of Cable Chart to next marker, k7 (13, 19, 24), (p1, k1) 4 times, p2.

Work 22 more rows in pattern as set, working first and last 10 stitches in rib as set, working Cable Chart between markers, and working remaining stitches in reverse stockinette stitch. Work measures approximately 3" (7.5cm) from hem fold line; side slit borders are complete.

Next Row (RS) Purl to marker, work next row of Cable Chart to next marker, purl to end.

Work 9 rows in pattern as set, working stitches at each edge in reverse stockinette stitch.

Next Row (RS) P1, p2tog, work in pattern to last 3 stitches, p2tog, p1.

Repeat these 10 rows twice more—150 (162, 174, 184) stitches.

Continue in pattern until the work measures 14½" (37cm) from hem fold line or desired length to underarm, ending with a wrong-side row. Make a note of which row of the Cable Chart you have ended on.

shape armholes

Bind off 7 (12, 15, 19) stitches at the beginning of the next 2 rows—136 (138, 144, 146) stitches.

Next Row (RS) P1, p2tog, work in pattern to last 3 stitches, p2tog, p1.

Work 1 row in pattern.

Repeat these 2 rows 6 (7, 9, 10) times more—122 (122, 124, 124) stitches.

Continue in pattern until the work measures 24½ (25, 25, 25½)" (62.2 [63.5, 63.5, 64.8]cm) from hem fold line (armhole measures 10 (10½, 10½, 11)" [25.5 (26.5, 26.5, 28)cm]), ending with a wrong-side row. Make a note of which row of the Cable Chart you have ended on.

Bind off 11 stitches at the beginning of the next 4 rows—78 (78, 80, 80) stitches.

Bind off 12 stitches at the beginning of the next 2 rows. Bind off remaining 54 (54, 56, 56) stitches.

BACK

Using smaller needle, cast on 136 (148, 160, 170) stitches.

Work 13 rows in stockinette stitch, ending with a right-side row.

Next Row (WS) Knit all stitches. This row forms a fold line for the hem.

Set-Up Row (RS) Using larger needles, cast on 10 stitches, k2, *p1, k1, repeat from * 3 times more, p7 (13, 19, 24), place marker, work row 1 of Cable Chart twice, place marker, purl remaining 7 (13, 19, 24) stitches, cast on 10 stitches—156 (168, 180, 190) stitches.

The 10 stitches cast on at each end form borders for the side slits, and will be worked in a rib pattern.

LEFT FRONT

Note: Short-row bust darts are unsuitable for this design, as they will cause the cable pattern to misalign at the shoulders.

Using smaller needle, cast on 69 (75, 81, 86) stitches.

Work 13 rows in stockinette stitch, ending with a right-side row.

Next Row (WS) Knit all stitches. This row forms a fold line for the hem.

Set-Up Row (RS) Using larger needles, cast on 10 stitches, k2, *p1, k1, repeat from * 3 times more, p7 (13, 19, 24), place marker, work Row 1 of Cable Chart, p1—79 (85, 91, 96) stitches.

Continue working with the larger needles.

Next Row (WS) K1, work Row 2 of Cable Chart to marker, k7 (13, 19, 24), *p1, k1, repeat from * 3 times more, p2.

Work 22 more rows in pattern as set. Work measures approximately 3" (7.5cm) from hem fold line; side slit borders are complete.

Next Row (RS) Purl to marker, work next row of Cable Chart, p1.

Work 9 rows in pattern as set, working stitches at each edge in reverse stockinette stitch.

Next Row (RS) P1, p2tog, work in pattern to end.

Repeat these 10 rows twice more—76 (82, 88, 93) stitches. Continue in pattern until the work measures 14½" (37cm) from hem fold line or desired length to underarm, ending with a wrong-side row. Be sure to end on the same row of the Cable Chart as Back at underarm.

shape armhole

Bind off 7 (12, 15, 19) stitches at the beginning of the next row— 69 (70, 73, 74) stitches.

Work 1 row in pattern.

Next Row (RS) P1, p2tog, work in pattern to end.

Repeat these 2 rows 6 (7, 9, 10) times more—62 (62, 63, 63) stitches.

Continue in pattern until work is 19 (21, 25, 27) rows shorter than Back at beginning of shoulder shaping (work measures approximately 22 [22¼, 21¾, 22]" [56 (56.5, 55.2, 56)cm] from hem fold line), ending with a right-side row.

shape neckline

Next Row (WS) Bind off 14 stitches, work in pattern to end— 48 (48, 49, 49) stitches.

Decrease Row 1 (RS) Work in pattern to last 3 stitches, p2tog, p1.

Decrease Row 2 (WS) K1, k2tog, work in pattern to end.

Repeat these 2 rows 4 (3, 2, 1) times more—38 (40, 43, 45) stitches.

Work Decrease Row 1.

Work 1 row in pattern.

Repeat these 2 rows 3 (5, 8, 10) times more—34 stitches.

Work should now measure same as Back to beginning of shoulder shaping.

Next Row (RS) Bind off 11 stitches, work in pattern to end.

Work 1 row in pattern.

Repeat these 2 rows once more. Bind off remaining 12 stitches.

RIGHT FRONT

Note: Short-row bust darts are unsuitable for this design, as they will cause the cable pattern to misalign at the shoulders.

Using smaller needle, cast on 69 (75, 81, 86) stitches.

Work 13 rows in stockinette stitch, ending with a right-side row.

Next Row (WS) Knit all stitches. This row forms a fold line for the hem.

Set-Up Row (RS) Using larger needles, p1, work Row 1 of Cable Chart, place marker, purl to end, cast on 10 stitches—79 (85, 91, 96) stitches.

Continue working with the larger needles.

Next Row (WS) P2, *k1, p1, repeat from * 3 times more, purl to marker, work Row 2 of Cable Chart, p1.

Work 22 more rows in pattern as set. Work measures approximately 3" (7.5cm) from the hem fold line; side slit borders are complete.

Next Row (RS) Work in pattern to marker, purl to end.

Work 9 rows in pattern as set, working stitches at each edge in reverse stockinette stitch.

Next Row (RS) Work in pattern to last 3 stitches, p2tog, p1.

Repeat these 10 rows twice more—76 (82, 88, 93) stitches. Continue in pattern until the work measures 14½" (37cm) from hem fold line or desired length to underarm, ending with a right-side row; be sure to make Right Front 1 row longer than Left Front to this point.

shape armhole

Bind off 7 (12, 15, 19) stitches at the beginning of the next row— 69 (70, 73, 74) stitches.

Next Row (RS) Work in pattern to last 3 stitches, p2tog, p1.

Work 1 row in pattern.

Repeat these 2 rows 6 (7, 9, 10) times more—62 (62, 63, 63) stitches.

Continue in pattern until work is 18 (20, 24, 26) rows shorter than Back at beginning of shoulder shaping, ending with a wrong-side row.

shape neckline

Next Row (RS) Bind off 14 stitches, work in pattern to end—48 (48, 49, 49) stitches.

Decrease Row 1 (WS) Work in pattern to last 3 stitches, ssk, k1.

Decrease Row 2 (RS) P1, p2tog, work in pattern to end.

Repeat these 2 rows 4 (3, 2, 1) times more—38 (40, 43, 45) stitches.

Work 1 row in pattern.

Work Decrease Row 1.

Repeat these 2 rows 3 (5, 8, 10) times more—34 stitches.

Note: Work should now measure 1 row longer than Back at beginning of shoulder shaping.

Next Row (WS) Bind off 11 stitches, work in pattern to end.

Work 1 row in pattern.

Repeat these 2 rows once more. Bind off remaining 12 stitches.

SLEEVES (MAKE 2)

Using smaller needle, cast on 73 (75, 77, 79) stitches.

Work 13 rows in stockinette stitch, ending with a right-side row.

Next Row (WS) Knit all stitches. This row forms a fold line for the hem.

Set-Up Row (RS) Using larger needles, p6 (7, 8, 9), place marker, work Row 1 of Cable Chart, place marker, purl remaining 6 (7, 8, 9) stitches.

Continue working with the larger needles.

Work 11 rows in pattern, working Cable Chart between markers and working remaining stitches in reverse stockinette stitch.

Increase Row (RS) P1, m1, work in pattern to last stitch, m1, p1.

Work 5 (5, 3, 3) rows in pattern.

Repeat these 6 (6, 4, 4) rows 10 (4, 27, 24) times more—95 (85, 133, 129) stitches.

Sizes L, 1X, 3X Only

Work Increase Row.

Work 3 (3, -, 1) rows in pattern.

Repeat these 4 (4, -, 2) rows 10 (19, -, 4) times more—117 (125, -, 139) stitches.

All Sizes

Continue in pattern until the work measures 17½" (44.5cm) from hem fold line or desired length to underarm, ending with a wrong-side row.

sleeve cap

Bind off 7 (12, 15, 19) stitches at the beginning of the next 2 rows—103 (101, 103, 101) stitches.

Decrease Row (RS) P1, p2tog, work in pattern to last 3 stitches, p2tog, p1.

Work 1 row in pattern.

Repeat these 2 rows 18 (23, 22, 27) times more—65 (53, 57, 45) stitches.

Work Decrease Row as above.

Next Row (WS) K1, k2tog, work in pattern to last 2 stitches, ssk, k1.

Repeat these 2 rows 10 (7, 8, 5) times more.

Bind off remaining 21 stitches.

COLLAR

Using larger needles, cast on 29 stitches.

Row 1 (RS) K3, p5, k2, purl to end.

Row 2 and 4 (WS) Knit to last 10 stitches, p2, k5, p3.

Row 3 (RS) K3, p2, MB, p2, k2, purl to end.

Row 4 (WS) Knit to last 10 stitches, p2, k5, p3.

These 4 rows set pattern for collar.

Work 8 more rows in pattern.

Working in pattern as set, shape Collar as follows:

Short Row 1 (RS) Work in pattern to last 5 stitches, W&T.

Short Row 2 (WS) Work in pattern to end.

Work 4 rows in pattern.

Repeat these 5 rows until shaped edge of Collar (edge without bobbles) is long enough to fit around neckline without stretching. Do not work short rows in last 1½" (3.8cm) of collar. End with Row 4 of pattern. Bind off all stitches.

FINISHING

button band

Using smaller needles, cast on 13 stitches.
Row 1 (RS) K2, *k1, p1, repeat from * to last stitch, k1.
Row 2 (WS) K1, *p1, k1, repeat from * to end.
Repeat these 2 rows until band is long enough to reach from hem fold line to beginning of neckline shaping on Left Front when slightly stretched.
Bind off all stitches.
Position band so that the wrong side of the band overlaps the right side of the Left Front by 2 stitches.
Sew in place using backstitch.

buttonhole band

Determine placement of buttons, placing one close to the neckline edge, and spacing others as desired. (It is a good idea to place one at the fullest part of your bust, to prevent gapping when sweater is worn!) Use pins to mark button placement.
Work as for Button Band, working buttonholes to correspond to button placement.
When desired location of buttonhole is reached, work buttonhole as follows:
Buttonhole Row (RS) K2, k1, p1, k1, p1, yo, k2tog, k1, p1, k1, p1, k1.

Sew in place on Right Front, overlapping right front edge by 2 stitches (as for Left Front).

collar hem

Using larger needles and with right side facing, pick up and knit 28 stitches along cast-on end of Collar.
Row 1 (WS) Purl all stitches.
Row 2 (RS) Knit all stitches.
Row 3 (WS) Knit all stitches.
Row 4 (RS) Switch to smaller needles and knit all stitches.
Row 5 (WS) Purl all stitches.
Bind off all stitches.
Repeat for bound-off end of Collar.

assembly

Block all pieces, folding hems on Back, Fronts, Sleeves, and Collar to the wrong side of the work.
Sew the shoulder seams.
Sew the Sleeves into the armholes.
Sew the Sleeve seams and side seams, leaving the side seams open above the tops of the ribbed bands at the side edges.
Sew all hems in place using slip stitch. Be sure to sew loosely, so that the hems will not bind when the jacket is worn.
Sew the Collar to the neckline.
Sew on the buttons opposite the buttonholes.

Key

☐ K on RS, P on WS	◹	C3R
▨ P on RS, K on WS	◸	C3L
B MB	CCA	
RT	CCB	

Cable Chart

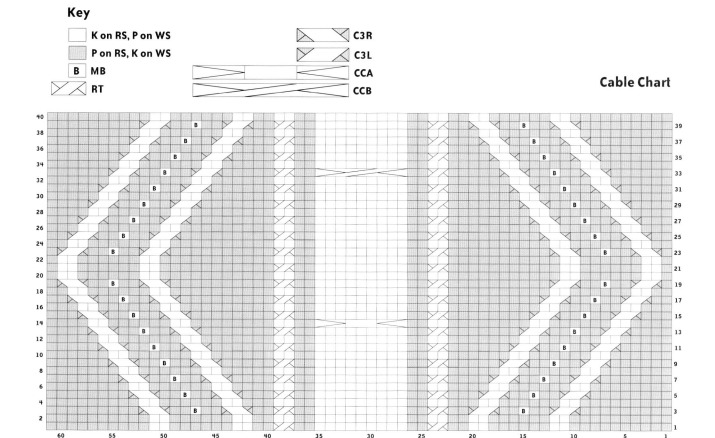

cable love
jacket

DIFFICULTY: 2
BY: TARA JON MANNING

This swingy tunic is the perfect bellygirl wear-with-all. Wear it on its own, pinned with something gorgeous, and let it swoosh as you walk. Or wear something lean underneath and don't close the jacket. We like the idea of wearing it pinned with a little camisole underneath so that if the wind catches it, nothing too personal gets exposed.

We love the pairing of lace and cables. We love the easy rolled edge and how it creates such a flattering vertical line. And we love the little horizontal band of lace and how it doesn't stop the eye long enough to cut you in half. Dammit, we are just full of cable love.

SIZES
L (1X, 2X, 3X)
Shown in size 1X

FINISHED MEASUREMENTS
Note: Chest and Lower Edge measurements are taken with the front edging overlapping the front edges of the cardigan.
Chest: 46 (50, 54, 58)" (117 [127, 137, 147.3]cm)
Lower Edge: 54 (58, 62, 66)" (137 [147.3, 157.5, 167.5]cm)
Length: 29 (29½, 30, 30)" (74 [75, 76, 76]cm)

MATERIALS

14 (15, 17, 18) balls Crystal Palace Crème; 60% wool, 40% Combed Silk; 124 yd (115 m) per 1¾ oz (50g) ball; #2030 Periwinkle

1 US #8 (5mm) circular needle, 32" (80cm) long, *or size needed to obtain gauge*
1 US #6 (4mm) circular needle, 32" (80cm) long
Note: *Though this sweater is worked back and forth in rows (rather than in the round), long circular needles are recommended because of the large numbers of stitches involved. For sections that have fewer stitches, such as the Band and Sleeves, you may prefer to use straight needles or a shorter circular needle.*
Cable needle
Row counter (optional)
Stitch markers
Stitch holders
Waste yarn
Tapestry needle

GAUGE
20 stitches and 28 rows = 4" (10cm) in stockinette stitch using larger needles

ABBREVIATIONS AND TECHNIQUES
See page 32.

STITCH PATTERNS
C4B (Cable 4 Back) Slip the next 2 stitches to the cable needle and hold to the back of the work, k2, k2 from the cable needle.
Band Pattern (Worked over 22 stitches)
Note: All slipped stitches should be slipped as if to knit.
Row 1 (RS) Slip 1, p1, k4, p3, *yo, p2tog; repeat from * once, p3, k4, p1, k1.
Rows 2 and 4 (WS) Slip 1, k1, p4, k2, p1, *yo, p2tog; repeat from * once, p1, k2, p4, k1, p1.
Row 3 (RS) Slip 1, p1, C4B, p3, *yo, p2tog; repeat from * once, p3, C4B, p1, k1.
Front Edge Pattern (Worked over 8 stitches)
Row 1 (RS) P2, C4B, p2.
Rows 2 and 4 (WS) K2, p4, k2.
Row 3 (RS) P2, k4, p2.
p2tog tbl Purl the next two stitches together through the back loops.

BAND
Using the larger circular needle, cast on 22 stitches.
Work 458 (498, 538, 578) rows in Band Pattern; you will end with Row 2.
Bind off all stitches but do not break the yarn; leave the last stitch on the needle.

LOWER BODY
Turn the work so that the long edge of the band nearest the stitch on the needle is facing up. With the right side facing, pick up and knit 229 (249, 269, 289) stitches (1 stitch in each slipped stitch) along the long edge of the band. Including the stitch remaining from the band bind-off, there are 230 (250, 270, 290) stitches.

Row 1 (WS) P58 (63, 68, 73), place marker, p114 (124, 134, 144), place marker, p58 (63, 68, 73).

Work 8 rows in stockinette stitch.

Increase Row (RS) *Knit to 1 stitch before marker, m1, k2, m1; repeat from * once, knit to end.

Work 9 rows in stockinette stitch.

Repeat these 10 rows 8 times more, then work Increase Row once more—270 (290, 310, 330) stitches.

Continue in stockinette stitch until the work measures 15" (38cm) from Row 1.

Bind off all stitches loosely.

UPPER BODY

Using the larger circular needle, with the right side facing, pick up and knit 230 (250, 270, 290) stitches along the upper long edge of the Band.

Work 4 rows in stockinette stitch.

divide fronts and back

Next Row (WS) P46 (50, 53, 56) stitches and place these stitches on a stitch holder, bind off the next 24 (26, 30, 34) stitches, p89 (97, 103, 109) (90 [98, 104, 110] stitches on the right needle) and place these stitches on a second stitch holder, bind off the next 24 (26, 30, 34) stitches, purl to end—46 (50, 53, 56) stitches remain on the needle.

RIGHT FRONT

Next Row (RS) K1, work the next 8 stitches in Front Edge Pattern, knit to last 3 stitches, ssk, k1.

This row sets the pattern for the Right Front, and begins the armhole shaping. The 8 stitches next to the front edge stitch are worked in Front Edge Pattern, and the remaining stitches are worked in stockinette stitch.

shape armhole

Work 1 row in pattern.

Next Row (RS) Work in pattern to last 3 stitches, ssk, k1.

Repeat these 2 rows 6 (7, 8, 11) times more—8 (9, 10, 13) stitches have been decreased at the armhole edge. AT THE SAME TIME, shape neckline as follows.

shape neckline

Work 3 rows in pattern.

Next Row (RS) Work 9 stitches in pattern, ssk, knit to end.

Repeat these 4 rows 12 (13, 15, 15) times more.

When all armhole and neckline shaping has been worked, 25 (27, 27, 27) stitches remain.

Continue in pattern until the armhole measures 9½ (10, 10½, 10½)" (24 [25.5, 26.5, 26.5]cm) from the initial bind-off. Place the 9 stitches at the front edge on hold on waste yarn and the remaining 16 (18, 18, 18) stitches on a stitch holder.

LEFT FRONT

Replace the held stitches of the Left Front on the needle with the right side facing and reattach the yarn at the underarm.

Decrease Row (RS) K1, k2tog, knit to last 9 stitches, work the next 8 stitches in Front Edge Pattern, k1.

This row sets the pattern for the Left Front, and begins the armhole shaping.

Note: Read ahead! Neckline and armhole shaping directions are worked at the same time.

shape armhole

Work 1 row in pattern.

Decrease Row (RS) K1, k2tog, knit to last 9 stitches, work in pattern to end.

Repeat these 2 rows 6 (7, 8, 11) times more—8 (9, 10, 13) stitches have been decreased at the armhole edge. AT THE SAME TIME, shape neckline as follows.

shape neckline

Work 3 rows in pattern.

Next Row (RS) Work in pattern to last 11 stitches, k2tog, work remaining 9 stitches in pattern.

Repeat these 4 rows 12 (13, 15, 15) times more.

When all armhole and neckline shaping has been worked, 25 (27, 27, 27) stitches remain.

Continue in pattern until the armhole measures 9½ (10, 10½, 10½)" (24 [25.5, 26.5, 26.5]cm) from the initial bind-off. Place the 9 stitches at the front edge on hold on waste yarn, and the remaining 16 (18, 18, 18) stitches on a stitch holder.

BACK

With the right side facing, replace the held stitches of the Back on the needle and rejoin the yarn at right underarm.

Decrease Row (RS) K1, k2tog, knit to last 3 stitches, ssk, k1.
Purl 1 row.

Repeat these 2 rows 7 (8, 9, 12) times more—74 (80, 84, 84) stitches remain.

Continue in pattern until the armhole measures 9½ (10, 10½, 10½)" (24 [25.5, 26.5, 26.5]cm) from the initial bind-off, ending with a wrong-side row.

Next Row (RS) K16 (18, 18, 18), bind off the next 42 (44, 48, 48) stitches, knit to end.

Join the Back to the Fronts at the shoulders using the three-needle bind-off (page 33).

NECKBAND

Replace the 9 held stitches of one front on the needle and work in pattern until the piece reaches the center of the back neckline.

Place the stitches on a stitch holder and work the held stitches of the other front in the same way.

Graft the two ends of the Neckband together and sew the lower edge of the piece to the back neckline edge.

SLEEVES (MAKE 2)

Using the larger needle, cast on 60 (63, 67, 72) stitches.
Beginning with a right-side row, work 10 rows in stockinette stitch.

Increase Row (RS) K1, m1, knit to last stitch, m1, k1.
Work 5 rows in stockinette stitch.

Repeat these 6 rows 17 (13, 9, 9) times more—96 (91, 87, 92) stitches.

Work Increase Row.

Work 3 rows in stockinette stitch.

Repeat these 4 rows 1 (7, 13, 13) times more—100 (107, 115, 120) stitches.

Continue in stockinette stitch until the Sleeve measures 18" (45.5cm) or desired length to underarm, ending with a wrong-side row.

shape sleeve cap

Bind off 12 (13, 15, 17) stitches at the beginning of the next 2 rows—76 (81, 85, 86) stitches.

Decrease Row (RS) K1, k2tog, knit to last 3 stitches, ssk, k1.
Purl 1 row.

Repeat these 2 rows 19 (21, 23, 23) times more—36 (37, 37, 38) stitches.

Work Decrease Row as above.

Next Row (WS) P1, p2tog tbl, purl to last 3 stitches, p2tog, p1.
Repeat these 2 rows 3 times more.

Bind off the remaining 20 (21, 21, 22) stitches.

FINISHING

assembly

Weave in all ends.
Sew Sleeves into armholes.
Sew sleeve seams.

front edging

With the right side facing, using the smaller needle, and beginning at the lower corner of the right front edge, pick up and knit 3 stitches for every 4 rows along the right front edge, back neckline edge, and left front edge. When you reach the Band, pick up 1 stitch in each cast-on or bound-off stitch. Work in stockinette stitch until the Edging measures 2 inches. Bind off all stitches loosely in pattern.

Weave in all ends and block the cardigan as desired.

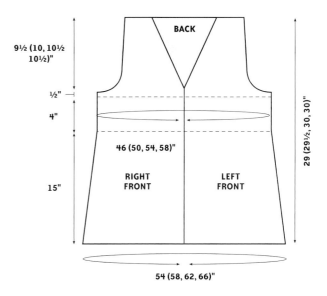

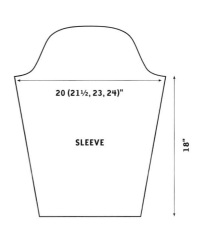

folly II

DIFFICULTY: 3

BY: JILLIAN MORENO FOR ACME KNITTING COMPANY

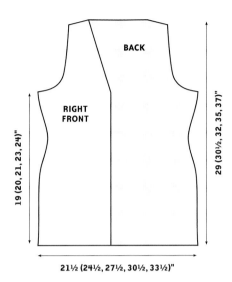

This sweater has it all: a little color, a little excess, a lot of tweedy yarn. This is not a sweater for the shy, faint of heart, or premenstrual. People will stare whenever you wear it. It's also one of the most flattering sweaters a belly/butt girl could wear . . . look at all those attention-getting flowers up by your face! How could you resist? And don't forget the waist shaping, which makes the flared hem look even flirtier.

Never worked a shawl collar before? Fret not. All those flowers will cover a multitude of knitting sins. And don't miss the groovy flower and button cufflinks.

SIZE

L (1X, 2X, 3X, 4X)

Shown in size 1X

FINISHED MEASUREMENTS

Chest: 43 (49, 55, 61, 67)" (109 [124.5, 139.7, 155, 170]cm)

Length: 29 (30½, 32, 35, 37)" (74 [78.5, 81, 88.5, 94]cm)

MATERIALS

Black Water Abbey Tweed; 100% wool; 220 yd (198m) per 4 oz (113 g) skein

7 (9, 10, 12, 13) skeins Chestnut (MC)

For Flowers:

1 skein Autumn (CC)

1 skein Gentian (purple, CC2)

1 skein Navy (CC3)

1 skein Wine (CC4)

1 US #6 (4mm) circular needle, 24" (60cm) long, *or size needed to obtain gauge*

1 US #5 (3.75mm) circular needle, 24" (60cm) long

1 set US #7 (4.5mm) straight needles

2 stitch markers

Safety pins

Tapestry needle

7 buttons, 1" (25mm) diameter (5 for button band, 2 for cufflinks)

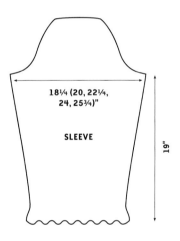

GAUGE

18 stitches and 26 rows = 4" (10cm) in stockinette stitch using the larger needles

ABBREVIATIONS AND TECHNIQUES

See page 32.

STITCH PATTERNS

Seed Stitch (Worked over an even number of stitches):

Row 1 (RS) *K1, p1; repeat from * to end.

Row 2 (WS) *P1, k1; repeat from * to end.

Repeat these 2 rows for Seed Stitch.

1x1 Rib (Worked over an even number of stitches):

Row 1 (K1, p1) to end.

Repeat Row 1 for 1X1 Rib.

BACK

Using the smaller needle and MC, cast on
98 (110, 124, 138, 152) stitches.
Work in Seed Stitch until the work measures 2½" (6.5cm).
Using the larger needle, work in stockinette stitch until the work measures 6 (7, 8, 10, 11)" (15 [18, 20.5, 25.5, 28]cm), ending with a wrong-side row.

waist shaping

Decrease Row (RS) K4, k2tog, knit to last 6 stitches, ssk, k4.
Work 9 rows in stockinette stitch.
Repeat these 10 rows 3 times more—90 (102, 116, 130, 144) stitches.
Increase Row (RS) K4, m1, knit to last 4 stitches, m1, k4.
Work 9 rows in stockinette stitch.
Repeat these 10 rows 3 times more—98 (110, 124, 138, 152) stitches.
Continue in stockinette stitch until the work measures 19 (20, 21, 23, 24)" (48.5 [51, 53.5, 58.5, 61]cm), ending with a wrong-side row.

shape armholes

Bind off 8 (10, 12, 13, 14) stitches at the beginning of the next 2 rows—82 (90, 100, 112, 124) stitches.
Decrease Row (RS) K1, k2tog, knit to last 3 stitches, ssk, k1.
Purl 1 row.
Repeat these 2 rows 7 (8, 10, 12, 12) times more—66 (72, 78, 86, 98) stitches.
Continue in stockinette stitch until the armhole measures 9 (9½, 10, 11, 12)" (23 [24, 25.5, 28, 30.5]cm), ending with a wrong-side row.

shape shoulders

Bind off 5 (6, 6, 8, 9) stitches at the beginning of the next 2 rows.
Bind off 6 (6, 7, 8, 9) stitches at the beginning of the next 2 rows.
Bind off 6 (7, 7, 8, 9) stitches at the beginning of the next 2 rows.
Bind off the remaining 32 (34, 38, 38, 44) stitches.

LEFT FRONT

Using the smaller needle and MC, cast on 44 (50, 58, 64, 72) stitches.
Work in Seed Stitch until the work measures 2½" (6.5cm).
Using the larger needles, work in stockinette stitch until the work measures 6 (7, 8, 10, 11)" (15 [18, 20.5, 25.5, 28]cm), ending with a wrong-side row.

waist shaping

Decrease Row (RS) K4, k2tog, knit to end.
Work 9 rows in stockinette stitch.
Repeat these 10 rows 3 times more—40 (46, 54, 60, 68) stitches.
Increase Row (RS) K4, m1, knit to end.
Work 9 rows in stockinette stitch.
Repeat these 10 rows 3 times more—44 (50,58, 64, 72) stitches.

Continue in stockinette stitch until the work measures 19 (20, 21, 23, 24)" (48.5 [51, 53.5, 58.5, 61]cm), ending with a wrong-side row.
Note: Read ahead! Neckline shaping and armhole shaping are worked simultaneously, starting on the next row.

shape armhole

Next Row (RS) Bind off 8 (10, 12, 13, 14) stitches, knit to end.
Purl 1 row.
Decrease Row (RS) K1, k2tog, knit to end.
Purl 1 row.
Repeat these 2 rows 7 (8, 10, 12, 12) times more. AT THE SAME TIME, shape neckline as follows.

shape neckline

Decrease Row (RS) Knit to last 3 stitches, ssk, k1.
Work 3 rows in stockinette stitch.
Repeat these 4 rows 10 (11, 14, 13, 17) times more.
When the armhole and neckline shaping has been worked, 17 (19, 20, 24, 27) stitches remain. Continue in stockinette stitch until armhole measures 9 (9½, 10, 11, 12)" (23 [24, 25.5, 28, 30.5]cm), ending with a wrong-side row.

shape shoulder

Bind off 5 (6, 6, 8, 9) stitches at the beginning of the next row.
Purl 1 row.
Bind off 6 (6, 7, 8, 9) stitches at the beginning of the next row.
Purl 1 row. Bind off the remaining 6 (7, 7, 8, 9) stitches.

RIGHT FRONT

Using the smaller needle and MC, cast on 44 (50, 58, 64, 72) stitches.
Work in Seed Stitch until the work measures 2½" (6.5cm).
Using the larger needles, work in stockinette stitch until the work measures 6 (7, 8, 10, 11)" (15 [18, 20.5, 25.5, 28]cm), ending with a wrong-side row.

waist shaping

Decrease Row (RS) Knit to last 6 stitches, ssk, k4.
Work 9 rows in stockinette stitch.
Repeat these 10 rows 3 times more—40 (46, 54, 60, 68) stitches.
Increase Row (RS) Knit to last 4 stitches, m1, k4.
Work 9 rows in stockinette stitch.
Repeat these 10 rows 3 times more—44 (50, 58, 64, 72) stitches.
Continue in stockinette stitch until the work measures 19 (20, 21, 23, 24)" (48.5 [51, 53.5, 58.5, 61]cm), ending with a right-side row.
Note: Read ahead! Neckline shaping and armhole shaping are worked simultaneously, starting on the next row.

shape armhole

Next Row (WS) Bind off 8 (10, 12, 13, 14) stitches, purl to end.
Decrease Row (RS) Knit to last 3 stitches, ssk, k1.
Purl 1 row.

Repeat these 2 rows 7 (8, 10, 12, 12) times more. AT THE SAME TIME, shape neckline as follows.

shape neckline
Decrease Row (RS) K1, k2tog, knit to end.
Work 3 rows in stockinette stitch.
Repeat these 4 rows 10 (11, 14, 13, 17) times more.
Once all armhole and neckline shaping has been worked, 17 (19, 20, 24, 27) stitches remain. Continue in stockinette stitch until the armhole measures 9 (9½, 10, 11, 12)" (23 [24, 25.5, 28, 30.5]cm), ending with a right-side row.

shape shoulder
Bind off 5 (6, 6, 8, 9) stitches at the beginning of the next row.
Knit 1 row.
Bind off 6 (6, 7, 8, 9) stitches at the beginning of the next row.
Knit 1 row. Bind off the remaining 6 (7, 7, 8, 9) stitches.

SLEEVES (MAKE 2)

ruffle
Using the larger needle and MC, cast on 176 (192, 216, 232, 256) stitches.
Beginning with a wrong-side row, work 3 rows in stockinette stitch.
Decrease Row (RS) (K2tog) to end—88 (96, 108, 116, 128) stitches.
Purl 1 row.
Decrease Row (RS) (K2tog) to end—44 (48, 54, 58, 64) stitches.
Work in stockinette stitch until the work measures 2" (5cm), ending with a wrong-side row.

cuff buttonholes
Next Row (RS) K5, bind off 3 stitches, knit to last 7 stitches, bind off 3 stitches, knit to end.
Next Row (WS) *Purl to bound-off stitches, cast on 3 stitches; repeat from * once, knit to end.
Work 2 rows in stockinette stitch.

Sizes L, 1X, 2X Only
Next Row (RS) K2, m1, knit to last 2 stitches, m1, k2.
Work 5 rows in stockinette stitch.
Repeat these 6 rows 8 (8, 2, -, -) times more—62 (66, 60, -, -) stitches.

All Sizes
Next Row (RS) K2, m1, knit to last 2 stitches, m1, k2.
Work 3 rows in stockinette stitch.
Repeat these 4 rows 9 (11, 19, 24, 25) times more—82 (90, 100, 108, 116) stitches.
Continue in stockinette stitch until the work measures 19" (48.5cm) or desired length to underarm, ending with a right-side row.

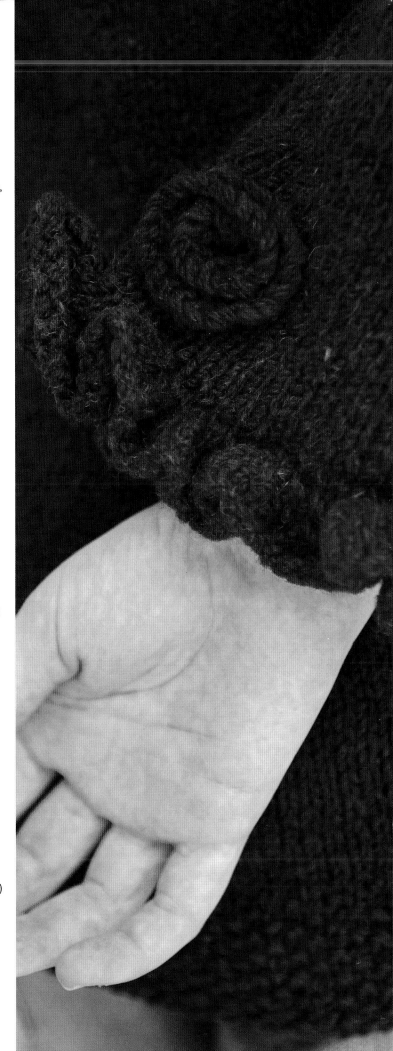

shape sleeve cap

Bind off 8 (10, 12, 13, 14) stitches at the beginning of the next 2 rows—66 (70, 76, 82, 88) stitches.

Next Row (RS) K1, k2tog, knit to last 3 stitches, ssk, k1. Purl 1 row.

Repeat these 2 rows 18 (19, 20, 22, 24) times more.

Bind off the remaining 28 (30, 34, 36, 38) stitches.

FINISHING

assembly

Block as desired.

Sew Back to Fronts at shoulders.

Sew sleeve caps into armholes.

Sew sleeve seams, leaving 3" (7.5cm) open at the lower edge.

Sew side seams.

shawl collar

Using smaller needle and MC, with the right side facing and beginning at the bottom of the neckline shaping, pick up and knit 4 stitches in every 5 rows along the right front neckline edge, place marker, pick up and knit 1 stitch in each bound-off stitch of the back neckline, place marker, pick up and knit 4 stitches in every 5 rows along the left front neckline edge, ending at the bottom of the neckline shaping.

Work in 1x1 Rib to second marker, W&T.

Work in 1x1 Rib to marker, W&T.

*Work across back neck stitches in 1x1 Rib to 1 stitch past marker, W&T. Repeat from * once.

**Work across back neck stitches in 1x1 Rib to 2 stitches past marker, W&T. Repeat from ** once.

Continue working short rows in 1x1 Rib, working each short row 1 stitch longer than the last, until all picked-up stitches have been worked.

Work 2 rows over all stitches in 1x1 Rib.

Work 4 rows in stockinette stitch, so that the right side of the stockinette stitch faces the right side of the sweater. (This will give the collar an edge that will curl under slightly when the collar is folded back.)

button band

Using the smaller needle and MC, with the right side facing, pick up and knit 3 stitches for every 4 rows along the left front edge.

Work 6 rows in Seed Stitch. Bind off all stitches in pattern.

buttonhole band

Try on the sweater and determine the best positions for the 5 buttons, placing one at the bottom, as shown. Mark the button placement near the right front edge using safety pins.

With the right side facing, using the smaller needle and MC, pick up and knit 3 stitches for every 4 rows along front edge of right front. Work 2 rows in Seed Stitch.

Next Row (WS) *Work in pattern to the position of a button, bind off 3 stitches; repeat from * 4 times more, work in pattern to end.

Next Row (RS) *Work in pattern to bound-off stitches, cast on 3 stitches; repeat from * 4 times more, work in pattern to end.

Work 2 more rows in Seed Stitch. Bind off all stitches in pattern.

Sew the lower edges of the collar to the top edges of the Button Band and Buttonhole Band. Sew on the buttons opposite the buttonholes.

flowers

Note: Leave 6" (15cm) yarn tails when casting on and binding off the flowers. These ends will be used to assemble and sew on the flowers.

Large Flower (Make 8 of each color):

Using double-pointed needles, cast on 20 stitches.

Knit 2 rows.

Next Row (Kfb) to end—40 stitches.

Knit 1 row.

Next Row (Kfb) to end—80 stitches.

Bind off all stitches.

Small Flower (Make 6 of each color):

Using double-pointed needles, cast on 10 stitches.

Knit 2 rows.

Next Row (Kfb) to end—20 stitches.

Knit 1 row.

Next Row (Kfb) to end—40 stitches.

Bind off all stitches.

Assembling Flowers

Thread the yarn tail from the bind-off onto the tapestry needle.

Fold the bound-off corner with the attached yarn tail down to the cast-on edge, forming a small triangle.

Wrap the rest of the piece around this triangle in a spiral, forming a flower.

Use the yarn tail to stitch the flower together at the bound-off edge.

cufflinks

Sew two small flowers to the backs of 2 buttons.

Insert the cufflinks through the sleeve buttonholes to hold the cuffs together.

attach flowers

Pin on the flowers in whatever pattern moves you. Try on the sweater to be sure the arrangement of flowers works when worn. Sew on flowers using the yarn tails from the cast-on.

Weave in all ends.

twisted
pullover

DIFFICULTY: 2
BY: LISA MARIE COLLINS

Sometimes color can say it all, but in this case it's color plus a subtle serving of texture that makes this sweater stand out. The V-neck has a little extra detail, so it works for all Bs. The hem is full of texture without being an unwanted horizontal, and look at those delicate squiggles that run top to bottom all over the sweater. Your eyes just can't sit still.

SIZE
L (1X, 2X, 3X)
Shown in size 1X

FINISHED MEASUREMENTS
Chest: 43 (47, 52½, 56½)" (109 [119.5, 133.4, 143.8]cm)
Length: 24 (25, 26, 26)" (61 [63.5, 66, 66]cm)

MATERIALS

8 (9, 11, 12) skeins Classic Elite Princess; 40% merino, 28% viscose, 10 cashmere, 7% angora, 15% nylon; 150 yd (137m) per 1¾ oz (50g) skein; Majesty's Magenta
1 set US #7 (4.5mm) straight needles, *or size needed to obtain gauge*
1 US #7 (4.5mm) circular needle, 16" (40.5cm) long
Cable needle
Stitch holder
Safety pin
2 Stitch markers
Tapestry needle

GAUGE
20 stitches and 31 rows = 4" (10cm) in stockinette stitch
20 stitches and 31 rows = 4" (10cm) in Body pattern (Rows 29–40 of Body Chart)

ABBREVIATIONS AND TECHNIQUES
See page 32.

STITCH PATTERNS
RT (Right Twist) Knit into the front of the second stitch on the left needle, but do not drop it from the left needle; knit into the first stitch on the left needle and drop both stitches from the left needle.

LT (Left Twist) Knit into the back of the second stitch on the left needle, but do not drop it from the left needle; knit the first and second stitches on the left needle together through their back loops.

RDD (Right Double Decrease) Slip the next 2 stitches to the cable needle and hold to the back of the work, behind the left needle; *insert the right needle into the first stitch on the left needle and into the first stitch on the cable needle, knit these 2 stitches together, repeat from * once.

LDD (Left Double Decrease) Slip the next 2 stitches to the cable needle and hold to the front of the work, in front of the left needle; *insert the right needle into the first stitch on the cable needle and into the first stitch on the left needle, knit these 2 stitches together, repeat from * once.

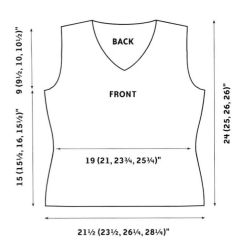

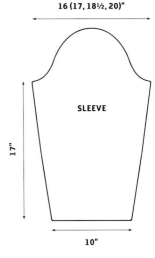

BACK

Note: It is very important to read the pattern before beginning! Multiple sets of directions (i.e., stitch pattern directions, shaping directions) are worked simultaneously.

Cast on 107 (117, 131, 141) stitches.

Row 1 (RS) K4 (2, 2, 7), work Row 1 of Body Chart to last 4 (2, 2, 7) stitches, knit to end.

Row 2 (WS) K2 (2, 2, 3), purl to last 2 (2, 2, 3) stitches (Row 2 of Body Chart), knit to end.

Continue in pattern as set, maintaining 2 (2, 2, 3) stitches at each edge in garter stitch.

Work Rows 1–28 once, then repeat Rows 29–40 until this piece is complete.

If you wish to omit the waist shaping that follows, continue in pattern as set until the work measures 15 (15½, 16, 15½)" (38 [39.5, 40.5, 39.5]cm), ending with a wrong-side row. Proceed to "Shape Armholes."

If you wish to add length below the waist, work more rows before beginning the waist shaping.

As written, the circumference of the sweater at the waist will be approximately 5" (12.5cm) less than the circumference of the sweater at the bust and hem, or approximately 38 (42, 47½, 51½)" (96.5 [106.5, 120.6, 130.8]cm).

After 30 rows of the Body Chart have been completed, work waist shaping as follows:

Waist Decrease Row (RS) K2 (2, 2, 3), ssk, work in pattern to last 4 (4, 4, 5) stitches, k2tog, knit to end.

Work 3 rows in pattern.

Repeat these 4 rows 4 times more, then work Decrease Row once more—95 (105, 119, 129) stitches.

Work 15 rows in pattern.

Waist Increase Row (RS) K2 (2, 2, 3), m1, work in pattern to last 2 (2, 2, 3) stitches, m1, knit to end.

Work 5 rows in pattern.

Repeat these 6 rows 5 times more—107 (117, 131, 141) stitches.

Continue in pattern as set until the work measures 15 (15½, 16, 15½)" (38 [39.5, 40.5, 39.5]cm), ending with a wrong-side row.

shape armholes

Bind off 5 (7, 7, 7) stitches at the beginning of the next 2 rows—97 (103, 117, 127) stitches.

Sizes 2X, 3X Only

Bind off 3 stitches at the beginning of the following 2 rows—- (-, 111, 121) stitches.

All Sizes

Armhole Decrease Row K1, k2tog, work in pattern to last 3 stitches, ssk, k1.

Work 1 row in pattern.

Repeat these 2 rows 0 (4, 7, 11) times more—95 (93, 95, 97) stitches.

Work Armhole Decrease Row.

Work 3 rows in pattern.

Repeat these 4 rows 4 (3, 2, 3) times more—85 (85, 89, 89) stitches.

Continue in pattern until the work measures 23 (24, 25, 25)" (58.5 [61, 63.5, 63.5]cm) (armhole measures 8 [8½, 9, 9½]" [20.5 (21.5, 23, 24)cm]), ending with a wrong-side row.

back neckline and shoulders

Work 32 (32, 34, 34) stitches in pattern, then place these stitches on a stitch holder; bind off the next 21 stitches, work in pattern to end—32 (32, 34, 34) stitches on needle.

left shoulder

Row 1 (WS) Work all stitches in pattern.

Row 2 (RS) Bind off 3 stitches, work in pattern to end.

Row 3 (WS) Work in pattern to last 2 stitches, p2tog tbl.

Row 4 (RS) Ssk, work in pattern to end.

Row 5 (WS) Work in pattern to last 2 stitches, p2tog tbl—26 (26, 28, 28) stitches.

Row 6 (RS) Work 15 (15, 17, 17) stitches in pattern, W&T.

Work in pattern to end.

Bind off all stitches.

Replace the held stitches of the right shoulder on the needle with the wrong side facing, and rejoin the yarn.

Row 1 (WS) Bind off 3 stitches, work in pattern to end.

Row 2 (RS) Work all stitches in pattern.

Row 3 (WS) P2tog, purl to end.

Row 4 (RS) Work in pattern to last 2 stitches, k2tog.

Row 5 (WS) P2tog, purl to end.

Row 6 (RS) Work all stitches in pattern.

Row 7 (WS) Work 15 (15, 17, 17) stitches in pattern, W&T.

Work in pattern to end.

Bind off all stitches.

FRONT

Begin as for Back, working through waist shaping if desired. The sweater shown has a shallow V-neckline, approximately 8½" (21.5cm) deep. The sweater may also be made with a deeper neckline, approximately 11" (28cm) deep. If you wish to work the sweater with the deeper neckline, the neckline shaping will begin before the armhole shaping begins, and the upper right and left sides of the Front will be worked separately. The sweater may also be worked with short-row bust shaping. As written, the short rows will add approximately 1" (2.5cm) of length to the sweater front. If additional length is desired, work more than one set of short rows as written below, working 2 to 4 straight rows (over all stitches) between sets of short rows. Note that after working short rows, the length of your work should be measured along the outer edges, beyond the ends of the short rows.

short-row bust shaping

When the work measures 12½ (13, 13, 13½)" (32 [33, 33, 34.5]cm), ending with a wrong-side row, work as follows:

Rows 1 and 2 Work in pattern to last 3 stitches, W&T.

Rows 3 and 4 Work in pattern to last 7 stitches, W&T.

Rows 5 and 6 Work in pattern to last 11 stitches, W&T.

Rows 7 and 8 Work in pattern to last 15 stitches, W&T.

Row 9 (RS) Work to end in pattern, working wraps together with wrapped stitches.

Row 10 (WS) Work all stitches in pattern, working remaining wraps together with wrapped stitches.

Read ahead to the neckline directions. If you are making the deep V-neckline, the directions will begin before the armhole shaping begins; if you are making the shallow neckline, the armhole shaping will begin first.

When the work measures 15 (15½, 16, 16½)" (38 [39.5, 40.5, 42]cm), ending with a wrong-side row, work armhole shaping as for Back. Armhole shaping will be worked at the same time as neckline shaping.

v-neckline

If working the deep neckline, begin working when the work measures 13 (14, 15, 15)" (33 [35.5, 38, 38]cm), before armhole shaping begins; if you are making the shallow neckline, begin when the work measures 15½ (16½, 17½, 17½)" (39.5 [42, 44.5, 44.5]cm) at the same time as armhole shaping. Neckline shaping begins on a right-side row.

Both deep and shallow V-necklines are worked in the same way for all sizes. When a set of two numbers appears in the directions that follow, they apply to the deep (shallow) necklines.

Set-Up Row (RS) Work to center stitch, place next stitch (center stitch) on hold on safety pin, place remaining stitches on stitch holder.

left front

Note: If working the deep neckline, do not forget to begin armhole shaping when the work measures 15 (15½, 16, 16½)" (38 [39.5, 40.5, 42]cm)!

Work 3 rows in pattern.

Neckline Decrease Row 1 (RS) Work in pattern to last 6 stitches, LDD, k2.

Repeat these 4 rows 1 (4) times more.

Work 7 (5) rows in pattern.

Work Neckline Decrease Row 1.

Repeat these 8 (6) rows 5 (2) times more.

When all neckline (for both deep and shallow necklines) and armhole shaping has been completed, 26 (26, 28, 28) stitches remain.

Continue in pattern until the work measures 23¾ (24¾, 25¾, 25¾)" (60.3 [62.8, 65.4, 65.4]cm), ending with a right-side row.

Next Row (WS) Work 15 (15, 17, 17) stitches in pattern, W&T.

Work in pattern to end.

Bind off all stitches.

right front

Replace the held stitches of the Right Front on the needle (leaving the center stitch on the safety pin) with the right side facing, and reattach the yarn. Work to the end of the row.

Work 3 rows in pattern.

Neckline Decrease Row 2 (RS) K2, RDD, work to end in pattern.

Repeat these 4 rows 1 (4) times more.

Work 7 (5) rows in pattern.

Work Neckline Decrease Row 2.

Repeat these 8 (6) rows 5 (2) times more.

When all neckline (for both deep and shallow necklines) and armhole shaping has been completed, 26 (26, 28, 28) stitches remain.

Continue in pattern until the work measures 23¾ (24¾, 25¾, 25¾)" (60.3 [62.8, 65.4, 65.4]cm), ending with a wrong-side row.

Next Row (RS) Work 15 (15, 17, 17) stitches in pattern, W&T.
Work in pattern to end.
Bind off all stitches.

SLEEVES (MAKE 2)

Cast on 49 stitches.
Work rows 1–22 of Sleeve Chart once, then repeat rows 23–34 until this piece is complete.
After 24 rows of Sleeve Chart have been completed, shape the sleeve as follows:
Increase Row (RS) K1, m1, work in pattern to last 2 stitches, m1, k1.
Work 7 (5, 5, 3) rows in pattern.
Repeat these 8 (6, 6, 4) rows 2 (11, 3, 24) times more, working increased stitches into pattern—55 (73, 57, 99) stitches.

Sizes L, 1X, 2X Only

Work Increase Row.
Work 5 (3, 3, -) rows in pattern.
Repeat these 6 (4, 4, -) rows 11 (5, 17, -) times more—
79 (85, 93, -) stitches.

All Sizes

Continue in pattern until the work measures 17" (43cm) or desired length to underarm, ending with a wrong-side row.

Shape Sleeve Cap

Bind off 5 (7, 7, 7) stitches at the beginning of the next 2 rows—
69 (71, 79, 85) stitches.

Sizes 2X, 3X Only

Bind off 3 stitches at beginning of following 2 rows—
- (-, 73, 79) stitches.

All Sizes

Decrease Row (RS) K1, ssk, work in pattern to last 3 stitches, k2tog, k1.
Work 1 row in pattern.
Repeat these 2 rows 6 (6, 7, 8) times more—55 (57, 57, 61) stitches.
Work Decrease Row.
Work 3 rows in pattern.
Repeat these 4 rows 4 times more—45 (47, 47, 51) stitches.
Work Decrease Row.
Work 1 row in pattern.
Repeat these 2 rows 6 (7, 7, 9) times more—31 stitches.
Use short rows to shape top of sleeve cap as follows:
*Work to last 2 stitches, W&T. Repeat from * once.
*Work to last 4 stitches, W&T. Repeat from * once.
*Work to last 7 stitches, W&T. Repeat from * once.
*Work to end of row, working wraps together with wrapped stitches. Repeat from * once.
Bind off all stitches.

FINISHING

assembly

Sew shoulder seams.

Sew the Sleeves into the armholes.

Sew the sleeve seams.

Sew the side seams, leaving the bottom 2" (5cm) open for side vents.

neckband

Using the circular needle, with the right side facing and beginning at the left shoulder seam, pick up and knit 2 stitches for every 3 rows down the left front neckline edge, place marker, knit the held center stitch, place marker, pick up and knit 2 stitches for every 3 rows along the right front edge, pick up and knit 2 stitches for every 3 rows and 1 stitch in each bound off stitch along the back neckline edge. Place marker and join to begin working in the round.

Round 1 (RS) *Yo, k2tog; repeat from * to 2 stitches before the first marker, ssk, k1, k2tog, **yo, k2tog; repeat from ** to end. Bind off all stitches loosely, decreasing 1 stitch before and after markers at center front (as in previous round).

Weave in ends.

Key

	K on RS, P on WS
	P on RS, K on WS
o	YO
/	K2tog
\	Ssk
△	S2KP
◢	P3tog
	RT
	LT
	Pattern Repeat

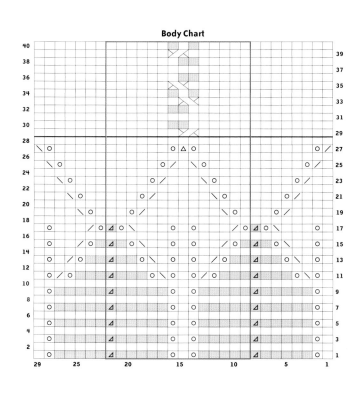

Body Chart

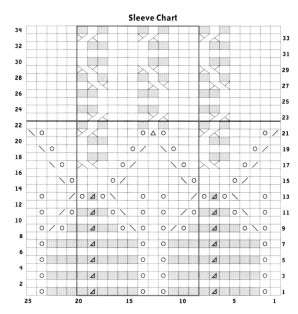

Sleeve Chart

mirage
pullover

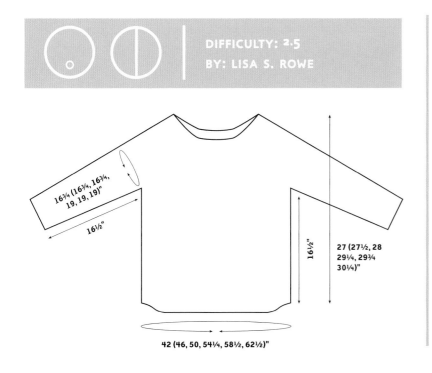

16¾ (16¾, 16¾, 19, 19, 19)"

16½"

16½"

27 (27½, 28 29¼, 29¾ 30¼)"

42 (46, 50, 54¼, 58½, 62½)"

DIFFICULTY: 2.5

BY: LISA S. ROWE

Cables do not mean complicated, especially when they're not real cables. A little clever directional decreasing and increasing gives this sweater the look of cables without adding bulk.

Mirage is an easy in-the-round knit featuring a sweetly feminine wide scoopy neckline that's a little deeper in the back. The mock cables and lace running up both sides act as side panels (you remember the visually slimming thing) and prevent you from knitting acres of uninterrupted stockinette and falling asleep at your needles.

SIZE
L (1X, 2X, 3X, 4X, 5X)
Shown in size 1X

FINISHED MEASUREMENTS
Chest: 42 (46, 50, 54½, 58½, 62½)" (106.5 [117, 127, 138, 149, 158.8]cm)
Length: 27 (27½, 28, 29¼, 29¾, 30¼)" (68.6 [70, 71, 74.3, 75.5, 76.8]cm)

MATERIALS

9 (10, 11, 12, 13, 14) skeins Classic Elite Classic Silk; 50% cotton, 30% silk, 20% nylon; 135 yd (123m) per 1¾ oz (50g) skein; #6947 Cobalt

1 US #7 (4.5mm) circular needle, 16" or 20" (40cm or 50cm) long, *or size needed to obtain gauge*
1 US #7 (4.5mm) circular needle, 32" (80cm) long
1 set US #7 (4.5mm) double-pointed needles
1 spare circular needle or set of double-point needles, US #7 (4.5mm) or smaller
Stitch markers—*be sure that one marker is a different size, color, or type from the others*
Split ring marker or safety pin
Waste yarn
Cable needle
Tapestry needle

GAUGE
19 stitches and 29 rows = 4" (10cm) in stockinette stitch
17 stitches = 3" (7.5cm) in Mock Cable pattern

ABBREVIATIONS AND TECHNIQUES
See page 32.

PATTERN NOTES
If you wish to work short row bust darts for this sweater, it is important that they are turned either within the stockinette stitch panel that forms the front of the sweater or within the reverse stockinette stitch columns on either side of this panel. It would look best to keep the number of short rows to a minimum, and to work them a few rows apart, instead of working all the short rows together (as they are usually worked in this book).

It is very important for the lower body and sleeves to end on the same pattern row. For this reason, as written, the sweater body and sleeves are the same length (16½" [42cm]) If you wish to lengthen or shorten the sleeves, they will need to be shortened or lengthened by a full pattern repeat. Because of this, you may wish to change the length of the body to accommodate the sleeve length you want. Join new balls of yarn at one of the reverse stockinette columns rather than in the middle of one of the stockinette stitch or pattern stitch panels. This will allow the ends to be woven in invisibly.

LOWER BODY

Using the longer circular needle, cast on 198 (218, 238, 260, 280, 300) stitches.

Knit 1 row.

Place marker and join, ensuring that the cast-on edge is not twisted. This marker will be referred to as the end-of-round marker.

Work 9 (9, 9, 13, 13, 13) rounds in garter stitch, ending with a purl round.

Set-Up Round *Pfb, k17 (17, 17, 23, 23, 23), pfb, k2 (2, 2, 3, 3, 3), [kfb] 6 (6, 6, 8, 8, 8) times, k3 (3, 3, 4, 4, 4), pfb, k17 (17, 17, 23, 23, 23), pfb, place marker, k50 (60, 70, 65, 75, 85), place marker; repeat from * once more, omitting last place marker—218 (238, 258, 284, 304, 324) stitches.

Next Round Work 59 (59, 59, 77, 77, 77) stitches of first round of the Body Chart for your size to first marker, knit to second marker, work first round of the Body Chart to third marker, knit to end of round.

Continue in pattern, working the charted pattern as set and all other stitches in stockinette stitch, until the work measures approximately 16½" (42cm) or desired length to underarm, ending with Round 2 or Round 8 (8, 8, 10, 10, 10) of the Chart. Note which round of the chart you have ended on. This is important because your sleeves will need to end on the same chart round if the pattern is to match up correctly in the yoke.

Set this piece aside and work the Sleeves. Do not remove the markers or break the yarn; begin the first sleeve with a new ball of yarn.

SLEEVES (MAKE 2)

Using double-pointed needles, cast on 48 (48, 48, 62, 62, 62) stitches.

Knit 1 row.

Divide stitches evenly between needles. Place marker and join, ensuring that the cast-on edge is not twisted. If desired, place a split ring marker or safety pin in your work to indicate the beginning of the round.

Work 9 (9, 9, 13, 13, 13) rounds in garter stitch, ending with a purl round.

Next Round K2 (2, 2, 5, 5, 5), m1, *k5 (5, 5, 4, 4, 4), m1; repeat from * to last 1 (1, 1, 5, 5, 5) stitches, knit to end— 58 (58, 58, 76, 76, 76) stitches.

Set-Up Round Work Round 1 of the Sleeve Chart for your size, beginning at the stitch marked with the red "X"; do not work the last 10 (10, 10, 13, 13, 13) stitches on the needles. Place a stitch marker at this point; this will now be the beginning of the round. Rearrange the stitches on the needles if desired. From this point, the rounds will begin with the first stitch of the Chart.

Note: The red box that encloses the 3 purl stitches between the last 2 panels in the Chart indicates the point at which the sleeve will be shaped in later rounds. The number of stitches between these panels will increase. The red "X" should be disregarded after the first time Round 1 of the Chart is worked.

Work 4 rounds in pattern. You will have just completed Chart Round 5.

Increase Round 1 Work in pattern to the beginning of the stitches marked by the red box, place marker, (pfb) twice, p1, place marker, work the last 17 (17, 17, 23, 23, 23) stitches of the Chart in pattern. From this point, the stitches enclosed by the newly placed markers will be represented in the chart by the stitches in the red box—60 (60, 60, 78, 78, 78) stitches.

Next Round Work in pattern to first marker, p2, k1, p2, work in pattern to end.

Repeat this round 4 times more.

Increase Round 2 Work in pattern to first marker, p1, pfb, kfb, p2, work in pattern to end—62 (62, 62, 80, 80, 80) stitches.

Work 5 rounds in pattern, working the newly increased stitches in stockinette stitch.

Increase Round 3 Work in pattern to first marker, p1, pfb, knit to last 3 stitches before second marker, kfb, p2.

Work 5 rounds in pattern, working the newly increased stitches in stockinette stitch.

Repeat these 6 rounds 10 times more—84 (84, 84, 102, 102, 102) stitches. There are 25 stitches in the stockinette stitch panel between the markers.

Continue in pattern until the sleeve measures 16½" (42cm) or desired length to underarm. Be sure to end with the same Chart Round you ended with for the Lower Body.

Purl the first 2 stitches of the next round, then break the yarn, leaving a 24" (61cm) tail. Place the next 17 (17, 17, 23, 23, 23) stitches on hold on waste yarn. Place the remaining 67 (67, 67, 79, 79, 79) stitches on hold on a spare circular needle or double-pointed needles; do not remove the markers that delineate the center panel.

When the second sleeve is complete, after the 17 (17, 17, 23, 23, 23) stitches have been placed on waste yarn, do not remove the remaining stitches from the working needle.

YOKE

Note: When shaping the Yoke, switch to a shorter circular needle when necessary.

Pick up the Lower Body and resume working with the attached ball of yarn as follows.

Joining Round *Work 19 (19, 19, 25, 25, 25) stitches in pattern, slip the next 2 stitches (purl stitches) to the cable needle and hold to the back of the work, place the next 17 (17, 17, 23, 23, 23) stitches on hold on waste yarn; purl the first stitch of one sleeve together with the first stitch from the cable needle, purl the next sleeve stitch together with the remaining stitch from the cable needle; work in pattern to the last 2 sleeve stitches, slip 2 stitches to the cable needle and hold them to the front of the work, work these 2 stitches together with the next 2 body stitches, work in pattern to the last 2 sleeve stitches, slip these stitches to the cable needle and hold to the front of the work; purl the first stitch of the front of the Lower Body together with the first stitch from the cable needle, purl the next Lower Body stitch together with the remaining stitch from the cable needle, work in pattern to the next marker, knit to the following marker; repeat from * once more—310 (330, 350, 388, 408, 428) stitches. The Lower Body and Sleeves are now joined on the long circular needle.

There are 8 markers on the needle. The end-of-round marker is at the back left shoulder. Including the end-of-round marker, there are 4 markers that rest between the stockinette stitch panels of the sweater front and back and the columns of reverse stockinette stitch that border the patterned side panels. Each sleeve also has 2 markers; these rest between the reverse stockinette stitch columns and the patterned panels. It is important that these markers are correctly placed before the raglan shaping begins.

Work 10 (10, 10, 13, 13, 13) rounds in pattern as set.

Next Round *Work in pattern to first marker, p2, k2tog, knit to 4 stitches before next marker, ssk, p2, work in pattern to next marker, k2tog, knit to 2 stitches before next marker, ssk; repeat from * once more—8 stitches have been decreased.

Work 1 round in pattern.

Repeat these 2 rounds 10 times more—222 (242, 262, 300, 320, 340) stitches; 3 stitches remain in the stockinette stitch panel of each sleeve.

In the next sequence of rounds, the remaining stitches of the center sleeve panel will be decreased away.

Round 1 *Work in pattern to first marker, p2, S2KP, p2, work in pattern to next marker, k2tog, knit to 2 stitches before next marker, ssk; repeat from * once more—214 (234, 254, 292, 312, 332) stitches.

Round 2 *Work in pattern to first marker, p5, work in pattern to next marker, knit to next marker; repeat from * once more.

Round 3 *Work in pattern to first marker, p2, p2tog, p1, work in pattern to next marker, k2tog, knit to 2 stitches before next marker, ssk; repeat from * once more—208 (228, 248, 286, 306, 326) stitches.

Round 4 Work all stitches in pattern.

Round 5 *Work in pattern to first marker, remove marker, (p2tog) twice, remove marker, work in pattern to next marker, k2tog, knit to 2 stitches before next marker, ssk; repeat from * once more—200 (220, 240, 278, 298, 318) stitches.

Four stitch markers remain, one on either side of the Front and Back stockinette stitch panels. Each of these panels has 22 (32, 42, 37, 47, 57) stitches. From this point, decreases will be worked on every round.

Next Round *Work in pattern to marker, k2tog, knit to 2 stitches before next marker, ssk; repeat from * once more—4 stitches have been decreased.

Repeat this round 1 (5, 9, 7, 11, 15) times more—192 (196, 200, 246, 250, 254) stitches. The front and back stockinette stitch panels each have 18 (20, 22, 21, 23, 25) stitches.

shape back neckline

The back neckline is shaped using short rows.

Row 1 (RS) Work in pattern to first marker (Left Front marker), W&T.

Row 2 (WS) Work in pattern to left back marker, p2tog tbl, purl to 2 stitches before right back marker, p2tog, work in pattern to right front marker, W&T.

Row 3 (RS) Work in pattern to right back marker, k2tog, knit to 2 stitches before left back marker, ssk, work 20 (20, 20, 26, 26, 26) stitches in pattern (to center of patterned panels), W&T.

Row 4 (WS) Work in pattern to left back marker, p2tog tbl, purl to 2 stitches before right back marker, p2tog, work 20 (20, 20, 26, 26, 26) stitches in pattern, W&T.

Row 5 (RS) Work in pattern to right back marker, k2tog, knit to 2 stitches before left back marker, ssk, W&T.

Row 6 (WS) P2tog tbl, purl to 2 stitches before right back marker, p2tog, W&T.

Row 7 (RS) Knit to end—182 (186, 190, 236, 240, 244) stitches. The back stockinette stitch panel has 8 (10, 12, 11, 13, 15) stitches.

NECKBAND

Round 1 **K3 (3, 3, 1, 1, 1), *k2tog, k8 (8, 8, 9, 9, 9); repeat from * to 5 (5, 5, 2, 2, 2) stitches before marker, k2tog, k3 (3, 3, 0, 0, 0), remove marker, knit to next marker, remove marker; repeat from ** once, but do not remove last marker—166 (170, 174, 216, 220, 224) stitches.

Rounds 2–4 Work in garter stitch (purl one round, knit one round), beginning with a purl round.

Round 5 *K6, k2tog; repeat from * to last 6 (2, 6, 0, 4, 0) stitches, knit to end—146 (149, 153, 189, 193, 196) stitches.

Rounds 6–8 Work in garter stitch, beginning with a purl round.

Round 9 *K5, k2tog; repeat from * to last 6 (2, 6, 0, 4, 0) stitches, knit to end—126 (128, 132, 162, 166, 166) stitches.

Turn work so that the wrong side is facing. Bind off all stitches knitwise. (Turning the work before binding off will allow the edges of the bind-off row to meet up more evenly once they are sewn together.)

FINISHING

Sew the short seams at the edges of the cast-on and bind-off rows.

Graft the held stitches of the Lower Body and Sleeves together at the underarms.

Weave in all ends and block the sweater as desired.

Mock Cable Charts

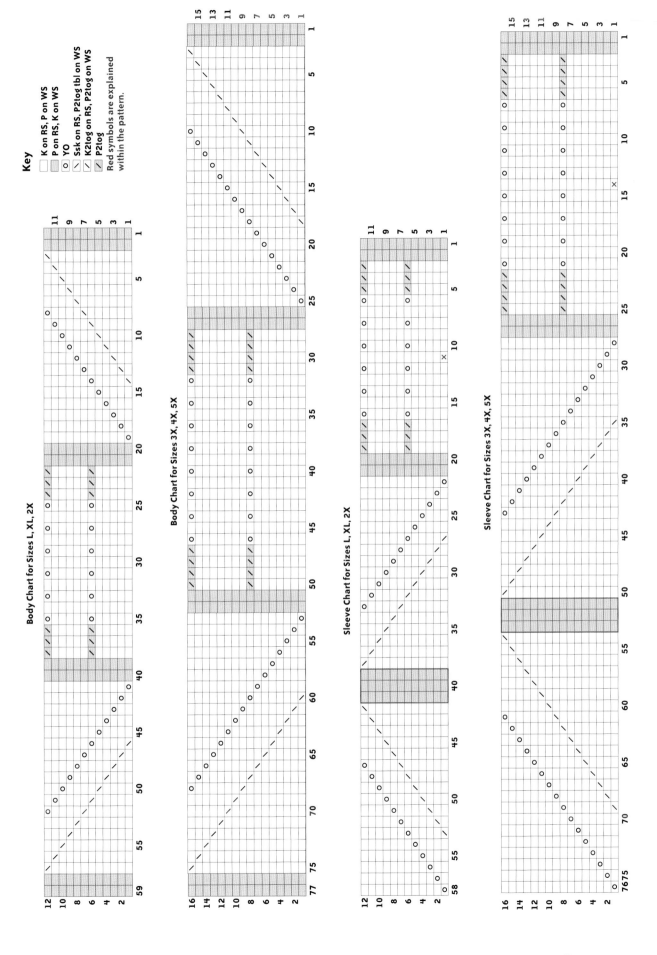

Key

K on RS, P on WS
P on RS, K on WS
◯ YO
╲ Ssk on RS, P2tog tbl on WS
╱ K2tog on RS, P2tog on WS
╱ P2tog
Red symbols are explained within the pattern.

Body Chart for Sizes L, XL, 2X

Body Chart for Sizes 3X, 4X, 5X

Sleeve Chart for Sizes L, XL, 2X

Sleeve Chart for Sizes 3X, 4X, 5X

no-gap wrap
pullover

We love clever, and this sweater is clever. Wraps, as we've said, are a flattering look for every Big Girl. But sometimes, wraps can gap and show off more than you planned. Plus there's an extra layer of fabric in the overlapped section that you may not want. Meet your solution.

This mock wrap sweater uses a diagonal openwork band to mimic the flattering diagonal lines of a wrap. A little extra openwork is sprinkled on the three-quarter length sleeves, for flavor and the suggestion of extra curviness. We love the sexy, wide V-neckline, too.

SIZES

L (1X, 2X, 3X, 4X)

Shown in size 1X

FINISHED MEASUREMENTS

Bust: 44 (47¾, 52, 55¾, 60)" (112 [121.5, 132, 141.5, 152.5]cm)

Length: 22½ (23, 23½, 24, 24½)" (57 [58.5, 59.5, 61, 62]cm)

MATERIALS

7 (8, 9, 10, 11) skeins Garnstudio Silke-Tweed; 52% silk, 48% lamb's wool; 219 yd (200m) per 1¾ oz (50g) skein; #12 Saffron (gold)

1 US #4 (3.5mm) circular needle, 40" (100cm) long, *or size needed to obtain gauge*

1 set US #4 (3.5mm) double-pointed needles

Optional: 1 US #4 (3.5mm) 16" (40cm) circular needle

Stitch holders or smooth waste yarn

Stitch markers

Tapestry needle

GAUGE

22 stitches and 32 rows = 4" (10cm) in stockinette or seed stitch pattern after blocking.

ABBREVIATIONS AND TECHNIQUES

See page 32.

STITCH PATTERNS

DLB (Diagonal Lace Band): (Ssk, yo) 3 times. On the next row or round, work these stitches in stockinette stitch.

Modified Seed Stitch Pattern (multiple of 6 stitches)

Note: When working modified seed stitch pattern, do not work a purled "seed" stitch if it falls next to a purled "seam" stitch, on an increase or decrease, or in the DLB. In these cases, knit the stitch instead.

Round 1 *P1, k5; repeat from * to end.

Rounds 2–6 Knit all stitches.

Round 7 K3, *p1, k5; repeat from * to last 3 stitches, p1, k2.

Rounds 8–12 Knit all stitches.

Repeat Rounds 1–12 for pattern.

PATTERN NOTES

If you wish to add short row bust shaping (directions for sizes C–DD cup may be found below), or if you wish to change the overall sweater length, you must follow these directions or the V-neck will not be centered. For each set of short rows or 2 added rows, you must move the start of the diagonal lace band (at the bottom edge) 1 stitch to the left. See Body Chart for how to do this if the diagonal band then crosses the side seam rather than the bottom edge.

To determine where to start short rows, see the worksheet on page 28.

Continue to work diagonal lace band and modified seed stitch patterns as established as you work short rows, and note that the diagonal band may meet the side "seam" and not the bottom hem, depending on your size and how many short row repeats you work. In size L and for a DD cup, the band will meet the side "seam" almost 3" (7.5cm) above the bottom hem. In size 1X and for a DD cup, the band will meet the "seam" 1½" (3.8cm) above the bottom hem. For larger sizes in all cup sizes, and for smaller sizes and C or D cups, the diagonal band will meet the bottom hem or will begin just a few rows up the side "seam."

C Cup: *Work to 3 stitches before side "seam," W&T. Repeat from * once more.

**Work to 3 stitches before last wrapped stitch, W&T; repeat from ** until 6 stitches on each side have been wrapped (12 rows total), then work across all stitches for 2 rows, picking up wraps and knitting or purling together with wrapped stitches.

D Cup: Repeat C cup directions once more.

DD Cup: Repeat C cup directions twice more.

LOWER BODY

Using the 40" (100cm) circular needle, cast on 242 (262, 286, 306, 330) stitches. Place marker and join to begin working in the round, being careful not to twist.

Round 1 P1 (left side "seam" stitch), k111 (117, 124, 130, 137), DLB, k2 (6, 11, 15, 20), place marker, p1 (right side "seam" stitch), k121 (131, 143, 153, 165).

Round 2 and all even-numbered rounds P1, k119 (129, 141, 151, 163), p1, k121 (131, 143, 153, 165).

Begin pattern as follows:

Size L Only

Round 3 P1, k4, work Round 1 of modified seed stitch pattern to 14 stitches before marker, p1, k4, DLB, k3, slip marker, p1, k3, work Round 1 of modified seed stitch pattern to 4 stitches before end of round, p1, k3.

Size 1X Only

Round 3 P1, k3, work Round 1 of modified seed stitch pattern to 18 stitches before marker, p1, k4, DLB, k3, p1, k3, slip marker, p1, k2, work Round 1 of modified seed stitch pattern to 3 stitches before end of round, p1, k2.

Size 2X Only

Round 3 P1, k3, work Round 1 of modified seed stitch pattern to 23 stitches before marker, p1, k4, DLB, k3, p1, k5, p1, k2, slip marker, p1, k2, work Round 1 of modified seed stitch pattern to 3 stitches before end of round, p1, k2.

Size 3X Only

Round 3 P1, k2, work Round 1 of modified seed stitch pattern to 27 stitches before marker, p1, k4, DLB, k3, p1, k5, p1, k6, slip marker, p1, k1, work Round 1 of modified seed stitch pattern to 2 stitches before end of round, p1, k1.

Size 4X Only

Round 3 P1, k1, work Round 1 of modified seed stitch pattern to 32 stitches before marker, p1, k4, DLB, k3, (p1, k5) 3 times, slip marker, p1, k1, work Round 1 of modified seed stitch pattern to 2 stitches before end of round, p1, k1.

All Sizes

Round 3 sets the pattern for the Front. From this point, continue in modified seed stitch pattern as set, moving the DLB pattern one stitch to the right on each odd-numbered round.

Work 5 rounds in pattern.

shape waist

Decrease Round *P1, k1, ssk, work to 3 stitches before marker, k2tog, k1; repeat from * once.

Repeat Decrease Round every 8th round 3 (3, 2, 1, 0) times more, then every 10th round 1 (1, 2, 3, 4) time(s)—222 (242, 266, 286, 310) stitches.

Work 15 rounds in pattern.

Increase Round *P1, k2, m1, work to 2 stitches before marker, m1, k2; repeat from * once.

Repeat Increase Round every 10th round 4 (4, 3, 3, 2) times more, then every 12th round 0 (0, 1, 1, 2) time(s)—242 (262, 286, 306, 330) stitches. Work 13 (15, 13, 13, 11) rounds even, ending with an even-numbered round.

shape v-neck and armhole

Next Round Work in pattern to 7 stitches before DLB, place marker, work V-Neck Chart over next 21 stitches, place marker, work in pattern to end.

Work 1 round even.

Next Round Bind off 8 (10, 12, 14, 16) stitches, work in pattern to side seam marker, p1, place 121 (131, 143, 153, 165) stitches on holder for back.

The upper front will be worked back and forth on the remaining 113 (121, 131, 139, 149) stitches.

Next Row (WS) Bind off 8 (10, 12, 14, 16) stitches, purl to end—105 (111, 119, 125, 133) stitches.

Next Row (RS) K1, ssk (ssk, sssk, sssk, sssk), work in pattern to last 3 (3, 4, 4, 4) stitches, k2tog (k2tog, k3tog, k3tog, k3tog), k1—103 (109, 115, 121, 129) stitches.

Purl 1 row.

Next Row (RS) K1, ssk (ssk, ssk, sssk, sssk), work in pattern to center of V-neck (separation on V-Neck Chart), and place remaining 51 (54, 57, 60, 64) stitches on holder for right front—50 (53, 56, 58, 62) stitches remain for left front.

Working back and forth on left front stitches only, purl 1 row. Continuing seed stitch pattern as set and moving DLB pattern 1 stitch to the right every right-side row, shape neck by decreasing 1 stitch at neck edge every right-side row (as shown on V-Neck Chart), and AT THE SAME TIME shape armhole by working sssk 1 stitch from armhole edge every right-side row 0 (0, 0, 0, 2) times, then ssk every right-side row 4 (6, 7, 8, 7) times.

When 16 (16, 17, 17, 17) stitches remain (about 8 [8¼, 8½, 8¾, 9]" [20.5 (21, 21.5, 22, 23)cm] from start of armhole shaping), ending with a right-side row, shape shoulder as follows (WS) work 8 stitches, W&T, work to end (decreasing 1 stitch at neck edge). Work 1 more row, picking up wrap and working it with wrapped stitch. Place remaining 15 (15, 16, 16, 16) stitches on holder. Break yarn, leaving a long tail.

RIGHT FRONT

With RS facing, join yarn to right front at V-neck, leaving a long tail. Beginning with Row 7, work V-Neck Chart as set, then work in pattern to last 3 (3, 3, 4, 4) stitches, k2tog (k2tog, k2tog, k3tog, k3tog), k1—50 (53, 56, 58, 62) stitches.

Purl 1 row.

Continuing modified seed stitch pattern as set and moving DLB 1 stitch to the left every right-side row, shape neck by decreasing 1 stitch at neck edge every right-side row (as shown on V-Neck Chart), and AT THE SAME TIME shape armhole by working k3tog 4 stitches before armhole edge every right-side row 0 (0, 0, 0, 2) times, then k2tog 3 stitches before armhole edge every right-side row 4 (6, 7, 8, 7) times.

When 17 (17, 18, 18, 18) stitches remain, shape shoulder as follows: on next right-side row, work 8 stitches (decreasing at neck edge), W&T, work to end.

Next Row Work to end (decreasing at neck edge), picking up wrap. Work 1 more row, then place remaining 15 (15, 16, 16, 16) stitches on holder. Break yarn, leaving a long tail.

BACK

Place 121 (131, 143, 153, 165) back stitches from holder onto needle. Continuing with modified seed stitch pattern as set, shape armhole as follows:

Next Row (RS) Bind off 7 (9, 11, 13, 15) stitches, work to end of row.

Next Row (WS) Bind off 7 (9, 11, 13, 15) stitches, purl to end of row—107 (113, 121, 127, 135) stitches.

Next Row K1, ssk (ssk, sssk, sssk, sssk), work to last 3 (3, 4, 4, 4) stitches, k2tog (k2tog, k3tog, k3tog, k3tog), k1—105 (111, 117, 123, 131) stitches.

Purl 1 row.

Next Row (RS) K1, ssk (ssk, ssk, sssk, sssk), work to last 3 (3, 3, 4, 4) stitches, k2tog (k2tog, k2tog, k3tog, k3tog), k1—103 (109, 115, 119, 127) stitches.

Decrease 2 stitches at each armhole edge every right-side row

0 (0, 0, 0, 2) times, then decrease 1 stitch at each armhole edge every right-side row 4 (6, 7, 8, 7) times—95 (97, 101, 103, 105) stitches.

Work even in pattern until the back measures 4 rows less than the front, ending with a wrong-side row.

Work back neck detail as follows:

Work 10 (10, 11, 11, 11) stitches in pattern, *yo, k2tog; repeat from * to last 9 (9, 10, 10, 10) stitches, work 2 stitches in pattern, W&T. Purl to last 7 (7, 8, 8, 8) stitches, W&T.

Work 2 stitches in pattern, *yo, k2tog; repeat from * to last 8 (8, 9, 9, 9) stitches, work in pattern to end, picking up wrap.

Next Row (WS) P15 (15, 16, 16, 16), bind off next 65 (67, 69, 71, 73) stitches for back neck, p15 (15, 16, 16, 16), picking up wrap. Place shoulder stitches on stitch holders.

RIGHT SLEEVE

Cast on 66 (70, 74, 78, 82) stitches. Divide stitches among 3 double-pointed needles and join to begin working in the round, being careful not to twist. Beginning with chart row as indicated for your size, work as follows:

Round 1 P1 (underarm "seam"), k2 (4, 6, 2, 10), p0 (0, 0, 1, 0), k0 (0, 0, 5, 0), place marker, work Sleeve Detail Chart, place marker, k2 (4, 6, 5, 10), p0 (0, 0, 1, 0), k0 (0, 0, 2, 0).

Round 2 and All Even-Numbered Rounds P1, knit to end.

Round 3 P1, k2 (1, 6, 8, 10), p0 (1, 0, 0, 0), k0 (2, 0, 0, 0), work Sleeve Detail Chart, k2 (2, 6, 8, 10), p0 (1, 0, 0, 0), k0 (1, 0, 0, 0).

Round 5 P1, k2 (4, 6, 8, 4), p0 (0, 0, 0, 1), k0 (0, 0, 0, 5), work Sleeve Detail Chart, k2 (4, 6, 8, 5), p0 (0, 0, 0, 1), k0 (0, 0, 0, 4).

Round 7 P1, k2 (4, 3, 5, 10), p0 (0, 1, 1, 0), k0 (0, 2, 2, 0), work Sleeve Detail Chart, k2 (4, 2, 2, 10), p0 (0, 1, 1, 0), k0 (0, 3, 5, 0).

Round 9 P1, k2 (4, 6, 8, 10), work Sleeve Detail Chart, k2 (4, 6, 8, 10).

Round 11 P1, k2 (4, 6, 8, 1), p0 (0, 0, 0, 1), k0 (0, 0, 0, 5), p0 (0, 0, 0, 1), k0 (0, 0, 0, 2), Sleeve Detail Chart, k2 (4, 6, 8, 2), p0 (0, 0, 0, 1), k0 (0, 0, 0, 5), p0 (0, 0, 0, 1), k0 (0, 0, 0, 1).

Continue modified seed stitch pattern as set and continue to follow chart; after chart is complete, continue modified seed stitch pattern as set. AT THE SAME TIME, beginning on chart row 47 (47, 45, 45, 43), shape sleeve as follows:

Increase round P1, k2, m1, work in pattern to last 2 stitches, m1, k2.

Repeat Increase Round every 4th round 3 (3, 2, 2, 1) times more, then every 6th round 9 (9, 10, 10, 11) times, changing to 16" (40cm) circular needle as desired—92 (96, 100, 104, 108) stitches.

Work 3 rounds in pattern.

shape cap

Next Round P1, bind off 7 (9, 11, 13, 15) stitches, work to end of round, purl "seam" stitch. Turn work.

Next Row (WS) Bind off 8 (10, 12, 14, 16) stitches, purl to end of row—77 stitches.

Working back and forth and continuing seed stitch pattern as set, work 2 rows even.

Decrease Row (RS) K1, ssk, work to last 3 stitches, k2tog, k1.

Repeat Decrease Row every 4th row 2 (3, 4, 4, 5) times more, then every other row 10 (10, 9, 9, 8) times, then every row 9 (7, 7, 11, 11) times—33 (35, 35, 27, 27) stitches.

Work short rows as follows:

*Work to last 3 (4, 4, 4, 4) stitches, W&T. Repeat from * once more.

Sizes L, 1X, and 2X Only
**Work to last 7 (8, 8, -, -) stitches, W&T. Repeat from ** once more.

All sizes
Work to end of row, picking up wrap(s) and working them together with wrapped stitch(es). Bind off all stitches on next row, picking up wrap(s) at the same time.

LEFT SLEEVE
Work as for right sleeve, but replace boxed area on chart with box for left sleeve.

FINISHING
With right sides together, join shoulders using the three-needle bind-off (page 33).
Sew Sleeves into armholes.

v-neck
At the base of the V-neck, note that the first row of bars connecting the beginning of the right lace border to the left lace border are narrow: they are formed of only 2 yarn strands versus 2 entire stitches worked together to form the thick bars. Using the long yarn tail left here, and referring to the diagram on the body chart, reinforce these 3 bars so they match the other thick bars. Work in a similar manner at the edge of the back neck detail if needed.

Weave in all ends and block the sweater as desired.

14¼ (14½, 14¾, 15, 15¼)"

40¼ (44, 48¼, 52, 56¼)"

22½ (23, 23½, 24, 24½)"

44 (47¾, 52, 55¾, 60)"

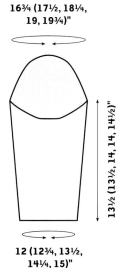

16¾ (17½, 18¼, 19, 19¾)"

13½ (13½, 14, 14, 14½)"

12 (12¾, 13½, 14¼, 15)"

BODY CHARTS

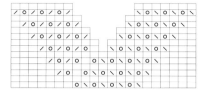
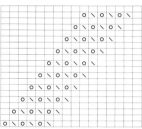

V-NECK CHART

This chart shows how to work the lace pattern at the dividing point for the V-neck. With the exception of the first 2 rows, the stitch pattern is worked on the right side rows only.

DIAGONAL LACE BAND CHART

This chart shows how the Diagonal Lace Band pattern is worked. The Seed Stitch Pattern is not shown.

LACE BAND AT SIDE SEAM

This chart shows the way the Diagonal Lace Band pattern should be started if it intersects with the side "seam" (see Pattern Notes).

Key

☐	K on RS, P on WS
▦	P on RS, K on WS
O	YO
\	Ssk
/	K2tog
◣	Sssk
◢	K3tog

SLEEVE DETAIL CHART

The chart below is for the Right Sleeve. When working the Left Sleeve, replace the section in the pink box below with the section in the pink box at the right.

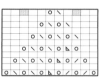

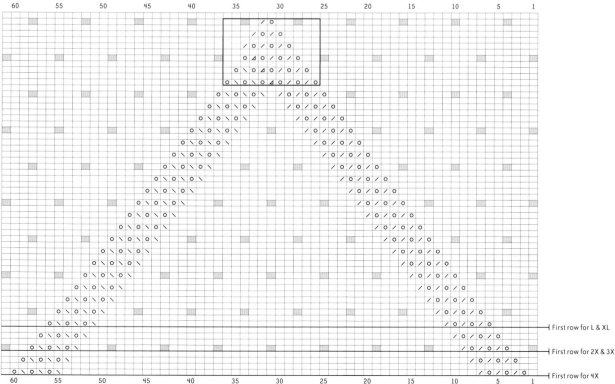

First row for L & XL
First row for 2X & 3X
First row for 4X

pastille

Like the delicate pastel-colored European sweet, this Pastille is full of flavor without being overpowering.

This sweater combines two different slip-stitch color patterns, creating the look of side panels (which you know we love). Because the mosaic pattern and the slip-stitch stripes knit to different gauges on the same needle, the central panels are longer and stretchier than the sides. This gives you more fabric in your belly zone, and less on the sides where you don't need or want it. The slightly flared shirttail hem is a little bit flirty and absolutely belly flattering, and the squared neckline is just low enough to show some skin without getting kinky.

Mosaic Chart

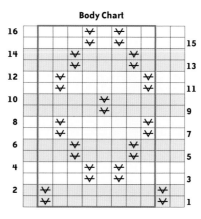

Body Chart

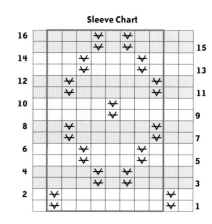

Sleeve Chart

Key

☐ Using MC, K on RS, P on WS
▨ Using CC, K on RS, P on WS
⋎ Sl 1 with yarn held to WS of work
☐ Pattern Repeat

SIZES
L (1X, 2X, 3X)
Shown in size 1X

FINISHED MEASUREMENTS
Chest: 42 (46, 50, 54)" (106.5 [117, 127, 137]cm)
Length: 22 (22½, 23, 24)" (56 [57.2, 58.5, 61]cm)

MATERIALS

Rowan Calmer; 75% cotton, 25% acrylic microfibre; 175yd (160m) per 1¾ oz (50g) ball
5 (5, 6, 7) balls #487 Refresh (pale blue, MC)
5 (5, 6, 7) balls #485 Kiwi (pale green, CC)
1 US #10 (6mm) circular needle, 24" (60cm) long, *or size needed to obtain gauge*
1 US #9 (5.5mm) circular needle, 24" (60cm) long
1 US #8 (5mm) circular needle, 16" (40cm) long
1 US #7 (4.5mm) circular needle, 16" (40cm) long
Note: Double-pointed needles may be substituted for circular needles.

Stitch markers
Stitch holders
Tapestry needle

GAUGE
28 stitches and 48 rows = 4" (10cm) in Stripe Pattern using large needles
22 stitches and 40 rows = 4" (10cm) in Chart Pattern using large needles
Note: If you wish to substitute a different yarn, the gauge listed on the ball band of the yarn used is 21 sts and 30 rows = 4" (10cm). You will likely need to use different needles if substituting a different yarn, so be sure to swatch.

ABBREVIATIONS AND TECHNIQUES
See page 32.

PATTERN NOTES
When working the slip-stitch patterns, all slipped stitches are slipped purlwise with the yarn held to the wrong side of the work.

FRONT

border

Using small 24" (60cm) circular needle and MC, cast on 131 (147, 159, 175) stitches.

Set-Up Row (WS) K44 (52, 58, 66), place marker, k43, place marker, k44 (52, 58, 66).

Join CC, but do not break MC.

Using CC, knit 2 rows.

Using MC, knit 2 rows.

body

Using large 24" (60cm) circular needles, continue as follows:

Row 1 (RS) Using CC, *k1, slip 1; repeat from * to marker, work Body Chart pattern to next marker, **slip 1, k1; repeat from ** to end.

Row 2 (WS) Using CC, *p1, slip 1; repeat from * to marker, work Body Chart pattern to next marker, **slip 1, p1; repeat from ** to end.

Row 3 (RS) Using MC, k2, *slip 1, k1; repeat from * to marker, work Body Chart pattern to next marker, **k1, slip 1; repeat from ** to last 2 stitches, k2.

Row 4 (WS) Using MC, p2, *slip 1, p1; repeat from * to marker, work Body Chart pattern to next marker, **p1, slip 1; repeat from ** to last 2 stitches, p2.

Rows 1–4 set the stitch patterns for the Front; the center panel is worked following the Body Chart, and the side panels are worked in a vertical stripe pattern. Work these patterns as set until the Front is complete.

Rows 5 and 6 Using CC, work in patterns as set.

If you wish to lengthen the body of the sweater, work more rows here before beginning the waist shaping. Be sure to end on a wrong-side CC row.

waist decrease

Note: The decreases and increases that shape the waist of this sweater will often result in 2 consecutive stitches of the same color. When this happens, work these stitches in pattern: For example, if there are 2 MC stitches together and you are working a MC row, knit both of these stitches. If you are working a CC row, slip these stitches.

When measuring your work, measure along the line formed by the decrease and increase pattern to achieve the most accurate measurement; the differing row gauges of the side and center panels will result in differing measurements if you measure elsewhere on the piece.

Row 7 (RS) Using MC, k2, *slip 1, k1; repeat from * 8 times more, k2tog, work in patterns to last 22 stitches, ssk, **k1, slip 1; repeat from ** 8 times more, k2—129 (145, 157, 173) stitches.

Rows 8–14 Work in patterns as set.

Row 15 (RS) Using MC, k2, *slip 1, k1; repeat from * 7 times more, slip 1, k2tog, work in patterns to last 21 stitches, ssk, **slip 1, k1; repeat from ** 8 times more, k1—127 (143, 155, 171) stitches.

Rows 16–20 Work in patterns as set.

Row 21 (RS) Using CC, *k1, slip 1; repeat from * 8 times more, k1, k2tog, work in patterns to last 21 stitches, ssk, k1, **slip 1, k1; repeat from ** to end—125 (141, 153, 169) stitches.

Rows 22–28 Work in patterns as set.

Row 29 (RS) Using CC, *k1, slip 1; repeat from * 8 times more, k2tog, work in patterns to last 20 stitches, ssk, **slip 1, k1; repeat from ** to end—123 (139, 151, 167) stitches.

Rows 30–34 Work in patterns as set.

Row 35 (RS) Using MC, k2, *slip 1, k1; repeat from * 7 times more, k2tog, work in patterns to last 20 stitches, ssk, **k1, slip 1; repeat from ** 7 times more, k2—121 (137, 149, 165) stitches.

Rows 36–42 Work in patterns as set.

Row 43 (RS) Using MC, k2, *slip 1, k1; repeat from * 6 times more, slip 1, k2tog, work in patterns to last 19 stitches, ssk, **slip 1, k1; repeat from ** 7 times more, k1—119 (135, 147, 163) stitches.

Continue in patterns as set until the work measures 6 (6, 7, 8)" (15 [15, 18, 20.5]cm), ending with a wrong side CC row.

bust increase

Row 1 (RS) Using MC, k2, *slip 1, k1; repeat from * 6 times more, slip 1, RLI, work in patterns to last 17 stitches, LLI, **slip 1, k1; repeat from ** to last stitch, k1—121 (137, 149, 165) stitches.

Rows 2–6 Work in patterns as set.

Row 7 (RS) Using CC, *k1, slip 1; repeat from * 8 times more, m1, work in patterns to last 18 stitches, m1, **slip 1, k1; repeat from ** to end—123 (139, 151, 167) stitches.

Rows 8–14 Work in patterns as set.

Row 15 (RS) Using CC, *k1, slip 1; repeat from * 8 times more, RLI, work in patterns to last 18 stitches, LLI, **slip 1, k1; repeat from ** to end—125 (141, 153, 169) stitches.

Rows 16–20 Work in patterns as set.

Row 21 (RS) Using MC, k2, *slip 1, k1; repeat from * 7 times more, slip 1, m1, work in patterns to last 19 stitches, m1, **slip 1, k1; repeat from ** to last stitch, k1—127 (143, 155, 171) stitches.

Rows 22–28 Work in patterns as set.

Row 29 (RS) Using MC, k2, *slip 1, k1; repeat from * 7 times more, slip 1, RLI, work in patterns to last 19 stitches, LLI, **slip 1, k1; repeat from ** to last stitch, k1—129 (145, 157, 173) stitches.

Rows 30–34 Work in patterns as set.

Row 35 (RS) Using CC, *k1, slip 1; repeat from * 9 times more, m1, work in patterns to last 20 stitches, m1, **slip 1, k1; repeat from ** to end—131 (147, 159, 175) stitches.

Rows 36–42 Work in patterns as set.

Row 43 (RS) Using CC, *k1, slip 1; repeat from * 9 times more, RLI, work in patterns to last 20 stitches, LLI, **slip 1, k1; repeat from ** to end—133 (149, 161, 177) stitches.

Rows 44–48 Work in patterns as set.

Row 49 (RS) Using MC, k2, *slip 1, k1; repeat from * 8 times more, slip 1, m1, work in patterns to last 21 stitches, m1, **slip 1, k1; repeat from ** to last stitch, k1—135 (151, 163, 179) stitches.
Continue working in patterns until the work measures 13 (13, 13, 13½)" (33 [33, 33, 34.5]cm), ending with a wrong-side row.

Next Row (RS) Alternating stitches in each color, bind off 6 (10, 12, 16) stitches, work in patterns to end.

Next Row (WS) Bind off 6 (10, 12, 16) stitches, work in patterns to end—123 (131, 139, 147) stitches.

The armhole decreases are worked in the same way as the waist decreases; the position of the decreases in relation to the edge of the piece will vary slightly, depending on which color is being used for the row you are working, in order to maintain the stripe pattern.

Work the decreases 4 or 5 stitches from the edge of the piece, working a (k2tog) increase at the right side of the work and a (ssk) decrease at the left side of the work.

Decrease as described above on the next right-side row.

Work 1 wrong-side row in pattern.

Repeat these 2 rows 5 (7, 11, 15) times more—111 (115, 115, 115) stitches.

Continue in pattern until the work measures 16 (16½, 17, 18)" (40.5 [42, 43, 45.5]cm) (armhole measures 3 [3½, 4, 4½]" [7.5 (9, 10, 11.5)cm] from initial bind-off), ending with a wrong-side row.

shape neckline

Next Row (RS) Work 34 (36, 36, 36) stitches in pattern (to edge of center panel), join a second ball of yarn, k43 using the new ball of yarn and place these 43 stitches on a stitch holder, work in pattern to end. There are 2 sets of 34 (36, 36, 36) stitches. Working each set of stitches separately, continue in pattern until the work measures 19 (19½, 20, 21)" (48.5 [49.5, 51, 53.5]cm). Bind off all stitches.

Note: Do not worry if the armhole looks shallow. The sleeve cap extends into a wide saddle shoulder that will add 3" (7.5cm) to the armhole depth.

BACK

border

Using smaller needle and MC, cast on 127 (139, 147, 163) stitches.

Set-Up Row (WS) K14 (20, 24, 32), place marker, k99, place marker, k14 (20, 24, 32).
Join CC, but do not break MC.
Using CC, knit 2 rows.
Using MC, knit 2 rows.

body

Using large needles, continue as follows:

Row 1 (RS) Using CC, *k1, slip 1; repeat from * to marker, work Body Chart pattern to next marker, **slip 1, k1; repeat from ** to end.

Row 2 (WS) Using CC, *p1, slip 1; repeat from * to marker, work Body Chart pattern to next marker, **slip 1, p1; repeat from ** to end.

Row 3 (RS) Using MC, k2, *slip 1, k1; repeat from * to marker, work Body Chart pattern to next marker, **k1, slip 1; repeat from ** to last 2 stitches, k2.

Row 4 (WS) Using MC, p2, *slip 1, p1; repeat from * to marker, work Body Chart pattern to next marker, **p1, slip 1; repeat from ** to last 2 stitches, p2.

Rows 1–4 set the stitch patterns for the Back; the center panel is worked following the Body Chart, and the side panels are worked in a vertical stripe pattern. Work these patterns as set until the Back is complete.

Rows 5 and 6 Using CC, work in patterns as set.

If you wish to lengthen the body of the sweater, work more rows here before beginning the waist shaping. Be sure to end on a wrong side CC row.

waist decrease

Row 7 (RS) Using MC, k2, *slip 1, k1; repeat from * 1 (3, 3, 3) times more, k2tog, work in patterns to last 8 (12, 12, 12) stitches, ssk, **k1, slip 1; repeat from ** 1 (3, 3, 3) times more, k2—121 (133, 145, 161) stitches.

Rows 8–14 Work in patterns as set.

Row 15 (RS) Using MC, k2, *slip 1, k1; repeat from * 0 (2, 2, 2) times more, slip 1, k2tog, work in patterns to last 7 (11, 11, 11) stitches, ssk, **slip 1, k1; repeat from ** 1 (3, 3, 3) times more, k1—119 (131, 143, 159) stitches.

Rows 16–20 Work in patterns as set.

Row 21 (RS) Using CC, *k1, slip 1; repeat from * 1 (3, 3, 3) times more, k1, k2tog, work in patterns to last 7 (11, 11, 11) stitches, ssk, k1, **slip 1, k1; repeat from ** to end—117 (129, 141, 157) stitches.

Rows 22–28 Work in patterns as set.

Row 29 (RS) Using CC, *k1, slip 1; repeat from * 1 (3, 3, 3) times more, k2tog, work in patterns to last 6 (10, 10, 10) stitches, ssk, **slip 1, k1; repeat from ** to end—115 (127, 139, 155) stitches.
Rows 30–34 Work in patterns as set.
Row 35 (RS) Using MC, k2, *slip 1, k1; repeat from * 0 (2, 2, 2) times more, k2tog, work in patterns to last 6 (10, 10, 10) stitches, ssk, **k1, slip 1; repeat from ** 0 (2, 2, 2) times more, k2—113 (125, 137, 153) stitches.
Rows 36–42 Work in patterns as set.

Size L Only
Row 43 (RS) Using MC, k2, slip 1, k2tog, work in patterns to last 5 stitches, ssk, slip 1, k1—111 stitches.

Sizes 1X, 2X, 3X Only
Row 43 (RS) Using MC, k2, *slip 1, k1; repeat from * once, slip 1, k2tog, work in patterns to last 9 stitches, ssk, **slip 1, k1; repeat from ** twice more, k1— -(123, 135, 151) stitches.

All Sizes
Continue in pattern as set until the work measures 6 (6, 7, 8)" (15 [15, 18, 20.5]cm), ending with a wrong side CC row.

upper back increase

Size L Only
Row 1 (RS) Using MC, k2, slip 1, RLI, work in pattern to last 3 stitches, LLI, slip 1, k2—113 stitches.

Sizes 1X, 2X, 3X Only
Row 1 (RS) Using MC, k2, *slip 1, k1; repeat from * once, slip 1, RLI, work in patterns to last 7 stitches, LLI, **slip 1, k1; repeat from ** to last stitch, k1— -(125, 137, 153) stitches.

All Sizes
Rows 2–6 Work in patterns as set.
Row 7 (RS) Using CC, *k1, slip 1; repeat from * 1 (3, 3, 3) times more, m1, work in patterns to last 4 (8, 8, 8) stitches, m1, **slip 1, k1; repeat from ** to end—115 (127, 139, 155) stitches.
Rows 8–14 Work in patterns as set.
Row 15 (RS) Using CC, *k1, slip 1; repeat from * 1 (3, 3, 3) times more, RLI, work in patterns to last 4 (8, 8, 8) stitches, LLI, **slip 1, k1; repeat from ** to end—117 (129, 141, 157) stitches.
Rows 16–20 Work in patterns as set.
Row 21 (RS) Using MC, k2, *slip 1, k1; repeat from * 0 (2, 2, 2) times more, slip 1, m1, work in patterns to last 5 (9, 9, 9) stitches, m1, **slip 1, k1; repeat from ** to last stitch, k1—119 (131, 143, 159) stitches.
Rows 22–28 Work in patterns as set.
Row 29 (RS) Using MC, k2, *slip 1, k1; repeat from * 0 (2, 2, 2) times more, slip 1, RLI, work in patterns to last 5 (9, 9, 9) stitches, LLI, **slip 1, k1; repeat from ** to last stitch, k1—121 (133, 145, 161) stitches.
Rows 30–34 Work in patterns as set.

Row 35 (RS) Using CC, *k1, slip 1; repeat from * 2 (4, 4, 4) times more, m1, work in patterns to last 6 (10, 10, 10) stitches, m1, **slip 1, k1; repeat from ** to end—123 (135, 147, 163) stitches. Continue working in patterns until the work measures 13 (13, 13, 13½)" (33 [33, 33, 34.5]cm), ending with a wrong-side row.

shape armholes

Next Row (RS) Alternating stitches in each color, bind off 6 (10, 12, 16) stitches, work in pattern to end.

Next Row (WS) Bind off 6 (10, 12, 16) stitches, work in pattern to end—111 (115, 123, 131) stitches.

The armhole decreases are worked in the same way as for the Front. The decreases will encroach on the center panel; work the decreases and the edge stitches in the Stripe Pattern.

Decrease as described above on the next right-side row.

Work 1 wrong-side row in pattern.

Repeat these 2 rows 5 (7, 11, 15) times more—99 stitches.

Continue in pattern until the work measures 16 (16½, 17, 18)" (40.5 [42, 43, 45.5]cm) (armhole measures 3 [3½, 4, 4½]" [7.5 (9, 10, 11.5)cm] from initial bind-off), ending with a wrong-side row.

Continue in pattern until the work measures 19 (19½, 20, 21)" (48.5 [49.5, 51, 53.5]cm), ending with a wrong-side row.

Next Row (RS) Alternating stitches in each color, bind off 28 stitches, work in patterns to end.

Next Row (WS) Bind off 28 stitches, work in pattern to end—43 stitches.

Continue in patterns until the work measures 21 (21½, 22, 23)" (53.5 [54.6, 56, 58.5]cm). Place the remaining stitches on a stitch holder.

SLEEVES (MAKE 2)

border

Using smaller needle and CC, cast on 67 (67, 67, 75) stitches.

Set-Up Row (WS) K16 (16, 16, 20), place marker, k35, place marker, k16 (16, 16, 20).

Join MC, but do not break CC.

Using MC, knit 2 rows.

Using CC, knit 2 rows.

sleeve

Using larger needle, continue as follows:

Row 1 (RS) Using MC, *k1, slip 1; repeat from * to marker, work Sleeve Chart pattern to next marker, **slip 1, k1; repeat from ** to end.

Row 2 (WS) Using MC, *p1, slip 1; repeat from * to marker, work Sleeve Chart pattern to next marker, **slip 1, p1; repeat from ** to end.

Row 3 (RS) Using CC, k2, *slip 1, k1; repeat from * to marker, work Sleeve Chart pattern to next marker, **k1, slip 1; repeat from ** to last 2 stitches, k2.

Row 4 (WS) Using CC, p2, *slip 1, p1; repeat from * to marker, work Sleeve Chart pattern to next marker, **p1, slip 1; repeat from ** to last 2 stitches, p2.

Rows 1–4 set the stitch patterns for the Sleeve; the center panel is worked following the Sleeve Chart, and the side panels are worked in a vertical stripe pattern. Work these patterns as set until the Sleeve is complete.

Rows 5 and 6 Using MC, work in patterns as set.

shape sleeve

Row 7 (RS) Using CC, k2, *slip 1, k1; repeat from * 3 times more, k2tog, work in patterns to last 12 stitches, ssk, **k1, slip 1; repeat from ** 3 times more, k2—65 (65, 65, 73) stitches.

Rows 8–14 Work in pattern as set.

Row 15 (RS) Using CC, k2, *slip 1, k1; repeat from * twice more, slip 1, k2tog, work in patterns to last 11 stitches, ssk, **slip 1, k1; repeat from ** 3 times more, k1—63 (63, 63, 71) stitches.

Rows 16–20 Work in patterns as set.

Row 21 (RS) Using MC, *k1, slip 1; repeat from * 3 times more, k1, k2tog, work in patterns to last 11 stitches, ssk, k1, **slip 1, k1; repeat from ** to end—61 (61, 61, 69) stitches.

Rows 22–28 Work in patterns as set.

Row 29 (RS) Using MC, *k1, slip 1; repeat from * 3 times more, k2tog, work in patterns to last 10 stitches, ssk, **slip 1, k1; repeat from ** to end—59 (59, 59, 67) stitches.

Rows 30–36 Work in patterns as set.

Row 37 (RS) Using MC, *k1, slip 1; repeat from * 3 times more, RLI, work in patterns to last 8 stitches, LLI, **slip 1, k1; repeat from ** to end—61 (61, 61, 69) stitches.

Rows 38–42 Work in patterns as set.

Row 43 (RS) Using CC, k2, *slip 1, k1; repeat from * twice more, slip 1, m1, work in patterns to last 9 stitches, m1, **slip 1, k1; repeat from ** to last stitch, k1—63 (63, 63, 71) stitches.

Rows 44–50 Work in patterns as set.

Row 51 (RS) Using CC, k2, *slip 1, k1; repeat from * twice more, slip 1, RLI, work in patterns to last 9 stitches, LLI, **slip 1, k1; repeat from ** to last stitch, k1—65 (65, 65, 73) stitches.

Rows 52–56 Work in patterns as set.

Row 57 (RS) Using MC, *k1, slip 1; repeat from * 4 times more, m1, work in patterns to last 10 stitches, m1, **slip 1, k1; repeat from ** to end—67 (67, 67, 75) stitches.

Continue increasing in patterns, working 10 (12, 18, 20) more increase rows—87 (91, 103, 115) stitches.

Continue in patterns until the work measures 17 (17, 18, 18)" (43 [43, 45.5, 45.5]cm) or desired length to underarm, ending with a wrong-side row.

sleeve cap

Next Row (RS) Alternating stitches in each color, bind off 6 (10, 12, 16) stitches, work in pattern to end.

Next Row (WS) Bind off 6 (10, 12, 16) stitches, work in pattern to end—75 (71, 79, 83) stitches.

Sleeve cap decreases should be worked 2 or 3 stitches from the edge of the work as needed to maintain the stripe pattern. Work a (k2tog) at the beginning of each decrease row, and a (ssk) at the end. Decreases are worked on right-side rows only.

Work 6 (10, 8, 8) rows in pattern.

Decrease at each end of the next row as described above.

Work 5 (7, 7, 7) rows in pattern.

Repeat these 6 (8, 8, 8) rows 6 (4, 4, 1) times more—61 (61, 69, 79) stitches.

Sizes 2X, 3X Only

Decrease at each end of the next row as described above.

Work 5 rows in pattern.

Repeat these 6 rows -(-, 3, 8) times more—61 stitches.

All Sizes

Decrease at each end of the next row as described above.

Work 1 row in pattern.

Repeat these 2 rows 12 times more—35 stitches.

shoulder saddle

Continue to work the remaining 35 stitches in pattern until the work measures 5" (12.5cm) from the last decrease row. Bind off all stitches.

FINISHING

assembly

Block all pieces.

Sew the Sleeves to the Front and Back along the armhole edges.

Sew the sides of the saddles to the bound-off shoulder stitches of the Front and Back.

Sew the side edges of the Back neck to the ends of the saddles.

Sew the side seams and sleeve seams.

neckline edging

Using the small 24" (60cm) circular needle and MC, with the right side facing and beginning at the right back neckline edge, knit the 43 held stitches of the back neck, pick up and knit 22 stitches along the end of the left saddle and 12 stitches along the left front neckline edge, knit the 43 held stitches of the front neckline edge, pick up and knit 12 stitches along the right front neckline edge and 22 stitches along the end of the right saddle—154 stitches.

Purl 1 round.

Join CC but do not break MC. Work 2 rounds in garter stitch using CC and the large 16" (40cm) circular needle. Break CC. Using MC, work 2 rounds in garter stitch using the small 16" (40cm) circular needle.

Bind off all stitches.

Weave in all ends and block again if desired.

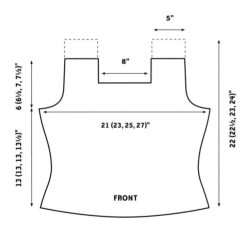

FRONT

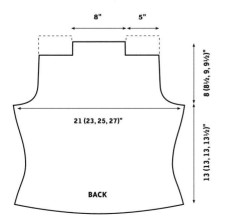

BACK

slipstream
pullover

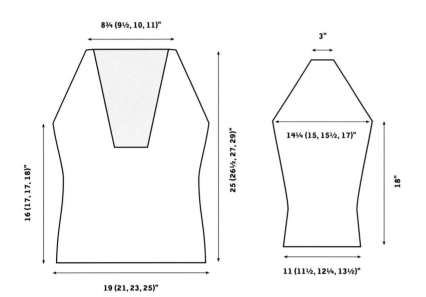

Allover use of shimmery metallic yarns is like a coastguard spotlight, it's true. So you probably think you shouldn't use them at all. Not so fast! What if you use them in key Big Girl spots—to outline the deep V-neck, to add shimmer to the side panels without going over the top, to make the cuffs and hem treatment sing. Slipstream is a little loose, a little easy, but still has sexy shape. And using the shimmery silk ribbon in the same color palette as the rest of the sweater tones down the spotlightness just a smidge, so you won't find random boats following you home.

SIZE
L (1X, 2X, 3X)
Shown in size 1X

FINISHED MEASUREMENTS
Chest: 42 (46, 50, 54)" (106.5 [117, 127, 137]cm)
Length: 25 (26½, 27, 29)" (63.5 [67.3, 68.5, 74]cm)

MATERIALS

7 (7, 8, 9) skeins Artyarns Ultramerino 6; 100% merino wool; 274 yd (250m) per 3½ oz (100g) skein; #244 pomegranate (MC)
3 (3, 3, 4) skeins Artyarns Silk Ribbon; 100% silk, 128 yd (117m) per ¾ oz (25g) skein; #115 variegated deep pink (CC)
1 set US #5 (3.75mm) straight needles, *or size needed to obtain gauge*
1 set US #2 (3mm) straight needles
1 US #5 (3.75mm) circular needle, 24" (60cm) long
Stitch markers
Stitch holder
Tapestry needle

GAUGE
22 stitches and 30 rows = 4" (10cm) in stockinette stitch using MC and larger needles

ABBREVIATIONS AND TECHNIQUES
See page 32.

STITCH PATTERN
Garter Slip Stitch Pattern (Worked over an even number of stitches)
Rows 1 and 2 Using CC, knit all stitches.
Row 3 (RS) Using MC, *k1, slip 1; repeat from * to last 2 stitches, k2.
Row 4 (WS) Using MC, k1, *p1, slip 1; repeat from * to last stitch, k1.
Rows 5 and 6 Using CC, knit all stitches.
Row 7 (RS) Using MC, k2, *slip 1, k1; repeat from * to end.
Row 8 (WS) Using MC, k1, *slip 1, p1; repeat from * to last stitch, k1.
Repeat Rows 1–8 for Garter Slip Stitch Pattern.

BACK

*Using MC and smaller needles, cast on 102 (114, 124, 136) stitches.

Knit 4 rows.

Using CC and larger needles, knit 2 rows.

Work Rows 1–8 of Garter Slip Stitch Pattern 3 times.

Using CC, knit 2 rows. Break CC.

Work in stockinette stitch using MC, beginning with a right-side row.

Continue until the work measures 5 (6, 6, 7)" (12.5 [15, 15, 18]cm), ending with a wrong-side row.

shape waist

Next Row (RS) K10, place marker, ssk, knit to last 12 stitches, k2tog, place marker, k10—100 (112, 122, 134) stitches.

Work 5 rows in stockinette stitch.

Next Row (RS) Knit to marker, ssk, knit to 2 stitches before next marker, k2tog, knit to end.

Repeat these 6 rows 3 times more—92 (104, 114, 126) stitches.

Work 17 rows in stockinette stitch.*

Next Row (RS) Knit to marker, slip marker, RLI, knit to next marker, LLI, slip marker, knit to end.

Work 3 rows in stockinette stitch.

Repeat these 4 rows 6 times more—106 (118, 128, 140) stitches.

Remove markers when working the next row and continue in stockinette stitch until the work measures 16 (17, 17, 18)" (40.5 [43, 43, 45.5]cm), ending with a wrong-side row.

shape raglan edges

Decrease Row 1 (RS) K3, ssk, knit to last 5 stitches, k2tog, k3.

Decrease Row 2 (WS) P3, p2tog, purl to last 5 stitches, p2tog tbl, p3.

Repeat these 2 rows 0 (2, 3, 3) times more—102 (106, 112, 124) stitches.

Work Decrease Row 1.

Purl 1 row.

Repeat these 2 rows 26 (26, 27, 31) times more—48 (52, 56, 60) stitches.

Bind off all stitches.

FRONT

Work as for the Back from * to *.

Next Row (RS) Knit to marker, slip marker, RLI, knit to next marker, LLI, slip marker, knit to end.

Work 3 rows in stockinette stitch.

Repeat these 4 rows 3 times more—100 (112, 122, 134) stitches.

shape neckline

Next Row (RS) Knit to marker, slip marker, RLI, k28 (34, 39, 45); place these 39 (45, 50, 56) stitches just worked on a stitch holder; bind off the next 24 stitches, knit to marker, LLI, slip marker, knit to end—39 (45, 50, 56) stitches.

Work 3 rows in stockinette stitch.

Next Row (RS) Knit to marker, LLI, slip marker, knit to end.

Repeat these 4 rows once more—41 (47, 52, 58) stitches.

The work measures approximately 14 (15, 15, 16)" (35.5 [38, 38, 40.5]cm).

Note: Read ahead! Neckline and raglan shaping directions are worked simultaneously.

Purl 1 row.

Next Row (RS) K1, k2tog, knit to end.

Work 7 (5, 5, 5) rows in stockinette stitch.

Repeat these 8 (6, 6, 6) rows 2 (10, 8, 9) times more.

Sizes L, 2X, 3X Only

Next Row (RS) K1, k2tog, knit to end.

Work 5 (-, 3, 3) rows in stockinette stitch.

Repeat these 6 (-, 4, 4) rows 5 (-, 3, 4) times more. AT THE SAME TIME, when the work measures 16 (17, 17, 18)" (40.5 [43, 43, 45.5]cm), ending with a wrong-side row, shape the raglan edge as follows:

Decrease Row 1 (RS) Knit to last 5 stitches, k2tog, k3.

Decrease Row 2 (WS) P3, p2tog, purl to end.

Repeat these 2 rows 0 (2, 3, 3) times more.

Work Decrease Row 1.

Purl 1 row.

Repeat these 2 rows 25 (25, 26, 30) times more—4 stitches.

Next Row (RS) Ssk, k2.

Purl 1 row.

Bind off the remaining 3 stitches.

Replace the held stitches of the left front on the needle with the wrong side facing and rejoin the yarn.

Work 3 rows in stockinette stitch.

Next Row (RS) Knit to marker, slip marker, RLI, knit to end.

Repeat these 4 rows once more—41 (47, 52, 58) stitches.

The work measures approximately 14 (15, 15, 16)" (35.5 [38, 38, 40.5]cm).

Note: Read ahead! Neckline and raglan shaping directions are worked simultaneously.

Purl 1 row.

Next Row (RS) Knit to last 3 stitches, ssk, k1.

Work 7 (5, 5, 5) rows in stockinette stitch.

Repeat these 8 (6, 6, 6) rows 2 (10, 8, 9) times more.

Sizes L, 2X, 3X Only

Next Row (RS) Knit to last 3 stitches, ssk, k1.

Work 5 (-, 3, 3) rows in stockinette stitch.

Repeat these 6 (-, 4, 4) rows 5 (-, 3, 4) times more. AT THE SAME TIME, when the work measures 16 (17, 17, 18)" (40.5 [43, 43, 45.5]cm), ending with a wrong-side row, shape the raglan edge as follows:

Decrease Row 1 (RS) K3, ssk, knit to end.
Decrease Row 2 (WS) Purl to last 5 stitches, p2tog tbl, p3.
Repeat these 2 rows 0 (2, 3, 3) times more.
Work Decrease Row 1.
Purl 1 row.
Repeat these 2 rows 25 (25, 26, 30) times more.
Next Row (RS) K2, k2tog.
Purl 1 row.
Bind off the remaining 3 stitches.

SLEEVES (MAKE 2)

Using MC and smaller needles, cast on 60 (64, 68, 74) stitches.
Knit 4 rows.
Using CC and larger needles, knit 2 rows.
Work Rows 1–8 of Garter Slip Stitch Pattern 3 times.
Using CC, knit 2 rows. Break CC.
Work in stockinette stitch using MC and larger needles, beginning with a right-side row.
Continue until the work measures 5" (12.5cm), ending with a wrong-side row.
Next Row (RS) K1, ssk, knit to last 3 stitches, k2tog, k2.
Purl 1 row.
Repeat these 2 rows 4 times more—50 (54, 58, 64) stitches.
Work 4 rows in stockinette stitch.
Next Row (RS) K1, RLI, knit to last stitch, LLI, k1.
Work 3 rows in stockinette stitch.
Repeat these 4 rows 13 (13, 13, 14) times more—78 (82, 86, 94) stitches.
Continue in stockinette stitch until the work measures 18" or desired length to underarm, ending with a wrong-side row.

shape raglan edges

Decrease Row 1 (RS) K3, ssk, knit to last 5 stitches, k2tog, k3.
Decrease Row 2 (WS) P3, p2tog, purl to last 5 stitches, p2tog tbl, p3.
Repeat these 2 rows twice more—66 (70, 74, 82) stitches.
Work Decrease Row 1.
Purl 1 row.
Repeat these 2 rows 24 (26, 28, 32) times more.
Bind off the remaining 16 stitches.

FINISHING

Sew the Sleeves to the Front along the raglan edges.

neckline edging

With the right side facing, using MC and larger needles, pick up 1 stitch in each bound-off stitch along the top of one sleeve and 3 stitches for every 4 rows along the adjoining vertical neckline edge. Cast on 2 stitches at the beginning and end of the next row; this forms seam allowances, which will later be sewn to the back and lower front neckline edges.

Maintaining 2 stitches at each edge in stockinette stitch, work Rows 2–8 of Garter Slip Stitch Pattern.
Work Rows 1–8 of pattern 3 times.
Knit 2 rows using CC.
Using smaller needles, knit 1 row using MC.
Bind off all stitches.
Work a second Edging in the same way along the opposite neckline and sleeve edges.

assembly

Sew the Back to the Sleeves along the raglan edges.
Sew the lower side edges of the neckline facings to the bound-off edge of the front neckline. Sew the upper side edges of the facings to the back neckline edge.
The bound-off edges of the neckline facing will be sewn together to create a V-neckline of the desired depth. Wait until the side panels have been knit and the sweater assembled completely before doing this, so that you can try the sweater on and accurately determine how deep the neckline should be.

side panels

Right Side Panel

With the right side facing, using the larger circular needle and MC, pick up and knit 3 stitches for every 4 rows along the back edge of the Left Sleeve and the left edge of the Back. (If necessary, decrease 1 stitch in the next row to achieve an even number of stitches.)
Work Rows 2–8 of Garter Slip Stitch Pattern.
Work Rows 1–8 of pattern 3 times.
Using MC, knit 2 rows.
Bind off all stitches loosely in pattern.

Left Side Panel

Work a side panel for the Right side of the sweater in the same way.

Sew the front edges of the panels to the edges of the Front and the Sleeves.
Try the sweater on to determine the best depth for the V-neckline, and sew the edges of the neckline edging together accordingly.
Weave in all ends and block the sweater as desired.

guatemalan
floral tunic

DIFFICULTY: 2
BY: SANDI LUCK

This pattern was inspired by a fragment of a lovely woven Guatemalan tunic displayed in a local coffee house, but the thing you'll notice first are the sleeves. They're flowy and perfect for upper-arm hiders! The dark side panels are visually slimming and give you a little break from the intarsia. The shape is fitted but easy, and the wide neckline? A great way to show some skin without going too low. Just make sure your bra straps sit wider than the neck, or wear a strapless bra. This kind of good-looking exposure is worth a special undergarment.

SIZES
L (1X, 2X, 3X)
Shown in size 1X

FINISHED MEASUREMENTS
Chest: 46 (50, 54, 58)" (117 [127, 137, 147]cm)
Length: 23½ (23¾, 24, 24)" (59.5 [60, 61, 61]cm)

MATERIALS

Rowan Wool Cotton; 50% merino wool, 50% cotton; 123yd (113m) per 1¾ oz (50g) ball
7 (7, 8, 8) balls #911 Rich (maroon, MC)
7 (7, 8, 8) balls #909 French Navy (CC1)
2 balls #951 Tender (pale pink, CC2)
1 ball #943 Flower (deep pink, CC3)
1 ball #907 Deepest Olive (CC4)
1 ball #960 Laurel (bottle green, CC5)
1 ball #910 Gypsy (deep mauve, CC6)
1 US #5 (3.75mm) circular needle, 32" (80cm) long, *or size needed to obtain gauge*
1 US #4 (3.5mm) circular needle, 32" (80cm) long, or a set of straight needles
1 US #3 (3.25mm) circular needle, 32" (80cm) long, or a set of straight needles
1 D-3 (3.25mm) crochet hook

Stitch markers
Stitch holder
Tapestry needle

GAUGE
24 stitches and 32 rows = 4" (10cm) in stockinette stitch using larger needle

ABBREVIATIONS AND TECHNIQUES
See page 32.

PATTERN NOTES
This pattern offers a choice of 2 different side panels. Choose the Shaped Side Panels (shown) to provide waist shaping, or work the Ribbed Side Panels to flatter a longer or less curvy torso.
If you wish to lengthen the top, add additional length to the main panels before beginning the intarsia design. Add additional length to the side panels before beginning any shaping.
This top is worked using the intarsia technique. A separate ball or length of yarn is used for each different colored section of the main panels. When switching yarns between the different areas of color, be sure to pick up the new color from underneath the previous color. This will ensure that the two strands of yarn are twisted around each other, which will prevent holes from forming at these joining points.

BACK
Using the medium-size needle and MC, cast on 102 (106, 106, 108) stitches.
Work 3 rows in stockinette stitch, beginning with a right-side row.
Using the large-size needle, continue as follows:
Next Row (WS) Knit all stitches. This row forms a turning ridge for the hem.

Begin working from the Chart, beginning and ending each row as indicated for your size.
Continue in pattern until you have completed Chart Row 184 (186, 188, 188).
Next Row (RS) K24, join a new ball of MC and bind off 54 (58, 60, 60) stitches, work in pattern to end.
Working both shoulders at the same time using the attached balls of yarn, work 3 more rows in stockinette stitch.
Bind off all stitches.

FRONT

Work as for the Back until Chart Row 132 (134, 128, 128) is complete.

Next Row (RS) Work 24 stitches in pattern, join a new ball of MC, and bind off 54 (58, 60, 60) stitches, work in pattern to end. Working both shoulders at the same time using the attached balls of yarn, work in pattern until all chart rows have been completed.

Bind off all stitches.

SLEEVES (MAKE 2)

With CC and the large-size needle, using the Crochet Cast-On (page 33), cast on 3 stitches.

Rows 1–6 Work in stockinette stitch, beginning with a right-side row.

Note: In the next row, you will pick up stitches along 2 edges of the fabric. This means that the small strip of fabric you have knit will have only 1 remaining free edge, and will look rather awkward if you are unfamiliar with this type of construction. It will make more sense as the sleeve progresses.

Row 7 (RS) K3; pick up and knit 4 stitches along the side edge of the fabric; remove the waste yarn from the cast-on edge, place the resulting live stitches on a spare needle, and knit these 3 stitches—10 stitches.

Row 8 (WS) Purl.

Row 9 (RS) K3, *yo, k1; repeat from * 3 times more, yo, k3— 15 stitches.

Row 10 (WS) Purl.

Row 11 (RS) K3, *yo, k1; repeat from * 8 times more, yo, k3— 25 stitches.

Row 12 (WS) P7, place marker, *p4, place marker; repeat from * twice more, p6.

Row 13 (RS) K3, yo, *knit to marker, yo, slip marker, k1, yo; repeat from * 3 times more, knit to last 3 stitches, yo, k3— 35 stitches.

Row 14 (WS) Purl.

Rows 15–30 Work as for Rows 13 and 14. When Row 30 is complete, there are 115 stitches.

Row 31 (RS) K3, yo, *knit to 2 stitches before marker, k2tog, yo, slip marker, k1, yo, ssk; repeat from * 3 times more, knit to last 3 stitches, yo, k3—117 stitches.

Row 32 and 34 (WS) Purl.

Row 33 (RS) K3, yo, *knit to marker, yo, slip marker, k1, yo; repeat from * 3 times more, knit to last 3 stitches, yo, k3— 127 stitches.

Rows 35–46 Work as for Rows 31–34. When Row 46 is complete, there are 153 stitches.

Rows 47, 49, and 51 (RS) K3, yo, *knit to 2 stitches before marker, k2tog, yo, slip marker, k1, yo, ssk; repeat from * 3 times more, knit to last 3 stitches, yo, k3.

Rows 48, 50, 52, and 54 (WS) Purl.

Row 53 (RS) K3, yo, *knit to marker, yo, slip marker, k1, yo; repeat from * 3 times more, knit to last 3 stitches, yo, k3— 169 stitches.

Rows 55–62 Work as for Rows 47–54. When Row 62 is complete, there are 185 stitches.

Row 63 (RS) K3, yo, *knit to 2 stitches before marker, k2tog, yo, slip marker, k1, yo, ssk; repeat from * 3 times more, knit to last 3 stitches, yo, k3.

Row 64 (WS) Purl.

Repeat Rows 63 and 64 7 (7, 9, 9) times more—201 (201, 205, 205) stitches.

Work short rows as follows:

Row 1 (RS) *Knit to 2 stitches before marker, k2tog, yo, slip marker, k1, yo, ssk; repeat from * 3 times more, knit to last 4 stitches, W&T.

Row 2 (WS) Purl to last 4 stitches, W&T.

Row 3 (RS) *Knit to 2 stitches before marker, k2tog, yo, slip marker, k1, yo, ssk; repeat from * 3 times more, k23, W&T.

Row 4 (WS) Purl to last marker, p25, W&T.

Row 5 (RS) *Knit to 2 stitches before marker, k2tog, yo, slip marker, k1, yo, ssk; repeat from * twice more, k23, W&T.

Row 6 (WS) Purl to second marker from turning point of last short row, p25, W&T.

Row 7 (RS) Knit to 2 stitches before marker, k2tog, yo, slip marker, k1, yo, ssk, knit to 1 stitch before next marker, W&T.

Row 8 (WS) Purl to 1 stitch before marker, W&T.

Row 9 (RS) Knit to end, picking up wraps and knitting them together with wrapped stitches.

Row 10 (WS) Purl all stitches, removing all markers, picking up remaining wraps and purling them together with wrapped stitches.

Next Row (RS) K1, *yo, k2tog; repeat from * to end. This row forms a turning row for the sleeve hem.

Work 3 rows in stockinette stitch.

Loosely bind off all stitches.

OPTION 1: SHAPED SIDE PANELS (MAKE 2)

Using the medium-size needle and CC1, cast on 42 (51, 60, 72) stitches.

Work 3 rows in stockinette stitch, beginning with a right-side row.

Using the large-size needle, continue as follows:

Next Row (WS) Knit all stitches. This row forms a turning ridge for the hem.

Work in stockinette stitch until the piece measures 3" (7.5cm) from the turning ridge, ending with a wrong-side row.

shape waist

Decrease Row (RS) K2, ssk, knit to last 4 stitches, k2tog, k2.

Work 3 rows in stockinette stitch.

Repeat these 4 rows twice more—36 (45, 54, 66) stitches.

Work Decrease Row.

Purl 1 row.

Repeat these 2 rows 6 times more—22 (31, 40, 52) stitches.

Work 6 rows in stockinette stitch.

Increase Row (RS) K3, m1, knit to last 3 stitches, m1, k3.

Work 5 rows in stockinette stitch.

Repeat these 6 rows 4 times more—32 (41, 50, 62) stitches.

Work Increase Row.

Work 7 rows in stockinette stitch.

Repeat these 8 rows once more—36 (45, 54, 66) stitches.

Continue in stockinette stitch until the work measures 14¼ (14½, 14½, 14¼)" (36.2 [37, 37, 36.2]cm) from the turning ridge, ending with a wrong-side row.

shape underarm

Next Row (RS) K12 (16, 19, 23) and place these stitches on a stitch holder, bind off the next 12 (13, 16, 20) stitches, knit to end—12 (16, 19, 23) stitches.

Sizes 1X, 2X, 3X Only

Next Row (WS) Purl to last 3 stitches, p2tog, p1.

Next Row (RS) K1, k2tog, knit to end.

Repeat these 2 rows—(1, 2, 4) times more— -(12, 13, 13) stitches.

All Sizes

Purl 1 row.

Next Row (RS) K1, k2tog, knit to end.

Repeat these 2 rows 9 (9, 10, 10) times more.

Bind off the remaining 2 stitches.

Place the held stitches on the needle with the wrong side facing and reattach the yarn.

Sizes 1X, 2X, 3X Only

Next Row (WS) P1, p2tog tbl, purl to end.

Next Row (RS) Knit to last 3 stitches, ssk, k1.

Repeat these 2 rows—(1, 2, 4) times more— -(12, 13, 13) stitches.

All Sizes

Purl 1 row.

Next Row (RS) Knit to last 3 stitches, ssk, k1.

Repeat these 2 rows 9 (9, 10, 10) times more.

Bind off the remaining 2 stitches.

OPTION 2: RIBBED SIDE PANELS (MAKE 2)

Using the small-size needles and CC1, cast on 45 (57, 67, 81) stitches.

Row 1 (RS) K2, *p1, k1; repeat from * to last 3 stitches, p1, k2.

Row 2 (WS) P2, *k1, p1; repeat from * to last 3 stitches, k1, p2.

Repeat these 2 rows until the work measures 14¼ (14½, 14½, 14¼)" (36.2 [37, 37, 36.2]cm), ending with a wrong-side row.

shape underarm

Next Row (RS) Work 15 (20, 24, 31) stitches in pattern and place these stitches on a stitch holder, bind off the next 15 (17, 19, 19) stitches, work in pattern to end—15 (20, 24, 31) stitches.

Work 1 row in pattern.

Next Row (RS) Bind off 5 (6, 10, 11) stitches, work in pattern to end—10 (14, 14, 20) stitches.

Sizes 1X, 2X, 3X Only

Work 1 row in pattern.

Next row (RS) Bind off—(4, 4, 6) stitches, work in pattern to end— -(10, 10, 14) stitches.

Size 3X Only

Work 1 row in pattern.

Next row (RS) Bind off 3 stitches, work in pattern to end—11 stitches.

All Sizes

Work 1 row in pattern.

Next Row (RS) K1, k2tog, work in pattern to end.

Repeat these 2 rows 6 (5, 3, 4) times more—3 (4, 6, 6) stitches.

Work 3 rows in pattern.

Next Row (RS) K1, k2tog, work in pattern to end.

Repeat these 4 rows 0 (1, 3, 3) times more.

Bind off the remaining 2 stitches.

Replace the held stitches on the needle with the right side facing.

Work 1 row in pattern.

Next Row (WS) Bind off 5 (6, 10, 11) stitches, work in pattern to end—10 (14, 14, 20) stitches.

Sizes 1X, 2X, 3X Only

Work 1 row in pattern.

Next row (WS) Bind off—(4, 4, 6) stitches, work in pattern to end— -(10, 10, 14) stitches.

Size 3X Only

Work 1 row in pattern.

Next row (WS) Bind off 3 stitches, work in pattern to end—11 stitches.

All Sizes

Next Row (RS) Knit to last 3 stitches, ssk, k1.

Work 1 row in pattern.

Repeat these 2 rows 5 (4, 2, 3) times more, then work the first of these 2 rows once more—3 (4, 6, 6) stitches.

Work 3 rows in pattern.

Next Row (RS) Knit to last 3 stitches, ssk, k1.

Repeat these 4 rows 0 (1, 3, 3) times more.

Bind off the remaining 2 stitches.

FINISHING

Work duplicate stitch as indicated on the Chart, and weave in ends.

Block all pieces.

Sew the Front and Back together at the shoulders.

Fold the sleeve hems along the turning ridges and sew them in place.

If you worked the Ribbed Side Panels, fold the hems of the Front and Back along the turning ridges and sew them in place.

Sew the Side Panels to the Front and Back, beginning at the lower edges and pausing once you have reached the level of the waist.

Sew the Sleeves to the armhole edges of the Front and Back, beginning at the center of the shoulder and pausing once you reach the points where the sleeves and side panels begin to overlap.

Lap the Sleeve edges over the Side Panel edges and sew them, together, to the Front and Back Panels, so that the Sleeve edges are sandwiched between the Side Panel edges and the Front and Back Panel edges.

If you worked the Shaped Side Panels, fold the hem of the lower edge along the turning ridge and sew in place.

Using MC, work 1 row of single crochet around the neckline edge.

If desired, work 1 row of single crochet along the armhole edge of the Side Panel using CC1.

Weave in any remaining ends.

Block the hems and seams if desired.

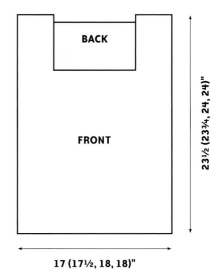

23½ (23¾, 24, 24)"

BACK

FRONT

17 (17½, 18, 18)"

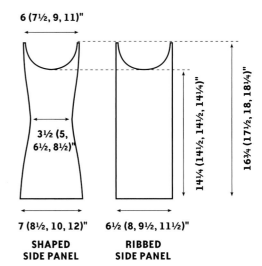

6 (7½, 9, 11)"

16¾ (17½, 18, 18¼)"

14¼ (14½, 14½, 14¼)"

3½ (5, 6½, 8½)"

7 (8½, 10, 12)"
SHAPED SIDE PANEL

6½ (8, 9½, 11½)"
RIBBED SIDE PANEL

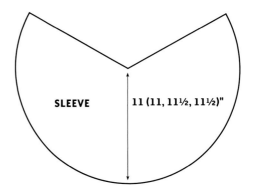

SLEEVE   11 (11, 11½, 11½)"

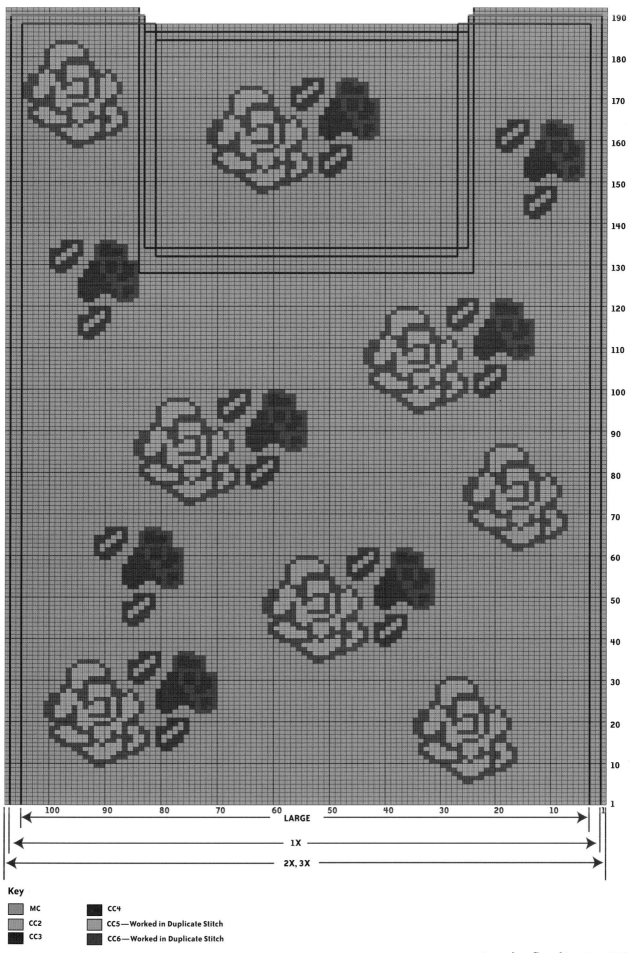

Key

MC	
CC2	
CC3	
CC4	
CC5—Worked in Duplicate Stitch	
CC6—Worked in Duplicate Stitch	

summer
chevron

DIFFICULTY: 2
BY: AUDREY ESCHRIGHT

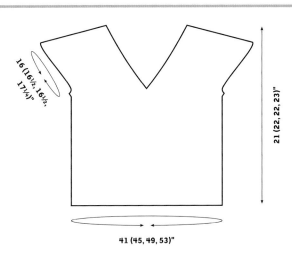

16 (16½, 16½, 17¾)"

21 (22, 22, 23)"

41 (45, 49, 53)"

Summer handknit tops for Big Girls can be hit or miss, with more miss than hit in our experience. That's why we love the plunging-V styling of this not-too-bare top. Sweet-but-not-tight sleeves give you just a bit of upper-arm privacy, and the cascading tonal colors are seriously flattering. Oh, by the way, the deep V? You get one on both sides. Righteous.

SIZES

L (1X, 2X, 3X)
Shown in size 1X

FINISHED MEASUREMENTS

Bust: 41 (45, 49, 53)" (104 [114, 124.5, 134.5]cm)
Length: 21 (22, 22, 23)" (53.5 [56, 56, 58.5]cm)
If you are between sizes, choose the smaller option. The diagonally knitted fabric has a lot of drape, so the sweater looks best if fit close to your actual bust measurement.

MATERIALS

Rowan Summer Tweed; 70% silk, 30% cotton; 118 yd (108m) per 1¾ oz (50g) skein
2 (2, 2, 3) skeins #525 Blueberry (faded blue, C1)
3 (3, 3, 4) skeins #510 Bouquet (purple/pink, C2)
2 (2, 2, 3) skeins #534 Delicious (faded purple, C3)

1 US #8 circular needle, 16" (40cm) long,
or size needed to obtain gauge
1 US #8 circular needle, 24" (60cm) long
1 US #8 circular needle, 32" (80cm) long
Stitch markers
Stitch holders or waste yarn
Tapestry needle

GAUGE

14 stitches and 16 rows = 4" (10cm) in stockinette stitch.

ABBREVIATIONS AND TECHNIQUES

See page 32.

STITCH PATTERNS

1x1 Rib (Worked over an even number of stitches)
Round 1 *K1, p1; repeat from * to end.
Repeat this round for 1x1 Rib.

TOP SECTION (NECKLINE AND TOP OF SLEEVES)

With the medium needle and C1, using the long-tail method, cast on 108 (112, 116, 120) stitches, placing a marker after every 27 (28, 29, 30) stitches to divide the work into 4 sections. Place marker and join, ensuring that the cast-on edge is not twisted. Knit 1 round.

Round 1 RLI, *knit to marker, LLI, slip marker, RLI; repeat from * 2 more times, knit to end of round, LLI—8 stitches increased.
Round 2 Knit all stitches.
Repeat these 2 rounds 7 times more—172 (176, 180, 184) stitches.
Using C2, work Round 1—180 (184, 188, 192) stitches.
Using C1, work Round 2.
Using C2, work Round 1—188 (192, 196, 200) stitches.
Using C1, work Round 2. Break C1.

Using C2, work Rounds 1 and 2, 7 (8, 9, 10) times more, changing to longer needle when desired—244 (256, 268, 280) stitches.
Using C3, work Round 1—252 (264, 276, 288) stitches.
Using C2, work Round 2.
Using C3, work Round 1—260 (272, 284, 296) stitches.
Using C2, work Round 2. Break C2.
Using C3, prepare for side shaping and set aside the left sleeve stitches as follows: k40 (43, 46, 49), place marker, slip the next 50 stitches onto a stitch holder or waste yarn, cast on 5 (6, 6, 7) stitches using the backward loop method, place marker, k40 (43, 46, 49), W&T.

LEFT SIDE SECTION

Row 1 (WS) Slip 1, purl to second marker, p40 (43, 46, 49), W&T.
Row 2 (RS) Slip 1, knit to 2 stitches before first marker, k2tog, k5 (6, 6, 7), k2tog tbl, k37 (40, 43, 46), W&T.
Row 3 (WS) Slip 1, purl to second marker, p38 (41, 44, 47), W&T.
Row 4 (RS) Slip 1, knit to 2 stitches before first marker, k2tog, k5 (6, 6, 7), k2tog tbl, k35 (38, 41, 44), W&T.
Row 5 (WS) Slip 1, purl to 1 stitch before next wrapped stitch, W&T.
Row 6 (RS) Slip 1, knit to 2 stitches before first marker, k2tog, knit to next marker, k2tog tbl, knit to 1 stitch before next wrapped stitch, W&T.
Repeat Rows 5 and 6 until 2 (3, 2, 3) stitches before first marker and after second marker remain unwrapped, ending with a wrong-side row.
Next row (RS) Slip 0 (1, 0, 1), k2tog, k5 (6, 6, 7), k2tog tbl, W&T.
Next row Slip 1, purl to 1 stitch before next wrapped stitch, W&T.
45 (50, 52, 57) stitches remain for the left side. Knit to the center back of the sweater, working wraps together with wrapped stitches.

RIGHT SIDE SECTION

K40 (43, 46, 49), place marker, slip the next 50 stitches onto a holder, cast on 5 (6, 6, 7) stitches using the backward loop method, place marker, k40 (43, 46, 49), W&T.
Work as for the Left Side Section. End by knitting to the center front of the sweater, working wraps together with wrapped stitches—90 (100, 104, 114) stitches.

BOTTOM BAND

Round 1 Knit all stitches, working wraps together with wrapped stitches.

Size L Only

Round 2 *Kfb, k1, (kfb) twice, k1; repeat from * to end—144 stitches.

Size 1X Only

Round 2 *K1, kfb; repeat from * to end—150 stitches.

Size 2X Only

Round 2 *Kfb, k1, kfb; repeat from * to last 2 stitches, k2—172 stitches.

Size 3X Only

Round 2 *Kfb, k1, kfb; repeat from * to end—190 stitches.

All Sizes

Round 3 Knit all stitches.
Work in 1x1 Rib for 7 rounds, or to desired finished length.
Bind off all stitches loosely in pattern.

SLEEVES (MAKE 2)

Note: Both sleeves are made in the same way.
Place the 50 held stitches of one sleeve onto the 16" (40cm) circular needle. Pick up and knit 3 (4, 4, 5) stitches along the cast-on edge at the underarm, place marker to denote beginning of round, pick up and knit 3 (4, 4, 5) more stitches along the cast-on underarm edge—56 (58, 58, 60) stitches.
Work in 1x1 Rib for 4 rounds.
Bind off all stitches loosely in pattern.

FINISHING

Weave in the ends. Mist with cold water and block lightly. Do this on a dress form if you have one available, to improve the fabric's drape over the bust and waist.

magic
halter

Sometimes a sweater is not just a sweater. This one is a sexy bra-strap-hiding device as well! (Check out the flap at the back that keeps the low back from being a lingerie peep show.) The rib and lace combo give this sexy halter a seriously strong vertical line. And bonus: you get flattering shaping with no extra math.

SIZES
L (1X, 2X, 3X)
Shown in size 1X

FINISHED MEASUREMENTS
Chest: Will stretch to comfortably fit 40 (44, 48, 52)" (101.5 [112, 122, 132]cm)
Length: 21½ (21½, 23, 24½)" (54.6 [54.6, 58.5, 62.2]cm)
Note: *Length is measured from the back of the neck to the lower edge when worn.*

MATERIALS

6 (6, 7, 8) balls Lang Opal; 58% nylon, 42% viscose; 168 yd (154m) per 1¾ oz (50g) ball; #0017 (pale green)
1 US #6 (4mm) circular needle, 32" (80cm) long, *or size needed to obtain gauge*
Stitch marker
Stitch holders or waste yarn
Tapestry needle
Sewing needle
Sewing thread matched to yarn color
2 shank buttons, ⅞" (22mm) diameter
2 small, flat buttons
2 small hook and eye closures
1 piece ¼" (6mm) wide elastic, approximately 34 (36, 38, 40)" (86 [91, 96.5, 101.5]cm) long
Note: *Purchase a longer piece of elastic than is called for; the length of the elastic will be adjusted during finishing.*

GAUGE
39 stitches and 40 rows = 4" (10cm) in 2x1 Rib, fabric relaxed
28 stitches and 40 rows = 4" (10cm) in 2x1 Rib, slightly stretched
35 stitches and 41 rows = 4" (10cm) in Openwork Rib, fabric relaxed

ABBREVIATIONS AND TECHNIQUES
See page 32.

PATTERN NOTES
The fabric formed by this yarn is very slinky, stretchy, and drapey. The top will look very small with the rib pattern relaxed and collapsed, but it will stretch to fit a range of sizes. The sizes listed here are recommended sizes only; each of the sizes can easily stretch an inch or three (2.5–7.5cm) larger than the measurements listed.
A stockinette stitch band along the outer edges of the back and upper body forms a casing for elastic, which gives the halter top the structure it needs to fit comfortably and securely. Before inserting the elastic, the top may appear limp and ill-fitting; don't worry! The elastic will work wonders.

STITCH PATTERNS
Openwork Rib (Worked in the round over a multiple of 6 stitches)
Rounds 1 and 3 *K2, p1; repeat from * to end.
Round 2 *K2, p1, yo, ssk, p1; repeat from * to end.
Round 4 *K2, p1, k2tog, yo, p1; repeat from * to end.
Repeat Rounds 1–4 for Openwork Rib.
2x1 Rib (Worked in the round over a multiple of 3 stitches)
Round 1 *K2, p1; repeat from * to end.
Repeat this round for 2x1 Rib.
2x1 Rib (Worked back and forth over a multiple of 3 stitches + 1)
Row 1 (RS) P1, *k2, p1; repeat from * to end.
Row 2 (WS) K1, *p2, k1; repeat from * to end.
Repeat these 2 rows for 2x1 Rib.
Seed Stitch (Worked back and forth over an odd number of stitches)
Row 1 K1, *p1, k1; repeat from * to end.
Repeat this row for Seed Stitch.

LOWER BODY

Cast on 276 (306, 336, 366) stitches. Place marker and join, ensuring that the cast-on edge is not twisted.

Work in Openwork Rib until the work measures 7" (18cm).

Work in 2x1 Rib until the work measures 10 (10, 11, 12)" (25.5 [25.5, 28, 30.5]cm).

Next Round Work 47 (53, 59, 65) stitches in Seed Stitch and place these stitches on a stitch holder or on a piece of waste yarn, continue in pattern to the end of the round—229 (253, 277, 301) stitches on the needle.

Remove the marker. From this point, the upper body will be worked back and forth in rows.

UPPER BODY

Row 1 (WS) Work all stitches in pattern.

Row 2 (RS) K3, (k2tog, k1) twice, k2tog, ssk, work in pattern to last 13 stitches, k2tog, (ssk, k1) twice, ssk, k3—221 (245, 269, 293) stitches.

Row 3 (WS) P8, p2tog, work in pattern to last 10 stitches, p2tog tbl, p8.

Row 4 (RS) K8, ssk, work in pattern to last 10 stitches, k2tog, k8.

Repeat Rows 3 and 4, 8 times more—203 (227, 251, 275) stitches remain. The work measures 12 (12, 13, 14)" (30.5 [30.5, 33, 35.5]cm).

divide for neckline

Next Row (WS) P8, p2tog, work 91 (103, 115, 127) stitches in pattern, kfb, work in pattern to last 10 stitches, p2tog tbl, p8—202 (226, 250, 274) stitches.

Next Row (RS) K8, ssk, work 91 (103, 115, 127) stitches in pattern, place the remaining 101 (113, 125, 137) stitches on hold on a stitch holder or on a piece of waste yarn.

LEFT FRONT

Row 1 (WS) Work in pattern to last 10 stitches, p2tog tbl, p8.

Row 2 (RS) K8, ssk, work in pattern to end.

Repeat these 2 rows 36 (42, 48, 54) times more, then work Row 1 once more—25 stitches.

Work 24 (18, 10, 10) rows in pattern, maintaining 9 stitches at outer edge in stockinette stitch.

place buttonholes

Buttonhole Row 1 (RS) Work 10 stitches in pattern, bind off 5 stitches, work in pattern to end.

Buttonhole Row 2 (WS) Work 10 stitches in pattern, cast on 5 stitches, work in pattern to end.

Work 8 rows in pattern.

Repeat these 10 rows once more.

Bind off all stitches.

RIGHT FRONT

Replace the held stitches of the Right Front on the needle with the right side facing, and rejoin the yarn at center front.

Row 1 (RS) Work in pattern to last 10 stitches, k2tog, k8.

Row 2 (WS) P8, p2tog, work in pattern to end.

Repeat these 2 rows 37 (43, 49, 55) times more—25 stitches.

Work 44 (38, 30, 30) rows in pattern, maintaining 9 stitches at outer edge in stockinette stitch.

Bind off all stitches.

BRA FLAP

Replace the held back stitches on the needle and rejoin the yarn.

Work 2" (5cm) in Seed Stitch.

Bind off all stitches loosely in pattern.

FINISHING

Fold the Bra Flap and the upper ½" (13mm) of the Lower Body toward the wrong side of the work, and pin in place. Sew the upper edge of the Bra Flap to the Lower Body approximately ¾" (2cm) from the fold, forming the back of the elastic casing. The rest of the Bra Flap remains free, and can be tucked over and into the back band of a strapless or halter bra when the top is worn.

Thread the elastic through this short casing, and draw it through so that equal lengths of elastic emerge on either end. Pin the ends of the elastic so that they stick out an inch or two past the ends of the straps; this is so that they will not be accidentally drawn inside the casing while the casing is being sewn.

Fold the stockinette bands in half lengthwise over the elastic. Sew the edges of this casing in place, beginning at the edges of the back casing and ending at the ends of the straps.

Overlap the ends of the straps approximately 3" (7.5cm) and pin them together. Try the top on, and adjust the length of the elastic so that it will hold the back of the top comfortably and securely in place. Use sewing thread to sew the elastic very securely in place inside the casing. Trim the ends of the elastic, and sew the ends of the casing closed.

Sew the large shank buttons to the outside of the right strap, opposite the buttonholes, sewing one small flat button to the inside of the strap at the back of each large button. Each pair of buttons (1 large button and 1 small button) should be sewn together through the thickness of the strap. This will prevent the larger, heavier buttons from pulling and stressing the delicate, stretchy fabric of the top.

With the buttons fastened, sew the hook of one hook and eye closure to the elastic casing near the end of the right strap, on the wrong side of the strap. Sew the eye to the left strap opposite the hook. Sew the second closure to the straps near the point where the end of the left strap sits under the right strap. These closures will keep the ends of the straps in place when the top is worn.

Weave in all ends and block as desired.

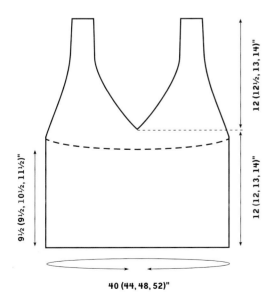

9½ (9½, 10½, 11½)"

12 (12½, 13, 14)"

12 (12, 13, 14)"

40 (44, 48, 52)"

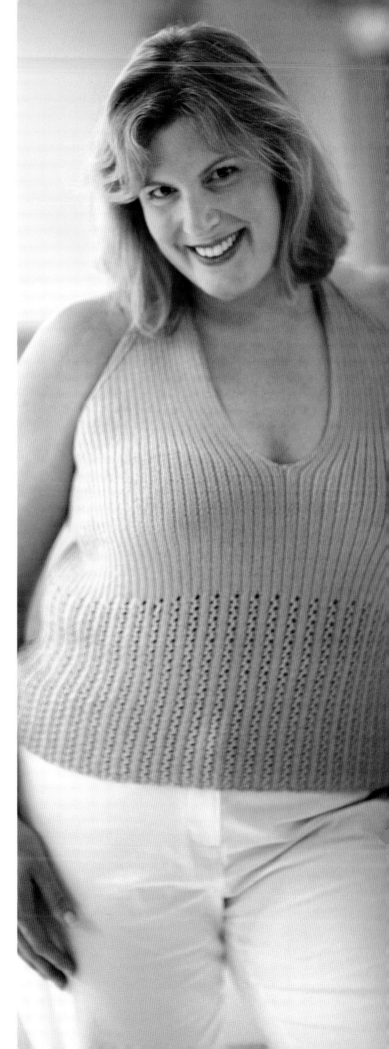

orange smoothie
tank

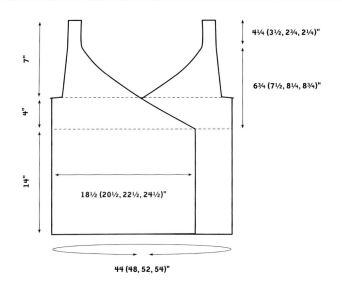

It's hot, and you can't go outside naked. What do you wear? Slip on an Orange Smoothie! It's ever so cool. You can adjust it to show exactly as much or as little skin as you like. It's fluid and flowy, so it's perfect for capturing the breeze on hot summer days. It's very girly thanks to the subtle lace pattern below your cleavage, and it's got a perfect fit-and-flare shape that suits the well-endowed very well indeed.

SIZES

L (1X, 2X, 3X)

Shown in size 1X

FINISHED MEASUREMENTS

Chest: 44 (48, 52, 56)" (112 [122, 132, 142]cm)

Length: Approximately 25" (63.5cm)

MATERIALS

10 (10, 11, 13) skeins Dalegarn Svale; 50% cotton, 40% viscose, 10% silk; 114 yd (104m) per 1¾ oz (50g) skein; #3608 (bright orange)

1 US #5 (3.75mm) circular needle, 24" (60cm) long or longer, *or size needed to obtain gauge*

Stitch markers

Stitch holders

1 button, 1" (25mm) in diameter

4 yd (3.7m)½" (13mm) ribbon

Yarn needle

Sewing needle

Sewing thread matched to yarn color

GAUGE

22 stitches and 34 rows = 4" (10cm) in stockinette stitch

ABBREVIATIONS AND TECHNIQUES

See page 32.

STITCH PATTERNS

S2K2togP (Slip 2, knit 2 together, pass the 2 slipped stitches over) Slip the next 2 stitches together, knitwise, as if to work a k2tog. K2tog, then pass both slipped stitches over the k2tog just worked—3 stitches have been decreased.

SskS2KP (Slip, slip, knit 2 together; slip 2, knit 1, pass the 2 slipped stitch over) Slip 2 stitches one at a time to the right needle; insert left needle into the fronts of these 2 stitches and knit them together through the back loops. Slip the remaining stitch back to the left needle; slip this stitch and the next stitch to the right needle together as if to work a k2tog. Knit the next stitch, then pass both slipped stitches over the stitch just knit—3 stitches have been decreased.

Lace Column Pattern (See chart; worked over a multiple of 11 stitches plus 3 stitches)

Row 1 (RS) K1, SKP, k4, (yo) twice, k4, *S2KP, k4, (yo) twice, k4, repeat from * to last 3 stitches, k2tog, k1.

Row 2 (WS) Purl all stitches, except knit into the second yo of each double yo.

Repeat these 2 rows for Lace Column Pattern.

LOWER BODY

Cast on 322 (355, 388, 421) stitches.

Set-Up Row (WS) P99 (110, 121, 132), place marker, p121 (132, 143, 154), place marker, p102 (113, 124, 135).

Work in Lace Column Pattern until the work measures 14" (35.5cm), or 4" (10cm) less than desired length to underarm, ending with a wrong-side row.

BUST

Note: Read ahead! Neckline and armhole shaping directions are worked simultaneously.

shape front edges

Set-Up Row (RS) K1, SKP, k4, (yo) twice, k4, S2K2togP, k2tog, k7, slip 1, *k10, slip 1, repeat from * to last 17 stitches, ssk, SskS2KP, k4, (yo) twice, k4, k2tog, k1—316 (349, 382, 415) stitches. This row sets the slip stitch pattern for the Bust section. Throughout this section, the stitches that were slipped on this row will be slipped on all subsequent right-side rows.

Row 1 (WS) P7, k1, purl to last 7 stitches, k1, p6.

Row 2 (RS) K1, SKP, k4, (yo) twice, k4, S2K2togP, k2tog, work in slip stitch pattern as set to last 17 stitches, ssk, SskS2KP, k4, (yo) twice, k4, k2tog, k1—6 stitches decreased.

Repeat these 2 rows 8 (15, 15, 15) times more, working short rows if desired (see below)—262 (253, 286, 319) stitches.

Size L Only

Row 3 (WS) P7, k1, purl to last 7 stitches, k1, p6.

Row 4 (RS) K1, SKP, k4, (yo) twice, k4, S2K2togP, work in slip stitch pattern as set to last 15 stitches, SskS2KP, k4, (yo) twice, k4, k2tog, k1—4 stitches decreased; 258 stitches.

Repeat Rows 1–4 as above 3 times more—228 stitches.

All Sizes

Bust section measures approximately 4" (10cm) (measured along side or back). Proceed to "Bind Off for Back."

AT THE SAME TIME: When the work measures 2" (5cm) from the beginning of the Bust section, ending with a wrong-side row, work short-row shaping as follows. These short rows will be worked first on the right cup, then on the left cup, beginning on a right-side row. After working the short rows, if you wish to measure the length of the garment, do so along the side edge, or along the back.

The short rows as written will add approximately 1¼" (3cm) of length to the center of each cup. If more length is desired, the short row sequence may be worked more than once.

If less length is desired, fewer short rows may be worked, or the short-row shaping may be omitted completely.

short-row bust shaping

Work in pattern, working decreases as set, to 24 stitches before first marker, W&T.

Purl to 1 stitch before last slipped stitch (first slipped stitch on right side), W&T.

Work in pattern to 26 stitches before first marker, W&T.

Purl to 3 stitches before last slipped stitch, W&T.

Work in pattern to 28 stitches before first marker, W&T.

Purl to 5 stitches before last slipped stitch, W&T.

Work in pattern to 30 stitches before first marker, W&T.

Purl to 7 stitches before last slipped stitch, W&T.

Work in pattern to 32 stitches before first marker, W&T.

Purl to 9 stitches before last slipped stitch, W&T.

Work in pattern, working wraps together with wrapped stitches, to 1 stitch before the last slipped stitch on the right side, W&T.

Purl to 24 stitches before marker, W&T.

Work in pattern to 3 stitches before last slipped stitch, W&T.

Purl to 26 stitches before marker, W&T.

Work in pattern to 5 stitches before last slipped stitch, W&T.

Purl to 28 stitches before marker, W&T.

Work in pattern to 7 stitches before last slipped stitch, W&T.

Purl to 30 stitches before marker, W&T.

Work in pattern to 9 stitches before last slipped stitch, W&T.

Purl to 32 stitches before marker, W&T.

Work to end in pattern, working wraps together with wrapped stitches and working decreases as set.

When working the next wrong-side row, work remaining wraps together with wrapped stitches.

bind off for back

Next Row (WS) P7, k1, purl to 8 stitches before first marker, place the 44 (51, 62, 73) stitches just worked on a stitch holder; bind off 140 (151, 162, 173) stitches (to 11 stitches past second marker), removing markers; p37 (44, 55, 66), k1, p6—44 (51, 62, 73) stitches. Right and Left Fronts will be worked separately.

RIGHT FRONT

Size 1X Only

Next Row (RS) K1, SKP, k4, (yo) twice, k4, S2K2togP, work in slip stitch pattern as set to end—49 stitches.

Next Row (WS) Purl to last 7 stitches, k1, p6.

Sizes 2X, 3X Only

Next Row (RS) K1, SKP, k4, (yo) twice, k4, S2K2togP, k2tog, work in slip stitch pattern as set to end.

Next Row (WS) Purl to last 7 stitches, k1, p6.

Repeat these 2 rows -(-, 5, 17) times more— -(-, 44, 19) stitches.

All Sizes

Row 1 (RS) K1, SKP, k4, (yo) twice, k4, S2K2togP, k2tog, work in slip stitch pattern as set to end.

Rows 2 and 4 (WS) Purl to last 7 stitches, k1, p6.

Row 3 (RS) K1, SKP, k4, (yo) twice, k4, S2K2togP, work in slip stitch pattern as set to end.

Sizes 2X, 3X Only

Next Row (RS) Work in slip stitch pattern as set to last 17 stitches, ssk, SskS2KP, k4, (yo) twice, k4, k2tog, k1.
Next Row (WS) P6, k1, purl to end.
Repeat these 2 rows—(-, 5, 17) times more——(-, 44, 19) stitches.

All Sizes

Row 1 (RS) Work in slip stitch pattern as set to last 17 stitches, ssk, SskS2KP, k4, (yo) twice, k4, k2tog, k1.
Rows 2 and 4 (WS) Purl to last 7 stitches, k1, p6.
Row 3 (RS) Work in slip stitch pattern as set to last 15 stitches, SskS2KP, k4, (yo) twice, k4, k2tog, k1.
Row 4 (WS) Purl to last 7 stitches, k1, p6.
Repeat these 4 rows 5 (6, 5, 0) times more—14 stitches.

strap

Work the strap as for the Right Front strap.

FINISHING

When the left strap is complete, pin the ends of the straps to the back edge of the tank, and try the tank on, pinning it closed so that the Right Front overlaps the Left. Use safety pins to mark the best places for the straps to fasten to the back edge, and mark the point at the base of the Bust section on the inside of the Right Front where the Left Front edge will sit when the tank is closed.
If necessary, adjust the lengths of the straps, then bind off the strap stitches.
Sew the ends of the straps in place.
Sew a button to the inner Right Front; when the tank is worn, the button can be buttoned through an eyelet on the Left Front.
Weave in all ends.
Block the tank as desired.
Thread the ribbon through the topmost row of eyelets on the Lower Body of the tank. Try the tank on and arrange the ribbon as desired, then sew the ribbon to the right front edge of the tank, so that it will not slip when worn.

Row 4 (WS) Purl to last 7 stitches, k1, p6.
Repeat these 4 rows 5 (6, 5, 0) times more—14 stitches.

strap

Row 1 (RS) K1, SKP, k4, (yo) twice, k4, k2tog, k1.
Row 2 (WS) P7, k1, p6.
Repeat these 2 rows until the strap measures 11¼ (10½, 9¾, 9¼)" (28.5 [26.5, 24.8, 23.5]cm), or desired length. Break the yarn, leaving a 12" (30.5cm) tail, and place stitches on a stitch holder.

LEFT FRONT

Replace the held stitches of the Left Front on the needle with the right side facing, and reattach the yarn.

Size 1X Only

Next Row (RS) Work in slip stitch pattern as set to last 15 stitches, SskS2KP, k4, (yo) twice, k4, k2tog, k1—49 stitches.
Next Row (WS) P6, k1, purl to end.

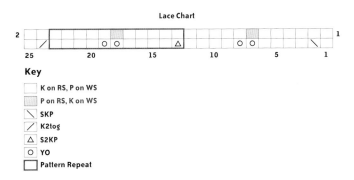

Lace Chart

Key

☐	K on RS, P on WS
▨	P on RS, K on WS
╲	SKP
╱	K2tog
△	S2KP
○	YO
☐	Pattern Repeat

goddess
shawl

This shawl, with its beads, intarsia borders and back panel, and subtle cable pattern, will hug you in a cocoon of silky love. You'll need to pay careful attention to the pattern as you knit, but the result will be an heirloom that will make you feel like a goddess.

Knitting begins with a narrow strip at the back neck, proceeds to the triangular beaded Gusset, and expands from there to become a semicircular shawl. When the shawl is at its full length, customizable short rows are added at the sides to make the shawl as wide as you want.

The inspiration for this design, with its sensually undulating lines, came from organic forms found in nature.

SIZES

L (1X, 2X)

FINISHED MEASUREMENTS

Width: 76 (86, 96)" (193 [218.5, 244]cm)

Length: 38" (96.5cm)

MATERIALS

Blue Sky Alpacas Alpaca Silk; 50% alpaca, 50% silk; 146 yd (133m) per 1¾ oz (50g) skein

13 (14, 15) skeins #131 Kiwi (pale green, MC)

3 skeins #132 Ginger (pale gold, CC)

1 set US #4 (3.5mm) double-pointed needles

2 US #4 (3.5mm) circular needles, 24" (60cm) long, *or size needed to obtain gauge*

1 US #4 (3.5mm) circular needle, 48" (120cm) long

1 crochet hook in a size close to the size of the needles

Approximately 705 (740, 775) size 6 seed beads (Be sure to buy extra beads!) Sample shawl used Berry-lined light topaz AB beads available at Earth Faire.

Dental floss threader (see note) or big-eye beading needle

Waste yarn

Small stitch holder

Cable needle

GAUGE

22 stitches and 34 rows = 4" (10cm) in stockinette stitch

ABBREVIATIONS AND TECHNIQUES

See page 32.

STITCH PATTERNS

B (Add Bead) Slide a bead up the yarn to the right needle, then work the next stitch. The bead will remain on the horizontal strand of yarn between the last 2 stitches.

C3B (Cable 3 Back) Slip next stitch to cable needle and hold to back of work, k2, p1 from cable needle.

C3F (Cable 3 Back) Slip next 2 stitches to cable needle and hold to front of work, p1, k2 from cable needle.

C5B (Cable 5 Back) Slip next 3 stitches to cable needle and hold to back of work, k2, slip the last stitch (a purl stitch) to the left needle and purl this stitch, k2 from cable needle.

Seed Stitch (Worked over an odd number of stitches)

Row 1 *K1, p1; repeat from * to last stitch, k1.

Repeat this row for Seed Stitch.

PATTERN NOTES

This shawl is worked using the intarsia technique. A separate ball of yarn is used for each different colored section of the shawl. When switching yarns between the different sections, be sure to pick up the new color from underneath the previous color. This will ensure that the two strands of yarn are twisted around each other, which will prevent holes from forming at these joining points.

The beading technique used for this shawl requires that beads be strung onto the yarn before knitting starts. Sivia uses dental floss threaders for stringing because they are cheap and easy to find in drug stores. Dental floss threaders are what people use to thread floss around their braces and bridges. It is semi-rigid plastic and is made up of an eye and a needle end. To use it for threading beads onto yarn, pass the knitting yarn through the loop of the threader and pick up beads with the working end of the needle. Then, slide the beads over the loop and onto the yarn. Always string a few more beads than you will need.

UPPER BORDER AND UPPER GUSSET

Divide one skein of CC into two balls of equal size. These two balls will be used for the seed stitch border, and should not be strung with beads.

Thread approximately 293 (295, 297) beads onto a second skein of CC.

With the beaded ball of CC and a short circular needle, cast on 9 stitches using the Crochet Cast-On (page 33).

Row 1 (RS) K5, p1, k1, B, k2.

Row 2 (WS) P3, k6.

Repeat these 2 rows 29 times more, then work Row 1 once more; 61 rows have been worked.

Place all stitches on a stitch holder; do not break the yarn.

Using the same circular needle, with the right side facing, pick up and knit 47 stitches (3 stitches for every 4 rows) along the beaded edge of the work.

Set-Up Row (WS) P3, *k2, p1; repeat from * to last 5 stitches, k2, p3.

Row 1 (RS) K2, B, k1, *p2, k1 tbl; repeat from * 4 times more, p1, W&T.

Even-Numbered Rows 2–10 (WS) K1, *p1, k2; repeat from * to last 3 stitches, p3.

Row 3 (RS) K2, B, k1, *p2, k1 tbl; repeat from * 3 times more, p1, W&T.

Row 5 (RS) K2, B, k1, *p2, k1 tbl; repeat from * twice more, p1, W&T.

Row 7 (RS) K2, B, k1, *p2, k1 tbl; repeat from * once more, p1, W&T.

Row 9 (RS) K2, B, k1, p2, k1 tbl, p1, W&T.

Row 11 (RS) K2, B, k1, p1, W&T.

Row 12 (WS) K1, p3.

When working the next row, pick up all wraps and work them together with the wrapped stitches.

Row 13 (RS) K2, B, k1, *p2, k1 tbl; repeat from * to last 5 stitches, p2, k1, B, k2.

Row 14 (WS) P3, *k2, p1; repeat from * 4 times more, k1, W&T.

Odd-Numbered Rows 15–23 (RS) P1, *k1 tbl, p2; repeat from * to last 3 stitches, k1, B, k2.

Row 16 (WS) P3, *k2, p1; repeat from * 3 times more, k1, W&T.

Row 18 (WS) P3, *k2, p1; repeat from * twice more, k1, W&T.

Row 20 (WS) P3, *k2, p1; repeat from * once more, k1, W&T.

Row 22 (WS) P3, k2, p1, more, k1, W&T.

Row 24 (WS) P3, k1, W&T.

Row 25 (RS) P1, k1, B, k2.

When working the next row, pick up all wraps and work them together with the wrapped stitches.

Row 26 (WS) P3, *k2, p1; repeat from * to last 5 stitches, k2, p3.

Rows 27–30 Work in pattern as set.

Row 31 (RS) Work 22 stitches in pattern, S2KP, work in pattern to end—45 stitches.

Row 32 (WS) Work in pattern as set.

Row 33 (RS) Work 21 stitches in pattern, S2KP, work in pattern to end—43 stitches.

Rows 34–67 Continue to work in this way, decreasing at the center of the piece every right-side row, until 9 stitches remain.

Row 68 (WS) P3, k1, p1, k1, p3.

Row 69 (RS) K2, B, ssk, k1 tbl, k2tog, B, k2—7 stitches.

Row 70 (WS) P7.

Row 71 (RS) P1, C5B, p1.

Row 72 (WS) K1, p2, k1, p2, k1. Do not break the yarn.

SHAWL BODY

In the next row, stitches will be picked up along the edge of the work, and the patterns for the body of the shawl will be established. Place the 9 held stitches of the upper border on a double-pointed needle and join one of the small balls of CC.

Set-Up Row (RS) Using a short circular needle and the attached small ball of CC, *k1, p1; repeat from * once more, k1, p2tog, k2tog; using MC, pick up and knit 48 stitches (4 stitches for every 5 rows) along the adjacent edge of the Gusset; using the attached, beaded ball of CC, P1, k1, B, k1, k1 tbl, k1, B, k1, p1; using a second short circular needle and a second ball of MC, pick up and knit 48 stitches along the remaining edge of the Gusset; remove the waste yarn from the cast-on edge of the upper border and place the resulting 9 live stitches on a double-pointed needle; attach the second small ball of CC and work these border stitches onto the circular needle as follows: k2tog, p2tog, **k1, p1; repeat from ** once, k1.

There are 117 stitches on the needle, and 5 balls of yarn are attached. The first and last 7 stitches of the row form the borders of the shawl. They will be worked in Seed Stitch throughout, using the small, unbeaded balls of CC. The two sections worked in MC will be referred to as the Shawl Body sections, and the central section, worked using the beaded ball of CC, will be referred to as the Gusset.

It will be easier to work the first part of the shawl if the stitches are distributed over two circular needles, with the Gusset stitches passed back and forth between needles as they are worked on every row. This will also help keep the joins between the different colors even on each side of the Gusset panel. After Row 24, when the Gusset panel increases are complete, all stitches will be transferred to the 47" (120cm) circular needle.

Set-Up Row (WS) Work border in Seed Stitch using CC; using MC, k3, *p4, k2, p1, k2; repeat from * 4 times more; using CC, k1, p5, k1; using MC, **k2, p1, k2, p4; repeat from ** 4 times more, k3; work border in Seed Stitch using CC.

Row 1 (RS) Work border in Seed Stitch using CC; using MC, work Row 1 of Body Chart 1; using CC, work Row 1 of Gusset Chart; using MC, work Row 1 of Body Chart 2; work border in Seed Stitch using CC—147 stitches.

Work through Rows 2–24 of Charts as set. When Row 24 is complete, there are 233 stitches.

Rows 25 and 26 of the Gusset Chart set the pattern for the remainder of the Gusset; repeat these 2 rows over the Gusset stitches until the shawl is complete. When working the next row, work all stitches onto the 47" (120cm) circular needle.

Next Row (RS) Work border in Seed Stitch using CC; using MC, work Row 1 of Body Chart 3; using CC, work Gusset stitches in pattern; using MC, work Row 1 of Body Chart 4; work border in Seed Stitch using CC.

Work through Rows 2–52 of Charts 3 and 4 as set. When Row 52 is complete, there are 353 stitches.

Work all stitches in pattern, increasing every eighth row as set and working new stitches into the cable pattern as shown by the green boxes in Body Charts 3 and 4.

Continue working in this way until 16 more increase rows have been worked. There are 673 stitches in total. Each pattern repeat wedge (counted from the right edge of one cable at its widest point to the right edge of the next cable) has 62 stitches.

Work 1 wrong-side row after this last increase row has been worked.

short rows

The short rows that follow will allow you to increase the width of the shawl without increasing its length. Continue working yarn over increases as set; the increase rows will be indicated within the short row directions.

As the short rows are worked in 8-row increments across each wedge, the same row of the cable pattern will be worked for every cable within the current short row.

When working each row after the first short row, pick up the wrap from the previous row and work it together with its wrapped stitch.

Row 1 (RS) Work in pattern to 12 stitches past the first cable, W&T.

Even-Numbered Rows 2–8 (WS) Work in pattern to end.

Rows 3 and 5 (RS) Work in pattern to 10 stitches past the previous wrapped stitch, W&T.

Row 7 (RS) Work in pattern to 10 stitches past the previous wrapped stitch, working increases as set; W&T—675 stitches.

Row 9 (RS) Work in pattern to 12 stitches past the second cable, W&T.

Rows 10–16 Work as for Rows 2–8—679 stitches.

Row 17 (RS) Work in pattern to 12 stitches past the third cable, W&T.

Rows 18–24 Work as for Rows 2–8—685 stitches.

Row 25 (RS) Work in pattern to 12 stitches past the fourth cable, W&T.

Rows 26–32 Work as for Rows 2–8—693 stitches.

Row 33 (RS) Work in pattern to 12 stitches past the fifth cable, W&T.

Rows 34–40 Work as for Rows 2–8—703 stitches.

Row 41 (RS) Work all stitches in pattern.

Row 42 (WS) Work in pattern to 12 stitches past the first cable, W&T.

Rows 43 and 45 (RS) Work in pattern to end.

Rows 44 and 46 (WS) Work in pattern to 10 stitches past the previous wrapped stitch, W&T.

Row 47 (RS) Work in pattern to end, working increases as set—705 stitches.

Row 48 (WS) Work in pattern to 10 stitches past the previous wrapped stitch, W&T.

Row 49 (RS) Work in pattern to end.

Row 50 (WS) Work in pattern to 12 stitches past the second cable, W&T.

Rows 51–57 Work as for Rows 43–49—709 stitches.

Row 58 (WS) Work in pattern to 12 stitches past the third cable, W&T.

Rows 59–65 Work as for Rows 43–49—715 stitches.

Row 66 (WS) Work in pattern to 12 stitches past the fourth cable, W&T.

Rows 67–73 Work as for Rows 43–49—723 stitches.
Row 74 (WS) Work in pattern to 12 stitches past the fifth cable, W&T.
Rows 75–81 Work as for Rows 43–49—733 stitches.
Row 82 (WS) Work all stitches in pattern.
The short rows for size A are now complete. For sizes B (C), work Rows 1–82, 1 (2) times more, with the following difference: When working the second set of short rows, increase rows will be worked on the fifth row (instead of the seventh) of each set of 8 short rows from Rows 1–40, and on the fourth row (instead of the sixth) of each set of 8 short rows from Rows 42–81. For size C, when working the third set of short rows, increase rows will be worked on the third row of each set of 8 short rows from Rows 1–40, and on the second row of each set of 8 short rows from Rows 42–81.
Be careful never to work a W&T within the 5-stitch column formed by the eyelet motif; if necessary, turn the short row after more or fewer stitches to avoid this.
When all short rows are complete, there will be 733 (793, 853) stitches.
Continue in pattern without further increases until you have completed this row in each cable motif: C3B, p1, C3F. The two stockinette stitch "arms" of the cable pattern should be 3 stitches apart before the lower border begins. When working the border, work the 7 stitches of the cable as follows: k2, p3, k2. Break all strands of yarn connected to the shawl.

BEADED BORDER

String approximately 408 (440, 472) beads onto a new ball of CC. Be sure to string a few extra beads.
Using this beaded ball of CC, work 2 rows in pattern.
Next Row (RS) Work in pattern, working (k1, B, k1) in each pair of adjacent knit stitches. This refers to the (k2) ribs within the rib pattern of the shawl body, to the stockinette stitch "arms" of the cables, and to the borders of the Gusset.
Work 1 wrong-side row in pattern.
Repeat these 2 rows twice more, then work 1 more right-side row.
Bind off all stitches very loosely in pattern.

FINISHING

Weave in all ends.
Submerge the shawl in lukewarm water and allow it to soak until thoroughly saturated.
Gently squeeze out the excess water, then roll the shawl in a towel to remove more water.
Lay the shawl flat, arranging it carefully to ensure that the edges, cables, and gusset edges are straight. You should be able to achieve the measurements given without pinning, but if desired, the shawl may be pinned out to even larger dimensions.
Allow the shawl to dry completely.

Body Chart 1

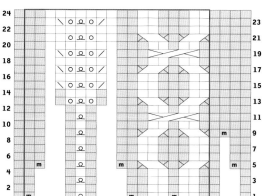

Body Chart 2

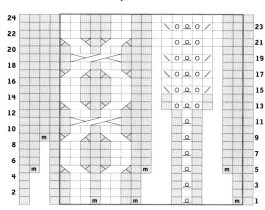

Body Chart 3

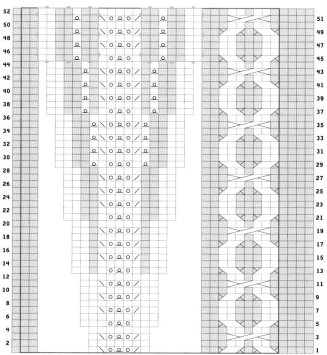

Body Chart 4

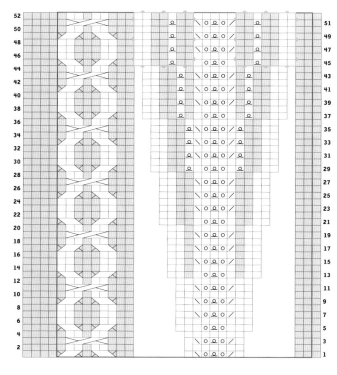

Cabled Shawl: Gusset Chart

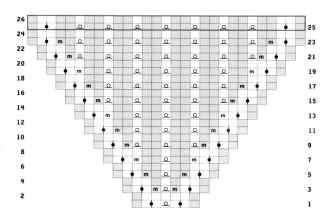

Key

☐	K	╲	Ssk
▨	P on RS, K on WS	●	B
m	M1	⧄	C3F
m	M1p	⧅	C3B
Ω	K tbl	⧓	C5B
O	YO	☐	Pattern Repeat
╱	K2tog	▨	Rib Pattern Repeat

perfection
wrap

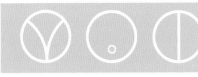
We Big Girls can run hotter than the average female, so a big, warm shawl isn't always appealing. What if we could knit ourselves something delicate, feminine, lacy, and not too warm? Something sized to be in proportion to our curvy selves, something drapey and barely there, but still eyecatching? We can have it all.

This wrap is knit in a silk-and-seacell blend yarn. It will block like a dream and will be a little cooler than a pure silk wrap. Sounds like perfection to us.

			＼	O			O	◢	O			O	╱					5
				＼	O	O	╱		＼	O		O	╱					3
				O	◢	O			O	◢	O							
				O	╱		＼	O	O	╱		＼	O					1

Key

☐	K on RS, P on WS
▨	P on RS, K on WS
O	YO
╱	K2tog on RS, P2tog on WS
＼	Ssk on RS, P2tog tbl on WS
◢	SK2P on RS, P3tog on WS
☐	Pattern Repeat

FINISHED MEASUREMENTS

Length: 90" (229cm)
Width: 30" (61cm)
Note: Measurements given for shawl after blocking.

MATERIALS

3 skeins Hand Maiden Sea Silk; 70% silk, 30% Seacell(r); 437 yd (400m) per 3½ oz (100g) skein; Glacier (ice blue-grey variegated)
1 set US #6 (4mm) straight needles, *or size needed to obtain gauge*
Tapestry needle

GAUGE

18 stitches and 24 rows = 4" (10cm) in pattern stitch after blocking
Note: *Exact gauge is not important for this project.*

ABBREVIATIONS AND TECHNIQUES

See page 32.

PATTERN NOTE

When working from the chart, odd-numbered rows are right-side rows, and even-numbered rows are wrong-side rows.

WRAP

Loosely cast on 135 stitches.
Knit 6 rows.
Work Rows 1–6 of the chart pattern until the work measures approximately 67" (170cm) without being stretched, ending with Row 6 of the chart pattern. The pattern repeat in the red box will be worked a total of 19 times in each row.
Knit 6 rows.
Bind off all stitches loosely in pattern.

FINISHING

Weave in all ends.
Lay the wrap flat and pin it out to the dimensions given. Using a spray bottle, spray the wrap with water until it is completely saturated.
Allow it to dry completely before removing the pins.

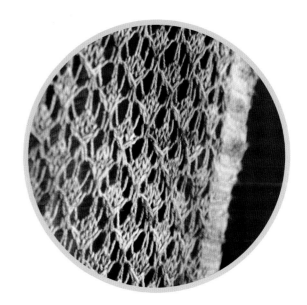

finagle

DIFFICULTY: 1
DESIGNED BY: AMY R. SINGER
KNIT BY: JILLIAN MORENO

Amy's not one to abide by rules, especially if they keep her away from yarn she loves. In this case, it was a rich, chunky, ultrasoft ruby wonder and there was no denying that she was going to wrap herself in it. But it's nowhere near approved Big Girl gauge . . . so how could she finagle it into this book? Simple. Make it into a luscious wrap, that's how. The simple textured rib looks great on both sides and is a blissfully mindless knit. Wrap it around your shoulders and secure it with a heavy-duty pin, or wear it as we've shown it—scarflike—and you won't even feel the cold. There's no greater vertical than the lush inches trailing down your bod. Knit it long enough to wrap around your neck once and just clear the floor. Yum.

(For those who know Amy can't knit with wool, a little backstory: The original yarn Amy found is a specialty cotton. To make sure we wouldn't drive you crazy looking for the impossible-to-find yarn, we chose a beautiful wool that is even prettier, softer, and more richly ruby than Amy's original lust object. Jillian knit the wrap you see here.)

FINISHED MEASUREMENTS
Length: 100" (254cm)
Width: 11" (28cm)

MATERIALS

10 skeins Filtes King Super; 100% merino wool; 128 yd (117m) per 3½ oz (100g) ball; #2181 (red)
1 set US #17 (12mm) straight needles, *or size needed to obtain gauge*
Tapestry needle

GAUGE
11 stitches and 12 rows = 4" (10cm) in Rib Pattern

ABBREVIATIONS AND TECHNIQUES
See page 32.

STITCH PATTERN
Rib Pattern (Worked over a multiple of 6 stitches)
Row 1 (RS) *K3, p3; repeat from * to end.
Row 2 (WS) *K1, p1; repeat from * to end.
Repeat these 2 rows for Rib Pattern.

WRAP
Note: This wrap is worked with 2 strands of yarn held together throughout. Leave long tails when switching balls; it will make it easier to weave in the ends neatly.
Using 2 strands of yarn held together, cast on 30 stitches.
Work in Rib Pattern until the work measures 100" (254cm).
Bind off all stitches loosely in pattern.

FINISHING
Weave in all ends and block as desired.
To weave in the ends, divide each strand of yarn into separate plies. Weave in groups of a few plies each, weaving the groups in different directions, to help distribute the bulk of the woven ends.

trellis diamond
socks

Handknit socks are a luxurious necessity for Big Girl calves . . . you can make them the right size and shape to fit you perfectly. These beauties feature a gorgeous lace pattern, the girliest of girl colors (we love the pink) and are too beautiful to keep hidden. Knit them taller and wear them with skirts. We just can't get enough.

SIZES
1 (2) (shown in size 2)

FINISHED MEASUREMENTS
Ankle circumference: Will stretch to fit up to 9½ (11)" (24 [28]cm)

MATERIALS
 2 skeins Lorna's Laces Shepherd Sock; 80% superwash wool, 20% nylon; 215 yd (197m) per 57g skein; Pink Blossom

1 set of 5 US #1 (2.25mm) double-pointed needles for size 1
1 set of 5 US #0 (2mm) double-pointed needles for size 2
1 spare needle, same size as working needles or smaller

1 C-2 (2.75mm) or D-3 (3.25mm) crochet hook
Smooth waste yarn (mercerized cotton works well)
Stitch markers

GAUGE
Size 1: 32 stitches = 4" (10cm) in stockinette stitch
Size 2: 38 stitches = 4" (10cm) in stockinette stitch

ABBREVIATIONS AND TECHNIQUES
See page 32.

PATTERN NOTE
If desired, the leg of the sock may be worked on a larger needle to accommodate a larger ankle.

CUFF
Using the crochet chain cast-on (page 33), cast on 60 (72) stitches. When using the working yarn to pick up stitches in the waste yarn crochet chain, be sure to start picking them up at the end of the chain, rather than the beginning, to make it easy to remove the provisional cast-on later. Divide the stitches evenly between the needles (15 [18] stitches on each needle) and join to begin working in the round, being careful not to twist.
Knit 7 rounds. These rounds form the hem facing.
Next Round *Yo, k2tog; repeat from * to end. This round forms a turning round for the picot hem.
Knit 6 rounds.
Joining Round Fold the hem facing along the turning round to the wrong side of the work. Unravel the crochet chain from the first few cast-on stitches and slip them to the spare needle, holding this needle behind the work so that each stitch on the spare needle is directly behind the corresponding stitch on the working needle. Knit the first stitch on the working needle together with the first stitch on the spare needle, then join the next stitches on each needle in the same way. Continue to work in this way, unraveling the chain from a few stitches at a time and working them together with the stitches on the working needle until all stitches have been worked—60 (72) stitches.

LEG
Begin working in pattern from the Leg Chart.
Continue in pattern until the work measures 7" (18cm) or the desired length to the top of the foot, ending with an even-numbered round. Make a note of which pattern round you have just completed.
Note: If you worked the leg using a larger needle than you plan to use for the foot, switch needles now.

HEEL FLAP
Work the first 16 (17) stitches of the next round onto one needle, then turn the work.
Slip one stitch, then purl 32 (34) stitches onto one needle. The heel flap will be worked back and forth over the 33 (35) stitches on this needle; the remaining 27 (37) stitches will be held on the other needles for the instep.
Row 1 (RS) *Slip 1, k1; repeat from * to last stitch, k1.
Row 2 (WS) Slip 1, p32 (34).
Repeat these 2 rows until the Flap measures 2½" (6.5cm), ending with a wrong-side row.
Note: The length of the Heel Flap should be the same as the measurement from the floor to the bottom of your ankle bone (taken standing flat on the floor). A longer or shorter Heel Flap may be worked in order to achieve the correct measurement.

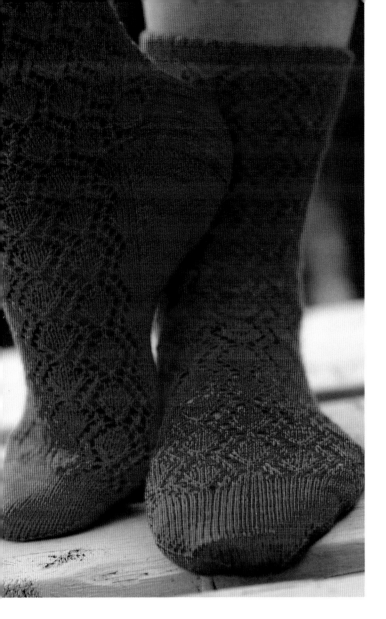

GUSSET

Knit the first 9 (10) heel stitches.

Using a new needle, knit the remaining 10 (11) heel stitches, then pick up and knit 1 stitch in each slipped stitch along the edge of the heel flap, and 1 stitch in the space between the top of the Heel Flap and the instep. This needle will be designated Needle 1.

Using a second and third needle, work the held stitches of the instep following the Instep Chart, beginning and ending at the points indicated for your size and beginning with the chart round that follows the last chart round you worked for the Leg. These needles will be designated Needles 2 and 3.

Using a fourth needle, pick up and knit 1 stitch in the space between the instep and Heel Flap and 1 stitch in each slipped stitch along the edge of the heel flap, then knit the first 9 (10) heel stitches. This needle will be designated Needle 4.

Round 1 Knit to last 3 stitches of Needle 1, k2tog, k1; work stitches of Needles 2 and 3 in pattern; k1, ssk, knit to end of Needle 4.

Round 2 Work all stitches in pattern.

Repeat these 2 rounds until 58 (70) stitches remain. There will be 16 (17) stitches on Needle 1, 27 (37) stitches divided between Needles 2 and 3, and 15 (16) stitches on Needle 4.

FOOT

Continue in pattern until the foot measures 2" (5cm) less than the desired length to the end of the toe, ending with an even-numbered Chart Round.

Knit 2 rounds.

TOE

Redistribute the stitches on the needles as follows:

Size 1: Slip 1 stitch from the end of Needle 1 to the beginning of Needle 2, and slip 1 stitch from the beginning of Needle 4 to the end of Needle 3.

Size 2: Slip 1 stitch from the beginning of Needle 2 to the end of Needle 1, and slip 1 stitch from the end of Needle 3 to the beginning of Needle 4.

Round 1 Knit to last 3 stitches of Needle 1, k2tog, k1; k1, ssk, knit to end of Needle 2; knit to last 3 stitches of Needle 3, k2tog, k1; k1, ssk, knit to end of Needle 4.

Round 2 Knit all stitches.

Repeat these 2 rounds 9 (11) times more—18 (22) stitches.

Slip the stitches on Needle 3 to Needle 2, and the stitches on Needle 4 to Needle 1. Graft the stitches on Needle 1 to the stitches on Needle 2.

FINISHING

Weave in ends. Block to open lace pattern.

Turn Heel

Row 1 (RS) Slip 1, k18 (19), ssk, k1. Turn work.

Row 2 (WS) Slip 1, p6, p2tog, p1. Turn work.

Row 3 (RS) Slip 1, k7, ssk, k1. Turn work.

Row 4 (WS) Slip 1, p8, p2tog, p1. Turn work.

Row 5 (RS) Slip 1, k9, ssk, k1. Turn work.

Row 6 (WS) Slip 1, p10, p2tog, p1. Turn work.

Row 7 (RS) Slip 1, k11, ssk, k1. Turn work.

Row 8 (WS) Slip 1, p12, p2tog, p1. Turn work.

Row 9 (RS) Slip 1, k13, ssk, k1. Turn work.

Row 10 (WS) Slip 1, p14, p2tog, p1. Turn work.

Row 11 (RS) Slip 1, k15, ssk, k1. Turn work.

Row 12 (WS) Slip 1, p16, p2tog, p1. Turn work.

Row 13 (RS) Slip 1, k17, ssk, k0 (1). Turn work.

Row 14 (WS) Slip 1, p17 (18), p2tog, p0 (1). Turn work— 19 (21) heel stitches remain.

Diamond Sock

Leg Chart

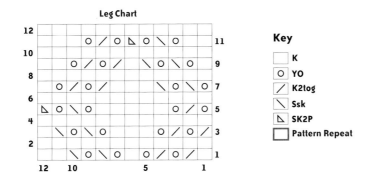

Key

☐	K
○	YO
╱	K2tog
╲	Ssk
◭	SK2P
☐	Pattern Repeat

Instep Chart

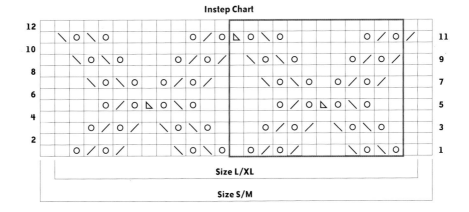

Size L/XL

Size S/M

indian summer
socks

With Big Girl ease built in to accommodate shapely ankles and calves, these grown-up-yet-girlish cuffed socks in three sizes give you a little extra sass below the knee. This pattern cleverly uses three needle sizes for different design details. Start with the biggest needle for the short-rowed lace cuff in contrasting yarn, then change to a smaller needle for upper leg ribbing and smallest needle for the ankle, heel, and foot. Beads give your feet just a bit of bling, and knitting them in is easy as pie.

SIZES

1 (2, 3) (shown in size 2)

FINISHED MEASUREMENTS

Foot/leg circumference: 8½ (9½, 10½)" (21.5 [24, 26.5]cm)

Leg from cuff to ankle: 5" (12.5cm)

MATERIALS

Fleece Artist Merino; 100% washable merino wool; 355 yd (325m) per 3½ oz (100g) skein

1 skein Indian Summer (pumpkin, MC)

1 skein Moss (CC)

1 US #3 (3.25mm) circular needle, 24" (60cm) long or pair of straight needles

2 US #2 (2.75mm) circular needles, 24" (60cm) long

3 US #1 (2.25mm) circular needles, 24" (60cm) long, *or size needed to obtain gauge*

56 size 5 triangle beads or size 5 or 6 seed beads. *Sample socks use size 5 Rococo silver-lined chartreuse triangle beads from Earth Faire.*

Dental floss threader or big-eye beading needle

Locking ring marker or safety pin

Two stitch markers

Tapestry needle

GAUGE

31 stitches and 45 rounds = 4" (10cm) in stockinette stitch on smallest needle.

ABBREVIATIONS AND TECHNIQUES

See page 32.

PATTERN NOTES

Bead (Bead 1 Stitch): Bring the yarn to the front of the work, slip the next stitch purlwise, slide a bead as close as possible to the right needle, return the yarn to the back of the work, leaving the bead in front of the slipped stitch.

For stringing beads, use a big-eye beading needle or a dental floss threader (used to thread floss around braces and bridges). Sivia uses dental floss threaders for stringing because they are cheap and easy to find in drug stores. A dental floss threader is semi-rigid plastic made up of a loop and a "joined" part. To use it for threading beads onto yarn, pass the knitting yarn through the loop of the threader and pick up beads with the opposite end of the threader, then slide the beads over the loop and onto the yarn.

RIGHT LACE CUFF

Thread 28 beads onto CC. Using the larger needle, cast on 56 stitches. Do not join; the cuff is worked back and forth in rows. Work 2 rows in garter stitch.

Bead Row (RS) *K2, Bead; repeat from * to last 2 stitches, k2.

right lace cuff short rows

Row 1 (WS) K4, W&T.

Row 2 (RS) K4. Turn work.

Row 3 (WS) K2, p4, W&T.

Row 4 (RS) K2, k2tog, yo, k2. Turn work.

Row 5 (WS) K2, p6, W&T.

Row 6 (RS) K3, k2tog, yo, k1, Bead, k1. Turn work.

Row 7 (WS) K2, p8, W&T.

Row 8 (RS) K2tog, yo, k2, (k2tog, yo) twice, k2. Turn work.

Row 9 (WS) K2, p10, W&T.

Row 10 (RS) K1, k2tog, yo, k2, (k2tog, yo) twice, k3. Turn work.

right lace cuff pattern

Odd-Numbered Rows 11–25 (WS) K2, purl to last 2 stitches, k2.

Row 12 (RS) K2, k2tog, yo, *k2, (k2tog, yo) twice; repeat from * to last 4 stitches, k2, Bead, k1.

Row 14 (RS) K5, *(k2tog, yo) twice, k2; repeat from * to last 3 stitches, k3.

Row 16 (RS) K2, *k2, (k2tog, yo) twice; repeat from * to last 6 stitches, k2, k2tog, yo, k2.

Row 18 (RS) K1, Bead, k1, *(k2tog, yo) twice, k2; repeat from * to last 5 stitches, k2tog, yo, k1, Bead, k1.

Row 20 (RS) K2, *(k2tog, yo) twice, k2; repeat from * to end of row.

Row 22 (RS) K3, k2tog, yo, *k2, (k2tog, yo) twice; repeat from * to last 3 stitches, k3.

Row 24 (RS) K1, Bead, k2tog, yo, *k2, (k2tog, yo) twice; repeat from * to last 4 stitches, k2, Bead, k1.

Repeat Rows 14–24 once.

Proceed to Leg and Foot.

LEFT LACE CUFF

Thread 28 beads onto CC. Using the larger needle, cast on 56 stitches. Do not join; the cuff is worked back and forth in rows. Work 2 rows in garter stitch.

Bead Row (RS) *K2, Bead; repeat from * to last 2 stitches, k2.

Next Row (WS) K2, purl to last 2 stitches, k2.

left lace cuff short rows

Row 1 (RS) K4, W&T.

Row 2 (WS) P2, k2. Turn work.

Row 3 (RS) K2, yo, ssk, k2, W&T.

Row 4 (WS) P4, k2. Turn work.

Row 5 (RS) K1, Bead, k1, yo, ssk, k3, W&T.

Row 6 (WS) P6, k2. Turn work.

Row 7 (RS) K2, (yo, ssk) twice, k2, yo, ssk, W&T.

Row 8 (WS) P8, k2. Turn work.

Row 9 (RS) K3, (yo, ssk) twice, k2, yo, ssk, k1, W&T.

Row 10 (WS) P10, k2. Turn work.

Row 11 (RS) K1, Bead, k2, (yo, ssk) twice, k2, (yo, ssk) twice, W&T.

Row 12 (WS) P12, k2. Turn work.

left lace cuff pattern

Row 13 (RS) K5, *(yo, ssk) twice, k2; repeat from * to last 3 stitches, k3.

Even-Numbered Rows 14–24 (WS) K2, p to last 2 stitches, k2.

Row 15 (RS) K2, yo, ssk, *k2, (yo, ssk) twice; repeat from * to last 4 stitches, k4.

Row 17 (RS) K1, Bead, k1, yo, ssk, *k2, (yo, ssk) twice; repeat from * to last 3 stitches, k1, Bead, k1.

Row 19 (RS) K2, *(yo, ssk) twice, k2; repeat from * to end.

Row 21 (RS) K3, *(yo, ssk) twice, k2; repeat from * to last 5 stitches, yo, ssk, k3.

Row 23 (RS) K1, Bead, k2, *(yo, ssk) twice, k2; repeat from * to last 4 stitches, yo, ssk, Bead, k1.

Repeat Rows 13–24 once, then work Row 13 once more.

LEG AND FOOT (RIGHT AND LEFT SOCKS)

Join in the Round

Using medium needles, purl 1 row.

Join for working in the round as follows: Distribute the 56 stitches over 2 medium needles, placing 28 stitches on each needle. Position the work so that the purl side is on the outside. (It will fold to the inside when the cuff is turned down.) To make the join at the start of the round more secure, swap the first and last stitches of the round by placing the last stitch of the round onto the first needle, and the first stitch of the round onto the second needle. Mark the beginning of round with a locking ring marker or safety pin.

Knit 4 rounds. Using MC and leaving an 8" (20.5cm) tail of CC, knit 1 round, increasing 8 (12, 16) stitches evenly spaced—64 (68, 72) stitches; 32 (34, 36) stitches on each needle.

leg rib pattern

Next Round *K1, p1; repeat from * to end.

Repeat this round for 2" (5cm).

Next Round Using smallest needles, *k3, p1; repeat from * to end.

Repeat this round for 3" (7.5cm). Total ribbing measures 5" (12.5cm).

For the right sock only, work 32 (34, 36) stitches past beginning of round. The heel for the right sock will be worked over the next 32 (34, 36) stitches. The heel for the left sock will be worked over the first 32 (34, 36) stitches of round. When the cuff is turned down, the asymmetrical opening of each sock is on the outside of the leg, with the longer point to the front of the sock.

HEEL FLAP (RIGHT AND LEFT SOCKS)

Work back and forth over 32 (34, 36) stitches as follows:

Row 1 *Slip 1, k1; repeat from * 15 (16, 17) times more.

Row 2 Slip 1, p31 (33, 35).

Work these 2 rows for 15 (16, 17) times more—32 (34, 36) rows have been worked.

Turn Heel (Right and Left Socks)

Row 1 (RS) K18 (19, 20), ssk, k1. Turn work.

Row 2 (WS) Slip 1, p5, p2tog, p1. Turn work.

Row 3 (RS) Slip 1, k6, ssk, k1. Turn work.

Row 4 (WS) Slip 1, p7, p2tog, p1. Turn work.

Row 5 (RS) Slip 1, k8, ssk, k1. Turn work.

Row 6 (WS) Slip 1, p9, p2tog, p1. Turn work.

Row 7 (RS) Slip 1, k10, ssk, k1. Turn work.

Row 8 (WS) Slip 1, p11, p2tog, p1. Turn work.

Row 9 (RS) Slip 1, k12, ssk, k1. Turn work.

Row 10 (WS) Slip 1, p13, p2tog, p1. Turn work.

Row 11 (RS) Slip 1, k14, ssk, k1. Turn work.

Row 12 (WS) Slip 1, p15, p2tog, p1. Turn work.
Row 13 (RS) Slip 1, k16, ssk, k0 (1, 1). Turn work.
Row 14 (WS) Slip 1, p16 (17, 17), p2tog, p0 (1, 1). Turn work.

Size 2 Only
Row 15 (RS) Slip 1, k18, ssk. Turn work.
Row 16 (WS) Slip 1, p18, p2tog. Turn work.

All Sizes
18 (20, 20) heel stitches remain.

GUSSET
(RIGHT AND LEFT SOCKS)

K18 (20, 20) heel stitches, pick up and knit 16 (17, 18) stitches along the right edge of the heel flap (1 stitch in each stitch that was slipped at the beginning of a row), pick up 1 stitch in the gap between the instep and heel flap and knit this stitch through the back loop, place marker, continuing with the same needle, k1, work 15 (16, 17) instep stitches in rib pattern as set; with second needle, work next 15 (16, 17) instep stitches in rib pattern, k1, place marker, pick up 1 stitch in the gap between the instep and heel flap and knit this stitch through the back loop, pick up and knit 16 (17, 18) stitches along left edge of heel flap, then knit the first 9 (10, 10) heel stitches again—84 (90, 94) stitches. The center of the heel is the new start of the round.
Round 1 Knit to first marker, k1, work in rib pattern to 1 stitch before next marker, k1, knit to end of round.
Round 2 Knit to 3 stitches before first marker, k2tog, k1, slip marker, k1, work in rib pattern to 1 stitch before next marker, k1, slip marker, k1, ssk, knit to end of round.
Repeat these 2 rounds until 64 (68, 72) stitches remain, or until the circumference of the sock fits your foot when you try on your sock. The total stitch count should be a multiple of 4.

FOOT
(RIGHT AND LEFT SOCKS)

Work even until the foot measures 1½ (1¾, 2)" (3.8 [4.5, 5]cm) less than the desired finished length.

TOE
(RIGHT AND LEFT SOCKS)

Work all stitches in stockinette stitch.
Round 1 *Knit to 3 stitches before marker, k2tog, k1, slip marker, k1, ssk; repeat from * once more, knit to end of round.
Round 2 Knit.
Repeat these 2 rounds until 28 stitches remain; 14 stitches on each needle. Redistribute the stitches so that the sole stitches are on one needle and the instep stitches are on the other needle as follows: With first needle k7, with second needle k14,

with first needle k7, then knit the next 7 stitches on the first needle again (this brings you to the end of the needle).
At each end of each needle, pass the last stitch over the next to last stitch—12 stitches on each needle. Break the yarn, leaving an 18" (45.5cm) tail. Graft the instep stitches to the sole stitches.

FINISHING

With the tail of CC, sew the sides of the lace cuff together invisibly for about ½" (13mm) from the top of the ribbing. Weave in ends.
Immerse the socks in lukewarm water and blot the excess water with a towel. On a flat surface, stretch the lace cuffs away from the sock legs to about 3½" (9cm). Allow to dry flat.

twisty-stitch
socks

It's easy to add a gusset to the back of your handknit socks to accommodate curvy calves, but few sock patterns do it as elegantly as these ingenious socks. The stitch is twisty, but not as thick as a cabled pattern, so they'll fit in your shoes with ease. And the thicker-than-traditional-sockweight yarn means these are a quick knit. Good thing, since Cascade 220 comes in about a billion colors and you just might want to knit a pair in every one.

FINISHED MEASUREMENTS

Foot circumference: 7" (18cm)
Foot length: 9" (23cm)
Calf circumference: 8" (20.5cm)
Leg length (from top of heel): 7" (18cm)

MATERIALS

2 skeins Cascade 220; 100% wool; 220 yd (201m) per 3½ oz (100g) skein; #9487 Blue
2 US #3 (3.25mm) circular needles, 24" (60cm)
Safety pin or split ring marker
Cable needle
Tapestry needle

GAUGE

24 stitches and 32 rows = 4" (10cm) in stockinette stitch.

ABBREVIATIONS AND TECHNIQUES

See page 32.

STITCH PATTERNS

C2F (Cable 2 Front) Slip next stitch to cable needle and hold to front of work, k1, k1 from cable needle.

C2B (Cable 2 Back) Slip next stitch to cable needle and hold to back of work, k1, k1 from cable needle.

C2FP (Cable 2 Front Purl) Slip next stitch to cable needle and hold to front of work, p1, k1 from cable needle.

C2BP (Cable 2 Back Purl) Slip next stitch to cable needle and hold to back of work, k1, p1 from cable needle.

PATTERN NOTES

When working from the charts, the rows below the red box are worked only once. The rows within the red box are repeated as needed. The last row in the chart sets the rib pattern for the cuff of the sock.

If you wish to increase the foot circumference, work Round 1 of the toe until you have the desired number of stitches. Be sure you end up with a multiple of 8 stitches + 4. Each additional 8 stitches will increase the circumference by approximately 1¼" (3cm).

TOE

Using the long-tail cast-on, cast on 8 stitches.

Rotate the work 180 degrees. With the right side facing and using the second circular needle, pick up and knit 1 stitch in the base of each cast-on stitch.

There will be 8 stitches on each circular needle. The needle you used for your cast-on will be designated Needle 1, and the needle you used to pick up stitches will be designated Needle 2. After the first few rounds have been worked, place a safety pin or split ring marker in your work to indicate the beginning of the round.

Round 1 *K1, kfb, knit to last 2 stitches on needle, kfb, k1; repeat from * once—4 stitches have been increased.

Round 2 Knit.

Repeat these 2 rounds 8 times more—52 stitches.

Continue in stockinette stitch until the toe measures 2" (5cm), or 7" (18cm) less than the desired length of the foot.

Fitting Note: The numbers in the instructions above are based on a foot that is 9" (23cm) in length and are calculated so that the main motif of the Front Panel will end on a specific row. If your foot is much longer or shorter than 9" (23cm), you can change the length by working more or fewer repeats of the Front Panel motif, but you may also need to change the length of the toe.

Each motif is 1½" (3.8cm) long. If you plan to add 1 motif to the length of the foot, you should work your toe until it is 8½" (21.5cm) less than the desired length of the foot. If you plan to subtract 1 motif from the length of the foot, work your toe until it is 5½" (14cm) less than the length of the foot.

The toe length should not be shorter than 1½" (3.8cm.)

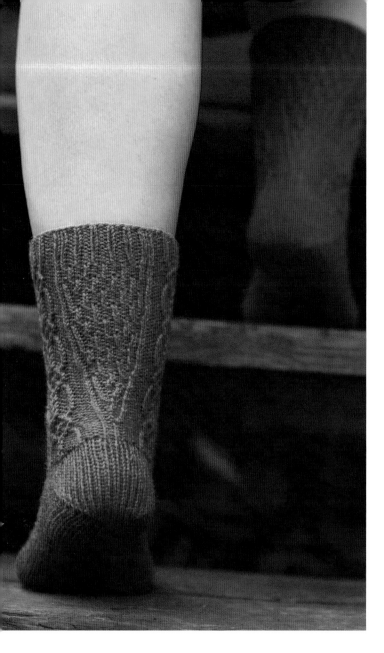

Row 2 (WS) Slip 1, purl to last stitch, W&T.
Row 3 (RS) Slip 1, knit to 1 stitch before last wrapped stitch, W&T.
Row 4 (WS) Slip 1, purl to 1 stitch before last wrapped stitch, W&T.
Repeat Rows 3 and 4 until there are 8 wrapped stitches at each end of the needle and 10 unwrapped stitches in the center.
Note: If you have increased the number of stitches in the foot, work an additional pair of short rows for every 8 stitches that have been added. For example, if you have 60 stitches (30 stitches on Needle 2), work Rows 3 and 4 until there are 9 wrapped stitches at each end of the needle and 12 unwrapped stitches in the center.
Next Row (RS) Slip 1, knit to first wrapped stitch, pick up the wrap and knit it together with the wrapped stitch, turn the work.
Next Row (WS) Slip 1, purl to first wrapped stitch, pick up the wrap and purl it together with the wrapped stitch, turn the work.
Repeat these 2 rows until all stitches have been worked, and all wraps have been worked together wth their respective stitches. Knit to the end of Needle 2.

LEG

Work 2 rounds in pattern, working Chart rounds 18–19 over the stitches on Needle 1, and knitting all stitches on Needle 2.
Next Round Work Round 20 of Front Panel Chart over the stitches on Needle 1; work Round 1 of Side Panel Chart over the first 12 stitches on Needle 2, work Round 1 of Back Gusset Chart over the next 2 stitches, work Round 1 of Side Panel chart over the last 12 stitches.
Note: If you have added stitches to the sock, work 2 additional purl stitches at the beginning and end of Needle 2 for every 8 stitches you have added.
Work in pattern, increasing as indicated within the Back Gusset Chart, until Round 57 of the Back Gusset Chart is complete. You will have just worked Round 15 of the Side Panel Chart and Round 20 of the Front Panel Chart—63 stitches.
Fitting Note: More or fewer increases may be worked within these 57 rounds to obtain a larger or smaller calf circumference. Each pair of increases will make a difference of approximately ⅓" (8mm) to the circumference.

CUFF

The last round of each chart sets the rib pattern for the cuff of the sock. Work 6 rounds in the rib pattern as shown.
Bind off all stitches very loosely.

FINISHING

Weave in all ends.
Block lightly on sock blockers or under a damp towel.

FOOT

Next Round Work Round 1 of Front Panel Chart over the stitches on Needle 1; knit all stitches on Needle 2.
Note: If you have increased the number of stitches in the sock, repeat the first and last 2 stitches of the Chart. For each 8 stitches you have increased, repeat each pair of stitches once. This will center the chart pattern over the stitches on Needle 1. Continue working in pattern as set through Chart Round 20. Work Rounds 7–20 once more, then work Rounds 7–16.
Next Round Work to the end of Needle 1; do not complete this round. You will have just completed Round 17 of the Chart.

HEEL

The heel will be worked back and forth over the stitches on Needle 2.
Row 1 (RS) Knit to last stitch, W&T.

Key

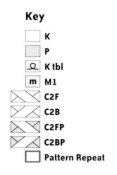

- ☐ K
- ▨ P
- Ω K tbl
- m M1
- ⧅ C2F
- ⧄ C2B
- ⧅ C2FP
- ⧄ C2BP
- ☐ Pattern Repeat

Side Panel

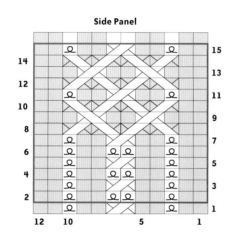

Gusset

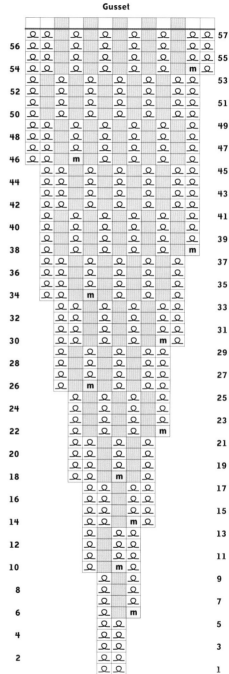

Front Panel

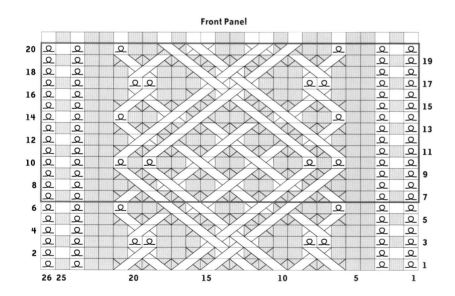

big
clutch

A girl can never have too many bags (you should see our closets!) But how many clutches—you know, the lean, sleek bag that holds your essentials but doesn't weigh you down—are proportioned to suit Big Girl bodies? This one is. Knit it in brights for summer. Make one in black with a bit of metallic shimmer, and it's the perfect evening bag. You have our permission to go nuts.

FINISHED MEASUREMENTS

Width: 14" (35.5cm)
Height: 5½" (14cm)
Gusset Depth: 1½" (3.8cm)

MATERIALS

Filatura di Crosa Millefili Fine; 100% Egyptian mercerized cotton; 136 yd (125m) per 1¾ oz (50g) skein
3 skeins #55 Red (MC)

1 skein # 284 Red Orange (CC1)
1 skein #167 Orange (CC2)
1 set US #2 (2.75mm) straight needles,
or size needed to obtain gauge
1 set US #2 (2.75mm) double-pointed needles
Lining fabric measuring 15" x 22" (38cm x 56cm)
Stiff canvas measuring 14" x 21" (35.5cm x 53.5cm)
Fusible double-sided interfacing measuring 14" x 21" (35.5cm x 53.5cm)
2 magnetic snaps
Tapestry needle
Sewing needle
Sewing thread

GAUGE

28 stitches and 40 rows = 4" (10cm) in stockinette stitch

ABBREVIATIONS AND TECHNIQUES

See page 32.

PATTERN STITCHES

Flap Pattern (Worked over a multiple of 6 stitches + 2 stitches)
Row 1 (RS) K1, *k1, slip 4, k1, repeat from * to last stitch, k1.
Row 2 (WS) P1, *p2, slip 2, p2, repeat from * to last stitch, p1.
Row 3 (RS) Knit.
Row 4 (WS) Purl.

Applied I-Cord
Using a double-pointed needle, cast on 3 stitches.
First Row K2, insert the tip of the left needle into the edge of the work and pick up a stitch, knit the last stitch on the left needle together with this picked-up stitch. Slide the 3 stitches just worked to the other end of the double-pointed needle, transfer this needle to your left hand, and bring the yarn around the back of the work, ready to begin working the next row.
Repeat this row for Applied I-Cord.

FLAP

Using straight needles and MC, cast on 116 stitches.
Knit 1 row.
Purl 1 row.
Using CC1, work Rows 1–4 of Flap Pattern.
Continuing in Flap Pattern, work as follows:
*4 rows MC
4 rows CC1
4 rows CC2
4 rows MC
4 rows CC1
Repeat from * twice more, then work as follows:
4 rows MC
4 rows CC1
4 rows CC2
4 rows CC1

BACK

Continuing in Flap Pattern, work as follows:
*4 rows CC2
4 rows CC1
4 rows MC
4 rows CC1
4 rows MC
Repeat from * 3 times more. Break CC1 and CC2; the rest of the bag will be worked using MC only.

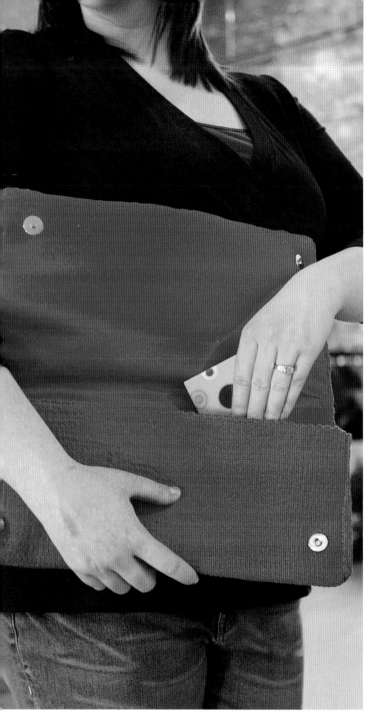

SIDE PANELS (MAKE 2)

Using MC, cast on 12 stitches.

Work 9 rows in stockinette stitch, ending with a wrong-side row.

Decrease Row (RS) K2tog, knit to last 2 stitches, k2tog.

Work 13 rows in stockinette stitch.

Work Decrease Row.

Work 23 rows in stockinette stitch.

Bind off all stitches loosely in pattern.

FINISHING

Weave in all ends.

Wet-block the pieces by immersing them in lukewarm water and allowing them to soak. Blot the excess water with a towel. Lay them flat. Pin out the main piece of the bag so that it measures 14" x 21" (35.5cm x 53.5cm), ensuring that the edges are straight. Allow the pieces to dry completely.

Using MC, work Applied I-Cord around the edge of the main piece (not the side panels).

assembly

Lay the lining fabric on a table with the wrong side facing. Place the fusible interfacing and canvas in the center of the lining fabric, with the interfacing sandwiched between the fabric and the canvas. There should be ½" (13mm) of lining fabric emerging from beneath the canvas around all edges. Fuse the fabric to the canvas.

Lay the main piece of the bag on a table with the wrong side facing. Center the fused canvas and fabric on top of the piece, with the lining facing up. Fold the edges of the lining fabric under the canvas. Pin the lining in place.

Attach the "male" halves of the magnetic snaps to the corners of the flap lining, approximately 1" (2.5cm) from each side edge and lower edge.

Sew the lining in place, sewing through all layers. Fold the bag in thirds to determine the best positions for the remaining halves of the snaps, and attach them.

Using MC, sew the side panels to the bag body, sewing the side panel edges between the lining edges and the I-Cord edging.

Stuff the bag with plastic bags to give it shape, then spritz with cold water. Crease the bottom and top of the bag and shape it as desired. Allow it to dry completely.

BOTTOM AND FRONT

Set-Up Row (RS) K4, *k2, kfb; repeat from * to last 4 stitches, k4—152 stitches.

Row 1 (WS) *P1, slip 1 with yarn held to back of work; repeat from * to end.

Row 2 (RS) *K1, slip 1 with yarn held to front of work; repeat from * to end.

Repeat these 2 rows until the work measures 6¾" (17.2cm) from the set-up row, ending with a wrong-side row.

Next Row (RS) P4, *p2, p2tog, repeat from * to last 4 stitches, p4—116 stitches.

Bind off all stitches.

felted
weekend bag

Key
CC1 Pretty Pink
CC2 Spring Green
CC3 Gourd

Here's a great way to get some crazy color in your life without having to wear it on any of your Bs: knit, felt, and then embroider this great big bag from Kristin Nicholas! Kristin's the queen of color and embroidery and has written some fabulous books on the subject. Our favorite is *Colorful Stitchery*, which is full of patterns and embroidery instruction if this stuff is new to you. It's not scary—promise.

This delectable bag is scaled up to suit our Big Girl frames, and is perfect for taking your gear to yoga, packing up your knitting, or just using as an everyday bag. You might want to make a few of them in different colors—Nashua Julia comes in a deluxe crayon box's worth of colors!

FINISHED MEAUREMENTS

Before Felting
Circumference: 72" (183cm)
Height: 20" (51cm)

After Felting
Circumference: 51" (129.5cm)
Height: 13" (33cm)
Note: *Results may vary depending on the characteristics of the washing machine used and of the yarn chosen (if a different yarn is substituted).*

MATERIALS

Nashua Handknits Julia; 50% wool, 25% alpaca, 25% mohair; 93 yd (85m) per 1¾ oz (50g) ball
10 balls #NHJ9235 Anemone (MC)
6 balls #NHJ8141 Pretty Pink (CC1)

1 ball #NHJ5185 Spring Green (CC2)
1 ball #NHJ1784 Gourd (CC3)
1 US #10 (6mm) circular needle, 32" (80cm) long, *or size needed to obtain gauge*
Stitch markers
Tapestry needle
Approximately 1yd (91cm) lining fabric
Sewing needle
Sewing thread
Plastic needlepoint canvas (optional; see finishing instructions)

GAUGE

13½ stitches and 20 rows = 4" (10cm) in stockinette stitch before felting

ABBREVIATIONS AND TECHNIQUES

See page 32.

BAG

Using CC1, cast on 110 stitches. Do not join.

Knit 46 rows (23 garter stitch ridges). Do not turn the work at the end of the last row.

Next Row Place marker, pick up and knit 23 stitches (1 stitch in each garter stitch ridge) along the side edge of the work adjacent to the end of the last row worked, place marker, pick up and knit 1 stitch in each stitch along the cast-on edge, place marker, pick up and knit 23 stitches along the remaining short edge of the work, place marker; this point will be the beginning of the round. Join to begin working in the round.

Work 8 rounds in garter stitch, beginning with a purl round. Break CC1.

Next Round Using MC, *p1, knit to 1 stitch before next marker, p1, knit to next marker; repeat from * once more.

Repeat this round until the work measures 18" (45.5cm) from the beginning of the MC section. Break MC.

Using CC1, work 10 rounds in garter stitch, beginning with a knit round.

Bind off all stitches.

HANDLES (MAKE 2)

Using CC1, cast on 98 stitches.

Work in garter stitch until the work measures 3½" (9cm).

Bind off all stitches.

FINISHING

At each corner of the bag, the column of purl stitches will form a slight crease. Fold the bag along each of these creases and sew the two thicknesses of fabric together near each fold, creating 4 seamed ridges on the inside of the bag.

felting

Fill the tub of your washing machine with hot water and a small amount of soap. Place the bag and handles in the machine along with an old pair of jeans (or another heavy garment) to provide additional agitation. Run the machine, checking on the bag every 5 minutes or so, until the bag reaches the desired size. Remove the bag and handles from the machine and rinse.

Shape the pieces as desired while they are wet. You may wish to lightly stuff the bag with plastic bags or some other material to help it maintain its shape while drying. Allow the pieces to dry completely.

Trim any loose ends.

assembly

Fold each handle in half lengthwise. Sew the edges of each handle together along the center 9½" (24cm), leaving the ends open.

Sew the ends of the handles to the bag, using the photo as a guide.

embroidery

Work 6 spider web circles as shown in color indicated.

Work chain stitch using CC2 around the outside of each spider web. These shapes need not be perfectly circular.

Work a french knot in the center of each spider web in CC2.

Work lazy daisy stitch around each double circle, working from the outside of each circle and building outward.

Work clusters of 3 french knots each, as shown in the diagram, using CC1 and CC3 as desired.

Work 5 lazy daisy stitches around 6 of the french knot clusters in desired colors.

lining

Lay the bag flat on a table and measure its height (including the bottom gusset) and width. Cut a piece of fabric that is 2" (5cm) longer than double the height of the bag and 1" (2.5cm) wider than the width of the bag.

Fold the fabric in half widthwise with the right sides together. Sew the side edges together, maintaining ½" (1.3cm) seam allowances. Fold the open edge of the lining over 1" (2.5cm) to the wrong side, and press.

If desired, cut the plastic needlepoint canvas to the size and shape of the rectangular bottom of the bag. For the bag shown, 2 pieces of plastic canvas were necessary to achieve the correct length. Sew the canvas to the inside bottom of the bag, overlapping the edges of the pieces if necessary.

Insert the lining into the bag and sew it in place around the upper edge.

Yarn Resources

The yarns chosen for this book should be available at your local yarn shop or online. If you cannot find them, or for more information and distribution of the yarns used for the projects, please contact the following companies:

art yarns

39 Westmoreland Avenue
White Plains, NY 10606
(914) 428-0333
www.artyarns.com

blue sky alpaca

PO Box 88
Cedar, MN 55011
(763) 753-5815
www.blueskyalpacas.com

cascade yarn

www.cascadeyarns.com

classic elite yarns

122 Western Avenue
Lowell, MA 01851-1434
(978) 453-2837
www.classiceliteyarns.com

cleckheaton yarn

Plymouth Yarn Company, Inc
PO Box 28
Bristol, PA 19007
(215) 788-0459
www.plymouthyarn.com

crystal palace

160 23rd Street
Richmond, CA 94804
(510) 237-9988
www.straw.com/cpy

dale of norway

IN THE UNITED STATES:
Dale of Norway Inc.
N16 W23390 Stoneridge Drive,
Suite A
Waukesha, WI 53188
(262) 544-1996

IN CANADA:
Estelle Designs
2220 Midland Avenue, Unit 65,
Scarborough, ON, Canada
M1P 3E6
(800) 387-5167

fleece artist

Hand Maiden Yarn
www.fleeceartist.com

garnstudio

www.garnstudio.com

jo sharp

JCA
35 Scales Lane
Townsend, MA 01469
(978) 597-8794

lang yarns

IN THE UNITED STATES:
Berroco Inc.
PO Box 367
14 Elmdale Road
Uxbridge, MA 01569
(508) 278-2527
www.berroco.com

IN CANADA:
Estelle Design & Sales Limited
Units 65/67
2220 Midland Avenue
Scarborough, ON M1P 3E6

lorna's laces

4229 North Honore Street
Chicago, IL 60613
(773) 935-3803
www.lornaslaces.net

noro

IN THE UNITED STATES:
Knitting Fever Inc.
315 Bayview Avenue
Amityville, NY 11701
(516) 546-3600
www.knittingfever.com

IN CANADA:
Diamond Yarns Ltd.
155 Martin Ross Avenue
Unit 3
Toronto, ON M3J 2L9
(416) 736-6111
www.diamondyarn.com

rowan

For a list of stores carrying Rowan yarns, please contact:

Westminster Fibers Inc.
4 Townsend West, Unit 8
Nashua, NH 03063
(603) 886-5041

tahki stacy charles
(filatura di crosa, tahki)

8000 Cooper Ave, Bldg 1
Glendale, NY 11385
(800) 338-YARN
www.tahkistacycharles.com

needful yarns

(866) 800-4700

IN THE UNITED STATES:
60 Industrial Parkway PMB #233
Cheektowaga, NY 14227

IN CANADA:
4476 Chesswood Drive Unit 10-11
Toronto, ON M3J 2B9

black water abbey yarns

Marilyn
PO Box 470688
Aurora, CO 80047-0688
(720) 320-1003

Yarn Substitution Chart

Yarn Weight Symbol & Category Names	1 SUPER FINE	2 FINE	3 LIGHT	4 MEDIUM	5 BULKY	6 SUPER BULKY
Type of Yarns in Category	Sock, Fingering, Baby	Sport, Baby	DK, Light Worsted	Worsted, Afghan, Aran	Chunky, Craft, Rug	Bulky, Roving
Knit Gauge Range* in Stockinette Stitch to 4 inches	27–32 sts	23–26 sts	21–24 st	16–20 sts	12–15 sts	6–11 sts
Recommended Needle in Metric Size Range	2.25—3.25mm	3.25—3.75 mm	3.75—4.5mm	4.5—5.5 mm	5.5—8mm	8 mm and larger
Recommended Needle U.S. Size Range	1 to 3	3 to 5	5 to 7	7 to 9	9 to 11	11 and larger

* GUIDELINES ONLY: *The above reflect the most commonly used gauges and needle or hook sizes for specific yarn categories.*

Inspirational Reading

big girl style books

Elements of Color, **by Johannes Itten, Wiley, 1970**

Color and Fiber, **by Patricia Lambert, Barbara Staepelaere, Mary Fry, Schiffer Publishing, 1986**

Colorworks, **by Deb Menz, Interweave Press, 2004**

Colorful Stitchery, **by Kristin Nicholas, Storey Publications, 2005**

Life Is Not a Dress Size, **by Rita Farro, Chilton, 1996**

Plus Style: The Plus Size Guide to Looking Great, **by Suzan Nanfeldt, Plume, 1996**

Well Rounded: Eight Simple Steps for Changing Your Life not Your Size, **by Catherine Lippincott, Pocket Books, 1997**

Fat!So?, **by Marilyn Wann, 10 Speed Press, 1998**

Learning Curves: Living Your Life in Full and with Style, **by Michelle Weston, Crown Publishers; 2001**

Fat Girl's Guide to Life, **by Wendy Shanker, Bloomsbury, 2004**

Does This Make Me Look Fat?, **by Leah Feldon, Villard, 2000**

What Not to Wear, **by Trinny Woodall and Susannah Constantine, Riverhead Books, 2002**

Figure It Out: The Real Woman's Guide to Great Style, **by Geri Brin and Tish Jett, Sixth and Spring Books, 2004**

The Science of Sexy: Dress to Fit Your Unique Figure with the Style System that Works for Every Shape and Size, **by Bradley Bayou, Gotham Publishing, 2006**

knitting books

Big Book of Knitting, **Katharina Buss, Sterling Publications, 1999**

Sweater Design in Plain English, **Maggie Righetti, St. Martin's Press, 1990**

Knitting in Plain English, **Maggie Righetti, St. Martin's Press, 1986**

Knitting for Dummies, **Pam Allen, Wiley Publishing, 2002**

Vogue Knitting, **Butterick Company, 1989**

Designing Knitwear, **Deborah Newton, Taunton Press, 1992**

Knitter's Handbook, **Montse Stanley, Reader's Digest, 1993**

Mary Thomas Guide to Knitting, **Mary Thomas, Dover, 1972**

Big Girl Knits, **Jillian Moreno and Amy R. Singer, Potter Craft, 2006**

Designer Bios

LIBBY BAKER finds escape from the chaos of everyday life in the rhythmic clacking of needles and fluid manipulation of fiber. She resides with her yarn and her family in Englewood, Colorado.

LISA MARIE COLLINS is the designer, knitter, and fiber-crazed individual behind Yo Mama Knits, a design company based in Vancouver, Canada. Lisa Marie chronicles her adventures in knitting, spinning, dyeing, and a bit of crochet, on her blog, www.yomamaknits.com.

AUDREY ESCHRIGHT experiments with anything she can get her hands on, including knitting, sewing, photography, and writing code, and lives in Portland, Oregon. *Find out more about her latest projects at www.lifeofaudrey.com.*

CHRISSY GARDINER is a knitwear designer, mother of two, and breastfeeding advocate living in Portland, Oregon. You can see more of her designs at her website, www.gardineryarnworks.com.

PAM GORDNIER learned to knit from her 6th-grade teacher and has had a project on the needles ever since. Pam lives in central New York with her husband, dog, and two horses, and works as a technician at Cornell University.

ANGELA HAHN learned to knit as a child. Just two years ago she rediscovered the joys of knitting and knitwear designing, and she has finally accepted that occasional ripping is required. She blogs at www.ahknits.typepad.com/knititude/

SIVIA HARDING is a designer with a growing following who dabbles in lace, beads, and most recently, socks. You can find her patterns for sale on her website (www.siviaharding.com) and at various online and brick and mortar yarn stores.

SHARON HILCHIE is a licensed pilot and electrical engineer who learned to knit from the same woman who taught her to fly sailplanes.

WENDY KNIGHT began knitting when she was four (thanks, Mum). She serendipitously landed a job in pattern writing at Patons in Melbourne, Australia, the same week she dropped out of university. Visit www.textandtextiles.com.au.

SANDI LUCK has been knitting for more than 30 years. Her math degree turned out to be useful after all for teaching those geeky technical knitting classes. You can find more of her designs at www.purlescenceyarns.com.

TARA JON MANNING finds inspiration for her work in nature, eastern arts, and the exploration of the connection between craft and spirituality. Tara pioneered the "mindful knitting" movement. Tara lives with her family in Boulder, Colorado. Visit www.tarahandknitting.com.

MANDY MOORE lives in Vancouver, BC with her small family of husband and cat. She is a technical editor for Knitty.com, and does technical editing for various knitting and crochet publications (including this book!). You can find her at yarnageddon.com.

KRISTIN NICHOLAS is a knitwear and stitchery designer who lives in western Massachusetts with her husband and daughter. She is the author of several books on knitting and embroidery. Her website address is www.kristinnicholas.com

JORDANA PAIGE has been designing knitwear since 2003. At 18 years old she founded her company, Jordana Paige. She offers a full range of knitting products at www.jordanapaige.com.

An avid knitter for twenty five years, **JOYCELYN POON** is a new designer. She spends her days editing children's cartoons for a Toronto-based animation studio and her nights watching Hong Kong action movies with her boyfriend and their three cats.

KRISTI PORTER is a knitting author, designer, teacher, and technical editor. She makes her home in La Jolla, California with her husband and two daughters, Zoe and Ella.

BRENDA PURDY knits and lives in Virginia.

LISA ROWE has dabbled at many careers but knitting is her true passion. In her "spare" time, Lisa also spins yarn, sews, weaves, leads Bible study, and writes fiction. www.europasw.com/lisa-rowe

AMY M. SWENSON, along with her partner, Sandra, owns and operates Make One Yarn Studio (www.make1yarns.com), a retail yarn shop in the heart of Calgary, Alberta. More of her design work can be found on Knitty.com, and in over 100 shops across North America under the pattern line IndiKnits (www.indiknits.com).

WENDY WONNACOTT lives in Sicily, Italy with her husband and daughter. More of her work can be found at The Garter Belt (www.thegarterbelt.com) and Knitty (www.knitty.com) Magazine.

Acknowledgments

Hugs, thanks, and love to Linda Roghaar for the big push on the swing that made this whole thing happen and for the handholding we needed when we needed it. Thanks also to Ann and Kay who encouraged us to seek out our own Linda. We love you guys.

Thanks to the entire team at Potter Craft for their support and guidance. Special thanks to our tag-team editors: Mona Michael, Erin Slonaker, and Courtney Conroy, and of course, Rosy Ngo.

Bowing deeply at the waist, we offer our thanks to Lise Varrette (and Matthew) who took our pile of inspiration images and ideas and turned them into beautiful photographs.

Our photoshoot team consisted of two kickass, talented women. Rikki Zucker did the gorgeous makeup on all the models (and on our author photo). She also started knitting as a result, and we love that about her. Jacquie Blackman (already a knitter) came out of nowhere to offer her help and was, without question, the most invaluable person on the set every single day.

Our beautiful models, Alana Bridgewater, Meghan Bradley, Melissa MacMullin, and Tamarah—thank you for your professionalism and hard work. Who said models have it easy?

To Addition-elle, who provided almost all the non-knit clothing you see in this book, thank you! Addition-elle is a great shop for Canadian Big Girls.

We shot this book on location all around Toronto. Special thanks to the beach locations: the Naked Sheep; the cool house with the great porch (you might recognize it from the movie Mean Girls); Kensington Market locations: Lettuce Knit, Boomerang, and King's Vegetarian Restaurant; and the Distillery District.

Huge thanks to all the yarn companies that provided fabulous materials for our designers to work with. Their names and contact details are listed on page 155.

Speaking of the designers, we must stop here to give them a huge shoutout. Your creativity and willingness to make real the Big Girl knitwear concepts, blended with your own personal style, are what made this book what it is. We are proud to know and work with all of you. Thank you.

To Mandy Moore, our technical editor, who cares more about clarity and correctness than anyone we know, thank you. You are our third brain.

Erica Mulherin—lightning-fast, perceptive, and talented—your illustrations look the way we see ourselves in our mind's eye. Please come over and draw us every morning, okay?

So many knitters of all sizes spoke to us after the first book came out, and gave us their feedback, thoughts, suggestions, encouragement, and, most often, hugs. We hug you back. This book is for you.

The company and camaraderie of our friends keeps us from jumping off life's ledges. We send them love. Jillian thanks Jane, Carla, Maggie, Rob, Matt, Barbara, Glenda, Amy, Lynne, Suzanne, Debela, Fran, Latifa, Shannon, and some days any and everyone who sends a kind word in her direction. Amy thanks Stephanie, Denny, Jen, Aleta, Nathania, Scout, the Lettuce Knit S&B girls and boys, and the readers of Knitty magazine.

No book would get written, no stitch knitted without the love and support of our nearest and dearest. Jillian thanks Andy, Isobel, and Henry for giving her a reason to smile every day. Amy thanks Philly and the bunnies for still being there after this book, and Jood, Mom, and Dad, for their unflagging support.

In true Chip-and-Dale fashion, Jillian and Amy thank each other. And are happy to report that they're still friends after book #2. Whew.

Index

a

advanced projects. *See* level 3 projects

b

bags
 Big Clutch, 148–51
 Felted Weekend Bag, 152–55
Belly girl info, 10, 15, 16
Belly girl projects
 Big Clutch, 148–51
 Boo, Too, 50–55
 Bountiful Bohus, 34–38
 Cable Love Jacket, 68–71
 Felted Weekend Bag, 152–54
 Finagle, 134–35
 Folly II, 72–77
 Guatemalan Floral Tunic, 108–13
 Hot Cocoa Jacket, 56–61
 Indian Summer Socks, 140–43
 Magic Halter, 118–21
 Mirage Pullover, 84–89
 Modular Spiral Jacket, 44–49
 No-Gap Wrap Pullover, 90–95
 Pastille, 96–102
 Peapod Aran Jacket, 62–67
 Plain Vanilla Pullover, 29–31
 Slipstream Pullover, 103–7
 Summer Chevron, 114–17
 Susie Hoodie, 39–43
 Trellis Diamond Socks, 136–39
 Twisted Pullover, 78–83
 Twisty-Stitch Socks, 144–47
Big Clutch, 148–51
Boo, Too, 50–55
Boob girl info, 10, 15, 16
Boob girl projects
 Big Clutch, 148–51
 Boo, Too, 50–55
 Felted Weekend Bag, 152–54
 Finagle, 134–35
 Indian Summer Socks, 140–43
 No-Gap Wrap Pullover, 90–95
 Orange Smoothie Tank, 122–25
 Plain Vanilla Pullover, 29–31

 Summer Chevron, 114–17
 Susie Hoodie, 39–43
 Trellis Diamond Socks, 136–39
 Twisted Pullover, 78–83
 Twisty-Stitch Socks, 144–47
books, recommended, 157
bottom-up short-row chart, 27
bottom-up waist shaping chart, 27
Bountiful Bohus, 34–38
B3 system, 9, 10
Butt girl info, 10, 15, 16
Butt girl projects
 Big Clutch, 148–51
 Boo, Too, 50–55
 Bountiful Bohus, 34–38
 Felted Weekend Bag, 152–54
 Finagle, 134–35
 Folly II, 72–77
 Guatemalan Floral Tunic, 108–13
 Hot Cocoa Jacket, 56–61
 Indian Summer Socks, 140–43
 Magic Halter, 118–21
 Mirage Pullover, 84–89
 No-Gap Wrap Pullover, 90–95
 Orange Smoothie Tank, 122–25
 Peapod Aran Jacket, 62–67
 Plain Vanilla Pullover, 29–31
 Slipstream Pullover, 103–7
 Summer Chevron, 114–17
 Susie Hoodie, 39–43
 Trellis Diamond Socks, 136–39
 Twisted Pullover, 78–83
 Twisty-Stitch Socks, 144–47

c

Cable Love Jacket, 68–71
cables and twists, 19
charts
 bottom-up short-row, 27
 bottom-up waist shaping, 27
 measurement, 11
 side panels, 22, 23
 yarn substitution, 156
 yarn yardage, 12
color, 15–18

color blocking, 17

d

designer bios, 158
duplicate stitch, 18

e

ease (fit), 13
easy projects. *See* level 1 projects
embroidery motifs, 18

f

Fair Isle motifs, 18
felted motifs, 18
Felted Weekend Bag, 152–54
Finagle, 134–35
fit, 13
Folly II, 72–77

g

Goddess Shawl, 126–31
Guatemalan Floral Tunic, 108–13

h

hems, 25–26
Hot Cocoa Jacket, 56–61

i

Indian Summer Socks, 140–43
intarsia, 18
intermediate projects. *See* level 2 projects

j

jackets
 Cable Love Jacket, 68–71
 Hot Cocoa Jacket, 56–61
 Modular Spiral Jacket, 44–49
 Peapod Aran Jacket, 62–67